SPIRITUAL VITAMINS
Volume 2

ALSO BY WINSTON WILSON

SPIRITUAL VITAMINS
Volume 1

SPIRITUAL VITAMINS

Volume 2

God's Call to Service,
Running or Redeeming?

WINSTON WILSON

BALBOA.
PRESS
A DIVISION OF HAY HOUSE

Balboa Press books may be ordered through booksellers or by contacting:
Balboa Press
A Division of Hay House
1663 Liberty Drive
Bloomington, IN 47403
www.balboapress.com
1-(877) 407-4847

ISBN: 978-1-4525-3999-7 (sc)
ISBN: 978-1-4525-3998-0 (e)
Library of Congress Control Number: 2011918296

All Scriptures are taken from the New International Version *(NIV) *
Unless otherwise stated. Copyright © 1973, 1978, 1984 By International Bible Society.

Other Scripture quotations are from the Kings James Version (KJV) of the Bible

American Standard Version (ASV) Copyright, 1901
By Thomas Nelson & Sons Copyright, 1929 By International Council of Religious Education

Printed in the United States of America
Balboa Press rev. date: 10/07/2011

I dedicate this book to

THE LORD OF GLORY

And to all its readers

Contents

Preface

This devotional book is based upon daily e-mail messages sent to my wife, friends and an ever widening circle of Christians both local and international.

The thoughts expressed in this book are taken from Jonah and I John. Jonah thought he could escape doing God's will by running away. He was soon to discover how determined God can be to get him to accomplish that mission. Running away from God will bring nothing but hardships in our lives as Jonah discovered. God controls the elements and in His providence He can unleash the forces of nature and circumstances against us so that we will reconsider our ways. Jonah learnt the hard way through chastening and scourging. He eventually surrendered to the will of God and went to the City of Nineveh and there proclaimed God's message to that city earmarked for destruction. That city repented and God extended His mercy to them and spared them. God has given us a serious assignment and that is to share this Good News with lost mankind. Dare we fail Him in the discharge of our duty? If Christ is Lord then we must do what He commands.

John on the other hand is inviting us to redeem the time. We have been brought into union with God through Christ and given eternal life. We live in a world that is hostile to God and everything that He values. We are called upon to walk in the light, to be a people separated unto God and His service. God has anointed us and we should walk in love towards each other. Prayer is an exercise in confident expectation in our God. God desires we enjoy our fellowship with Him and with each other. I pray that the thoughts expressed in this book will help to make your joy complete.

Winston Wilson

Thanks

It is a good thing to give thanks. Being thankful takes the focus from ourselves and put others on center stage. A thankful heart is one great way to reduce stress and anxiety for it elevates our spirits as we become other centered. Being thankful forces the mind into another mode and extracts and cultivates in our inner being a grateful spirit that beams and sparkles.

Being thankful allows us to see the good in others and to express it to them. I express my thanks and appreciation to my sister Audrey for going through this manuscript several times and for her helpful notes and suggestions. I am grateful to my editor, Dr. William (Billy) Hall for his advice and who painstakingly went through this document and helped to make it what it is. I am thankful for all my e-mail partners who encouraged me and blessed me with their gracious responses. Without them this book would have gone into limbo.

I am most thankful to my Lord and Savior Jesus Christ who got me up every morning and filled my mind with new messages. Even when my mind is blank and lacking in direction He comes through and thoughts begin to emerge to the praise of His glory. I am indeed thankful for God's faithfulness. I am thankful for the discipline He has put in my spirit and of course His patience with me. I am thankful for all the experiences He has brought in my life to enrich, empower and to enlighten. It is from our experiences that the Word of God becomes living and active and meaningful. With a grateful heart I can say, *"Thus far has the LORD helped me"* I Samuel 7:12 and for that I am thankful.

Winston Wilson

God's Call

"The word of the LORD came to Jonah son of Amittai: "Go to the great city of Nineveh and preach against it, because its wickedness has come up before me" Jonah 1:1-2.

REFLECTION

There is no greater privilege and responsibility given to man than to preach "Christ crucified" (I Corinthians 1:23). Every Christian has been chosen for the purpose of fulfilling that broad responsibility of preaching God's word.

Jonah's call was to do a specific task. How does one qualify to hear such a call? Isaiah heard the call of God after he had a vision of God; after his lips were cleansed; after his guilt was removed and after his sins were atoned for. A sure way then of hearing from God is to read and obey His Word and to be a person of prayer. Doing these things will ensure a clean and wholesome lifestyle and will result in active service in and out of the church.

When God's message comes to you it becomes a heavy burden until you deliver it faithfully; you cannot simply shrug it off or dismiss it. There will be no doubt in your inner being as to what God wants you to say or to do. It may be something He wants you to do on a specific occasion or it may be that which He wants to be your life's work.

The call of God will never conflict with the teachings of His Word. When the call of God comes to you, say like Samuel – *"Speak, for your servant is listening"* I Samuel 3:10. Listening to and obeying the voice of the Lord is crucial.

PRAYER

Lord, teach me to recognize your voice and to submit to your will always. Amen

WISDOM

Service to God has risks that are well worth taking!

Powerful Impressions

"The word of the LORD came to Jonah son of Amittai: "Go to the great city of Nineveh and preach against it, because its wickedness has come up before me"
Jonah 1:1-2.

REFLECTION

How can we know for sure if a powerful impression on our mind is of God? There are at least four possible sources of messages to the mind: (1) self, (2) demons, (3) angels, (4) God.

If we lend our minds to something we selfishly desire, we can deceive ourselves into believing that the message has been divinely revealed. Such 'revelations,' if believed, can only end in disaster and regret.

Christians are not immune to demonic activity and deception. Satan and his demons do operate as agents of light by imitating the ministry of the Holy Spirit. They are able to produce powerful impressions on the mind and so deceive the believer.

God sometimes communicates with us through His ministering spirits or angels. However, beware of the confusing work of the devil. In I John 4:1-3 we are warned "do not believe every spirit, but test the spirits to see whether they are from God." Because there are "deceiving spirits and things taught by demons" I Timothy 4:1.

Any message that fails to comply with the Word of God is false and must be rejected. Messages that conform to God's Word are indeed from God.

PRAYER

Lord, help me to always discern your voice speaking to me. Amen

WISDOM

God's Word is my best safeguard against the cunning wiles of the enemy.

Powerful Impressions

"The word of the LORD came to Jonah son of Amittai: "Go to the great city of Nineveh and preach against it, because its wickedness has come up before me" Jonah 1:1-2.

REFLECTION

God is, of course, the ultimate source of strong impressions on the human mind. He sometimes conveys His messages to us through angels. The prophets and apostles had numerous such encounters with God, and so do ordinary Christians, even today.

God also uses human messengers to convey His messages to us. In obedience to God's instructions, Isaiah the prophet told King Hezekiah that he would die. Hezekiah passionately pleaded with God to spare his life. As Isaiah was leaving the palace, God told him to go back and tell Hezekiah that fifteen years were to be added to his life.

God in His infinite wisdom, by various means deliberately communicates with us, His people, so that we may know His purpose and program for our lives.

Our minds are made fit and fertile for hearing God's messages when we think as Paul exhorts us to do in Philippians 4:8 - think on what is true, noble, right, pure, lovely, admirable, the excellent and the praise worthy.

God sometimes speaks to us in dramatic ways. At other times, it may be a conviction that becomes like a raging fire shut up in the bones (Jeremiah 20:9). When God speaks we cannot hold our peace (Acts 4:20).

PRAYER

Lord, help me to have a heart that will always hear your voice. Amen

WISDOM

Be still in His presence and you will hear His voice.

Powerful Impressions

*"**The word of the LORD came** to Jonah son of Amittai: "Go to the great city of Nineveh and preach against it, because its wickedness has come up before me"* Jonah 1:1-2.

REFLECTION

Sometime ago I was reading and meditating on the Word of God when without warning a powerful message from the passage grabbed my attention. It foretold of a dreadful event that would happen to me in the future and then after a period of time the matter would resolve itself. This message disturbed and distressed me mentally, emotionally and spiritually for weeks. Two years or so later the tragedy occurred. Having been forewarned by God prepared me to cope with the challenge.

God is now using this very experience as a means to strengthen others and to open up new areas of ministry that quite likely would not have been considered had not this event occurred.

God's word comes to us for various reasons. Sometimes it comes as a warning, or it may be a call to share our faith with a fellow worker, or a call to full time service. It could be a call to a specific area of ministry or a call to break off a relationship with an ungodly boyfriend or girlfriend.

The word of God still comes to you and me today and we can embrace it, ignore it or try to flee from it. God always gets His man in the end. Make it easy on yourself and submit to His will.

PRAYER

Lord, help me to cultivate the habit of recognizing your voice above the din of voices that try to get my attention. Amen

WISDOM

Don't wait on a powerful impression to do what the Bible clearly teaches.

Powerful Impressions

"The word of the LORD came to Jonah son of Amittai: "Go to the great city of Nineveh and preach against it, because its wickedness has come up before me" Jonah 1:1-2.

REFLECTION

God communicates His message not only to sanctified vessels but to unsavory characters.

Balaam was a false prophet yet He had powerful encounters with God. He predicted events regarding Israel's future Messiah. Though Balaam declared, *"I must speak only what God puts in my mouth"* Numbers 22:38, he was only in religion for gain. Jude confirms this in verse 11 of his book with the words, *"They have **rushed for profit** into **Balaam's error"*** Jude 11. Of false prophets Peter said, *"They have left the straight way and <u>wandered off to follow</u> the **way of Balaam** son of Beor, who <u>loved the wages of wickedness"</u>* II Peter 2:15.

Laban, in relating a dream he had to Jacob, his son-in-law said, *"But last night **the God of your father** said to me, 'Be careful not to say anything to Jacob, either good or bad"* Genesis 31:29.

The degenerate King Saul who prophesied in the name of the Lord in the time of Samuel (I Samuel 19:23) did not restrain his murderous intent to destroy David.

Paul spoke of men who for selfish ambition preached Christ out of envy and rivalry but were used of God to win souls for His Kingdom.

Strive always to be a vessel of honor for only such will be rewarded.

PRAYER

Lord, help me to incline my heart to always do your will sincerely. Amen

WISDOM

God is sovereign and free to do whatever pleases Him.

What's In A Name?

*"The word of the LORD came to **Jonah son of Amittai**: "Go to the great city of Nineveh and preach against it, because its wickedness has come up before me"* Jonah 1:1-2.

REFLECTION

In Bible times a name had significance and was even prophetic of a person's character. The angel Gabriel told Mary to name her Son 'Jesus' which means 'Savior' and Zechariah was told to name his son 'John' which means 'Jehovah has been gracious'. Amittai named his son 'Jonah' which means 'dove.'

The word 'dove' occurs 47 times in the Old Testament and ten times in the New. The dove is a clean bird and is first mentioned in the story of the flood. It was sent out to check if the land was ready for human habitation. The dove was offered by the poor as a sin offering, in the cleansing of lepers and for other ceremonial uncleanness.

The word 'dove' is used as a word of endearment and to describe the beauty of a woman's eyes and also her inward purity. The dove's mournful coo is symbolic of deep, inward sorrow and the affliction of the soul in the presence of God. The Psalmist desired to fly away like a dove to escape the sorrows that beset him. In the New Testament the dove is symbolic of The Holy Spirit.

We don't know why Amittai named his son Jonah. Was it because as a babe his son had beautiful eyes? Or was it prophetic that he would be a holy man of God? Or could it be that it was because he would try to flee from his commission to the Gentiles?

It is your character that gives true meaning and values to your name.

PRAYER

Lord, help me to give positive, spiritual meaning to my life. Amen

WISDOM

Be a person of worth.

Passing On The Truth

*"The word of the LORD came to **Jonah son of Amittai:** "Go to the great city of Nineveh and preach against it, because its wickedness has come up before me"* Jonah 1:1-2.

REFLECTION

Jonah, son of Amittai, is the same Jonah of II Kings 14:25. He is identified there as *"Jonah son of Amittai, the prophet from Gath Hepher."* What he predicted as the prophet of God came to pass in the days of Jeroboam son of Jehoash.

Now the meaning of Amittai is 'truth.' Jonah was the son of 'Truth.' This is something worth pondering. This precious virtue is fast disappearing from our families. There are far too many children from our homes who are not schooled in the truth of God's Word. We, as a people, are so busy grasping for the material, that imparting God's precious truth is slipping through the cracks in family life.

Jonah was 'schooled in truth' and that is more to be desired than the refinements of a 'pagan culture' that we desire our children to have today – a culture that we were denied when growing up. What value is there in having a sophisticated child who is ignorant of matters of the soul?

As a father, you owe your offspring God's truth. Jonah got it from his dad and was later called of God to be a prophet. Today, thousands of years later, Jonah son of Amittai is remembered and his short message is still being studied. Truth, God's truth, elevates the person, renews the spirit and prepares us for eternity.

PRAYER

Lord, help me to bring up my children to love, respect and honor your truth. Amen

WISDOM

What great joy there is for parents to lead their children to Christ!

God's Go

*"The word of the LORD **came** to Jonah son of Amittai: "**Go** to the great city of Nineveh and preach against it, because its wickedness has come up before me"* Jonah 1:1-2.

REFLECTION

When God **commissions** we must go and do as He says. When God brings to our consciousness the spiritual needs of others, and rouses our spirits or inflames the desires of our hearts, He is preparing us to 'go.'

God's strong commands are never aimless, but targeted, direct, and specific. Jonah had no doubt in his mind as to what God wanted him to do. He got a strong command. God's 'go' always requires immediate response because judgment is always pending; we should therefore go without delay to those to whom we are sent. God's go demands unconditional obedience.

Regrettably, the commissioned too often try to escape from their divine responsibilities, even with feeble excuses such as - 'I am a young Christian.' So What? Have you ever thought of Paul? Right after his conversion he began preaching that Jesus is the Christ. You don't have to be the son of a prophet to share the message with the lost. You have a testimony - start with that. A testimony is a most effective tool. Daily reading of the Word will accelerate your Christian growth and development and make you a better instrument in the hands of God.

If the call of God is upon your life, and if you are a Christian, then you ought to do His will - get up and go. Your Nineveh may be your office or your home or your school or the playfield or friends. The mission field is wherever there are persons lost in sin. It could even be just sending this message to someone who needs it.

PRAYER

Lord, help me to hear your voice and respond positively. Amen

WISDOM

We have a message of hope for the damned; let's not delay in telling it.

Nineveh's Heritage

*"The word of the LORD came to Jonah son of Amittai: "Go to the **great city of Nineveh** and preach against it, because its wickedness has come up before me"* Jonah 1:1-2.

REFLECTION

Jonah was sent to preach in the great city of Nineveh. The founder of that city was Nimrod, a mighty warrior. He built Babylon, Nineveh and other cities (Genesis 10:8-12). The ruins of this great Assyrian city are located in Iraq on the bank of the Tigris River. That great City was conquered by the Babylonians and its allies in 612B.C. The Prophet Nahum predicted the overthrow of Nineveh in very graphic language.

Nimrod the founder of these cities was an ungodly man. It was he who was the prime architect of the Tower of Babel. Is it not amazing how influential is the legacy of founding fathers? What will be the influence of your life's legacy to succeeding generations?

Nimrod was notorious for his cruelty and the Assyrians followed in his steps. Nahum, the prophet of God who predicted the destruction of Nineveh declared, *"From you, O Nineveh, has one come forth who plots evil against the LORD and counsels wickedness.* Nahum 1:11. Again he states, *"Woe to the city of blood, full of lies, full of plunder, never without victims!* Nahum 3:1.

Ah! What is true of a city is also true of a family. If we establish our homes on wickedness, then our evil will affect generations to come. But if we establish our homes on the foundation of truth and God, we will have the blessing of God on generations yet unborn.

PRAYER

Lord, help me to leave a legacy worthy of emulation. Amen

WISDOM

The path we choose is in our hands.

A Wicked City And God

*"The word of the LORD came to Jonah son of Amittai: "Go to the **great city of Nineveh** and preach against it, because its wickedness has come up before me"* Jonah 1:1-2.

REFLECTION

A great city is a great achievement. This is because a great city is a reflection of the human soul and as such is a manifestation of its inner workings. A great city is the melting pot of what constitutes the way of life for a people. A city then, though great may be anything but good.

The most powerful single element of a city is its religion. Depraved religion gives birth to corrupt moral behavior, marginalizes family life, produces a vile culture and gives birth to oppressive government. A city given over to idolatry is a city under the power of Satan. Corrupt religion breeds vices that are vile, repulsive and demonic.

God takes note of the activities of cities and visits them either in judgment or revival. There is a point when the cup of iniquity of a city becomes full and so is ripe for judgment. Then, such a city maybe overwhelmed by sudden destruction as was the case of Sodom.

There came a time when Nineveh came under God's scrutiny for judgment. God warns before He acts. Nineveh's cup had reached its capacity and judgment was pending. So He commissioned Jonah as His special agent for the task of preaching against its standard of morality.

What is the condition of my city? Is it the reflection of my soul? Should I divorce myself from the vices and violence that saturate it? Is my voice being heard? Should I try to isolate myself from its evils? Am I not God's salt and God's light in this corrupt and dark city?

PRAYER

Lord, help me to make a dynamic difference in my city. Amen

WISDOM

One person can make a great difference in a city.

God's Messenger

*"The word of the LORD came to Jonah son of Amittai: "Go to the great city of Nineveh and **preach against it**, because its wickedness has come up before me"*
Jonah 1:1-2.

REFLECTION

Preaching is a powerful tool that God uses to convey His message to lost mankind. The preacher in the hand of God can effect great change in the life of an individual, a community, a city or a nation. By the means of preaching, God, the Holy Spirit, uses human messengers to convict of sin, righteousness and coming judgment.

There is no Word more powerful to awaken a sin-benighted soul to the need of God's salvation than that which comes from the Bible. No matter how callous a soul might be, the Word of God can pierce that thick armor and make such a one into a tender hearted believer. The Word of God probes and awakens the conscience to the terror of God's judgment. The Word removes the superficial clothing of self- righteousness and leads us to become aware of our spiritual nakedness in the sight of God.

Jonah was God's human instrument to the sinners of Nineveh. His message was to be negative. He was to preach **against** the city of Nineveh. One cannot preach such a message with glee. One cannot preach of hell and not be conscious of its eternal horrors. One cannot preach of impending judgment and be dry-eyed. A preacher must enter the content and spirit of his message, whether speaking to an individual, or preaching to a congregation.

As a Christian, you are God's messenger. Are you delivering God's message to the lost?

PRAYER

Lord, help me to be a herald of your truth day by day. Amen

WISDOM

Christians are chosen by God to communicate Christ.

Your Conduct And God

*"The word of the LORD came to Jonah son of Amittai: "Go to the great city of Nineveh and preach against it, **because its wickedness has come up before me"***
Jonah 1:1-2.

REFLECTION

We should live to please God. We are stewards of our lives and our possessions. We are accountable to God for all we are and have. If we choose to live wisely God will bless us. If we choose to live wickedly God will reward us according to our deeds.

Fortunately for us, God is slow to anger and very patient with man, His fallen creature. So often, He gives us one more chance. If we entrust our lives to Him He will reward us abundantly.

Yet, God's mercy, grace, goodness and compassion must never be taken for granted. These are the 'tools' He uses to bring us to the knowledge of Himself. Despise them, or treat them contemptuously, or simply ignore them, and you will regret it. To shun God in this life is to ask for **Distress and Trouble**.

God is holy and He must deal with all flagrant disregards of His person and His favor. If we think He has forgotten our vile and hurtful behavior, we had better think again.

In Jonah's day, when Nineveh's day of reckoning was before God, when those wicked people were about to be visited, when they had their last chance of either to repent or be destroyed, they repented and were saved from destruction. The same can happen to you. Repent now, and experience God's forgiveness.

PRAYER

Lord, help me to repent today. Amen

WISDOM

Actions have consequences.

Running Away?

*"But **Jonah ran away from the LORD** and headed for Tarshish. He went down to Joppa, where he found a ship bound for that port. After paying the fare, he went aboard and sailed for Tarshish **to flee from the LORD"***
Jonah 1:3

REFLECTION

Jonah's attempted flight from God seems so foolish. Changing our geographical location does not in anyway affect the omnipresence of God. The Psalmist David contemplated doing that very thing hundreds of years earlier and penned these words, *"**Where can I go** from Your Spirit? **Where can I flee** from your presence? If I go up to the heavens, you are there; if I make my bed in the depths, you are there. If I rise on the wings of the dawn, if I settle on the far side of the sea, even there Your hand will guide me, Your right hand will hold me fast"* Psalm 139:7-10.

We cannot escape God's presence or judgment yet; many today seem to think they can. So many children, teenagers and adults foolishly use the cover of darkness to commit sin. But God sees as clearly in the night as He does in the day. There is nothing that can be hidden from God.

The spirit of disobedience produces spiritual distortions within, which in turn produces muddled and confused actions without. But sin is like that; it makes fools of all of us.

Consequently there is no one, who at one time or another, has not tried to escape from God and His call for service. We know it is foolish, yet we do it anyway.

PRAYER

Lord, help me to be obedient to you whatever the task. Amen

WISDOM

God sees all, knows all and is everywhere.

Planned Escape

*"But Jonah ran away from the LORD and headed for Tarshish. He went down to Joppa, where he found a ship bound for that port. After paying the fare, **he went aboard and sailed for Tarshish to flee** from the LORD"*
Jonah 1:3

REFLECTION

God gave Jonah a mission. He had no heart for it so he began to plan how he might get out of it. Two forces immediately came into operation to highjack the mind – the force of the old self and the force of the devil. Their task is to create barriers. They always seek to frustrate the will of God. They always seek to raise objections in the mind and to still the voice of conscience.

Therefore, because Jonah gave heed to these forces a battle raged in his mind. Jonah no doubt had fierce and exhausting struggles with God's command. To quell the clear and distinct call of God echoing in the soul is no easy undertaking. When the decision was finally made, Jonah sided with the old self and the devil.

Once the decision was made, he acted quickly. He decided to migrate. He took his life's savings and headed **down** to Joppa. While this 'down' has a lot to do with geographical location, there is a significant lesson in it for us. Departure from the will of God is always a **downward journey.**

Are you like Jonah planning to take a vacation from God's program and plan for your life? The first visible manifestation is usually a break from church attendance.

PRAYER

Lord, help me to fulfill the task you have put into my hands. Amen

WISDOM

Fleeing from God is folly.

Paying The Price

*"But Jonah ran away from the LORD and headed for Tarshish. He went down to Joppa, where he found a ship bound for that port. After **paying the fare**, he went aboard and sailed for Tarshish to flee from the LORD"*
Jonah 1:3

REFLECTION

Important decisions demand commitment. Jonah was committed to his course of action. **He paid the fare.**

The likelihood of his changing his mind at that point in time was highly unlikely. He was committed to a path of disobedience. He was prepared to take the risk of being out of the will of God. Like the prodigal, he was about to embark on a trip to a 'far country' and to start life afresh without God.

So many who once walked with God have now taken that 'Jonah Road.' Their minds have become so infatuated with the desire to escape their moral responsibility that no serious thought will now deter them from ever changing their minds. What looks so promising now to the deceived mind will become their most dreadful nightmare.

The allurements of the world, the flesh and the devil have a charm that conceals the barbed hook. What now looks so promising and full of hope will soon engulf the soul in painful misery and sorrow.

When God's will become unattractive to you then - beware! Grave danger is just ahead of you.

PRAYER

Lord, help me to please you always. Amen

WISDOM

God's will is always best.

Paying The Price

*"But Jonah ran away from the LORD and headed for Tarshish. He went down to Joppa, where he found a ship bound for that port. After **paying the fare**, he went aboard and sailed for Tarshish to flee from the LORD"*
Jonah 1:3

REFLECTION

Paying the fare will not get us there! Jonah paid the fare and departed for Tarshish – the wrong place. Departure for the wrong place is departure from the LORD. This process begins in the heart and gradually or sometimes swiftly engulfs our entire being as we try to escape our spiritual responsibilities.

Copping out is not peculiar to Jonah. It is a common problem in the Church and in Para-church organizations.

Once disloyalty to God surfaces, a trip to 'the port' of escape will become a logical option. It is there the 'fare' is paid to release one from necessary moral and spiritual obligation. The final step in backsliding is 'boarding' the ship to Tarshish.

The disobedient tends to get their theology quite muddled. Running away from responsibility generally breeds half baked and poorly thought out excuses. Running away from a problem only compounds it and creates additional ones. Taking a wrong turn at a crossroads takes us further away from our destination. We cannot run from God and expect to be free.

Are you running away from God's will for your life?

PRAYER

Lord, help me to confess to you my tendencies to backslide. Amen

WISDOM

Folly becomes evident in sober moments.

Perils Of The Backslider

*"Then the LORD sent a **great wind** on the sea, and such a **violent storm** arose that the **ship threatened to break up**"*
Jonah 1:4.

REFLECTION

Backsliding has perils. The moment the heart begins to backslide, the wheels of heaven are set in motion to restore such a one. God uses different methods to chasten us.

Any child of God who decides to walk contrary to God will be chastened. The chastening begins at the very moment of departure, but because of the mindset of the disobedient Christian the voice of God is not immediately heard and acknowledged. Jonah thought he had escaped God. Everything seemed to have been running smoothly for him when suddenly a violent storm, ordered by God, arose.

When God sets out to get you, He will use even the elements of nature to accomplish His purpose. The entire universe is at His command. Certainly, therefore, the winds are at His beck and call. Yes, God will sometimes use extreme measures to get our attention, as He did for Jonah.

Your 'violent storm' could be loss of a job, or a dreadful sickness, or death of a loved one, or unusual difficulty at work, or just anxiety and confusion. God can use whatever He chooses to unnerve you and make you feel the 'bottom' of your life is falling out.

God knows how to effectively get our attention when we go against His will and the mission He has assigned us.

Are you doing what God has called you to do?

PRAYER

Lord, help me to walk in obedience to your will for my life. Amen

WISDOM

Chastening is a sign that God loves us.

Moments Of Crisis

*"All the **sailors were afraid and each cried out** to his own god. And they threw the cargo into the sea to lighten the ship"*
Jonah 1:5a.

REFLECTION

Moments of crisis mark our lives and reveal our frail character. Life threatening events bring out the terror that resides in the heart of every person. Even someone trained to work on the high seas, when experiencing crisis, is likely to become terrified as the waters become turbulent. Someone trained for military combat can become terrified when thrust into real warfare. We are like that – made to fear naturally.

When we are faced with new and unaccustomed circumstances in life, over which we have no control, fear comes to the fore and in such circumstances we may not know how we will react. We learn things about ourselves when faced with situations that make us fear.

Fear shows us to be vulnerable and displays our limitation. In moments of fear we may embrace something false, if it gives us a sense of hope.

Because we all hold life to be precious, when endangered we reach out in hope. Each person on Jonah's ship reached out, in fear, as well as with hope, however true or false. With unabashed passion each man cried out to his god. In emergencies, religion becomes very personal, be it true or false. In emergencies even the shy lay aside their reservations and cry out loudly and excitedly to some source of hope for rescue.

Are you in an emergency? Then cry out – God will hear and respond. How wonderful to know that our God hears and cares, and rescues and redeems. In your moments of distress call upon Him and He will deliver you.

PRAYER

Lord, help me to trust you in moments of crisis. Amen

WISDOM

Behavior in crisis reveals who we are.

Moments Of Crisis

*"All the sailors were afraid and each cried out to his own god. And **they threw the cargo into the sea** to lighten the ship"*
Jonah 1:5a.

REFLECTION

Moments of crisis help us to make up our minds as to what is valuable. In such moments we decide what is precious. We go through life carrying so much 'cargo' that is of little value.

Jesus invited people who were burdened with the cares of this world to unburden themselves by coming to Him. When you come to Christ you will discover that burdens are lifted at the Throne of Grace and there you will find the calm that your heart longs for.

Is it not strange how a crisis can bring harmony in a home, or a community or a nation? Where there were tension and a lack of cooperation, in an emergency we tend to forget those differences and work together as one. Before a crisis we may have given 50% or less of ourselves in effort, but in a crisis we give 100%.

In a crisis the desire to promote 'self' and its interests evaporates into nothingness and team work generally becomes the order of the day. Crisis tends to bring to the fore potentials that we never knew we had within us and immediately it is put to work in creative ways. A crisis makes us realize that we need a Supreme Being in our lives who will aid us when we are vulnerable.

If you find your need of Him to be critical in a crisis, why don't you make Him a part of your life now?

PRAYER

Lord, help me to depend upon you in moments of crisis. Amen

WISDOM

God reigns in every crisis.

Copping Out?

*"All the sailors were afraid and each cried out to his own god. And they threw the cargo into the sea to lighten the ship. But **Jonah had gone below deck**, where he lay down and **fell into a deep sleep**"*
Jonah 1:5.

REFLECTION

Jonah was trying to escape by sea and by sleep! As the storm raged at sea, threatening life, Jonah was asleep below deck. On deck, there was panic among the sailors. 'A religious revival' was in progress. Each man was calling upon his god for deliverance. There was feverish activity as they hurled some of the cargo overboard to try to save themselves from a watery grave.

But Jonah, the backslider, was below deck, away from the pandemonium, fast asleep. He was not even conscious of the grave situation his life was in. All he wanted was to find a quiet spot to sleep. He found it, and sank into a deep sleep.

Some people find it easy to sleep when in trouble. Every opportunity they get they take a nap; thinking it would seem, that sleep is the antidote for their problems. Others may try to drown their problems with alcohol and drugs. Some people even exit this life by suicide. But for Jonah, sleep was the answer. You don't have to face the issues if you are asleep, do you?

But the truth is that no problem that is gnawing at your mind, emotions and spirit can be resolved through sleep, for when you awake, the problem is still there. Jonah, who was trying to escape from himself by relocating geographically, was trying to escape by sleep. Running away has diminishing returns. You have to face reality squarely in the face.

PRAYER

Lord, help me to face my problems and cast them on you. Amen

WISDOM

Real problem must be faced realistically.

A Rebuke

*"The captain went to him and said, "**How can you sleep?** Get up and call on your God! Maybe he will take notice of us, and we will not perish"*
Jonah 1:6.

REFLECTION

The ungodly sometimes have to rebuke the godly! How sad when a non-Christian rebukes a Christian. How sad when he who is the salt and light in the world fails in his moral obligations. How disappointing when everyone else is perplexed and desperate above deck, but below deck, the Christian is fast asleep.

Imagine the horror of the reality – while society is in the midst of a storm of social unrest, characterized by marriages falling apart, family life in disarray, communities divided, crime and violence stalking the land and fear overwhelming our people – Christians are asleep!

How can we be asleep when false religions and the cults are overrunning our country? How can we be asleep when ungodliness and irreverence are on the rise and God's Word is under attack?

The lesson from Jonah's experience is clear – it is an urgent call being made by many responsible people in the society for the Church to wake up and call urgently on God. Believers are being urged to petition God on behalf of the national ship which is being tossed about by strong winds of immorality, illegal drug dealing and gross iniquity.

Dare we sleep at such a time as this? How awake are you?

PRAYER

Lord, help me to perform my Christian duty at such a time as this. Amen

WISDOM

Rebuke by the ungodly is a divine weapon!

How Can You Sleep?

*"The captain went to him and said, "**How can you sleep**? Get up and call on your God! Maybe he will take notice of us, and we will not perish"*
Jonah 1:6.

REFLECTION

The soul loosed from its divine mooring is set adrift on the sea of life – spiritually endangered. In that situation, out of the will of God, we become like Samson without hair, and so weak. In that condition we become devoid of power, passion, drive, will and spiritual enthusiasm. We become listless and handicapped.

Soon, we are overtaken by deep spiritual slumber and spiritual dormancy, spiritual sloth and carnality. Disconnected from God we plunge to spiritual depths of apathy.

How can such spiritual decline happen to a Christian? It happens when we neglect fellowship and communion with God. Then our spirits become alienated and we lose our spiritual purpose and direction and hence fall into spiritual slumber and deep sleep. A dysfunctional Christian has no earthly use for the Kingdom of God, and so is rightly described as 'asleep'. Their sleep is not the sleep for rest, but the sleep of escape from duty and responsibility.

In such a spiritual condition, we need to heed the urgent cry: *"Get up and call on your God."* If you are sleepy or asleep the Apostle Paul counsels you, *"Wake up from slumber because our salvation is nearer now than when we first believed"* Romans 13:11.

PRAYER

Lord, help me to be always alert and active in your service. Amen

WISDOM

Keep in touch with God and you will never fall into spiritual slumber.

A Maybe God? No Never!

*"The captain went to him and said, **"How can you sleep?** Get up and call on your God! **Maybe he will** take notice of us, and we will not perish"*
Jonah 1:6.

REFLECTION

We have a God who can deliver? He is not a 'maybe God,' or a God of indifference to our agony or sorrow. He cares for the sparrows, the flowers and the very grass. He knows our distresses. He is aware of our needs and He takes no pleasure in afflicting us.

When we put our trust and confidence in Him, He will make Himself known to us in the midst of our 'storm.' When there is no way He will make one. He is the God who can provide water out of solid rock. He does deliver in the midst of the fiery furnace and in the den of fierce and hungry lions.

He does take notice of us when we feel threatened and fearful and does provide courage for us to come out victorious and unharmed.

Do not doubt the ability of our God when we pray. He has a proven track record. He is mighty to deliver from the hands of those who would harm us on a construction site. He is mighty to deliver us in the office from unscrupulous people, or on the streets where evil stalks, and preserve the family from going under.

God does take note of us wherever we are and does provide for whatever we need. Have faith in God in whatever circumstance you might find yourself today. Call upon Him, for He will answer in unexpected ways.

PRAYER

Lord, help me to trust you as a caring God. Amen

WISDOM

Confidence placed in God is not confidence misplaced.

Suspected

*"Then the sailors said to each other, "Come, **let us cast lots to find out** who is responsible for this calamity." They cast lots and the lot fell on Jonah"*
Jonah 1:7.

REFLECTION

Jonah was suspected before he was detected. Ever been in a situation where you suspect that somebody is responsible for the unusual events that have been occurring? There is the lurking feeling that someone is guilty of an offense with which God is very displeased with and that this person must be identified to prevent further disaster. That seemed to have been Jonah's case.

Sin is never a private matter. No sin affects only the offender. Jonah's sin endangered an entire ship - its goods, its crew and its passengers. The sin of the individual affects the community and so endangers many others.

Achan's sin, in the time of Joshua, affected an entire army and had them reeling in defeat. King David sinned and an entire nation felt the effect. The social implication of sin is enormous. It is like a deadly virus that enters the body and before long overwhelms the entire body. Sin allowed is sin encouraged.

The sailors suspected that something was not right and they acted quickly. Allow sin to fester and gangrene is on its way. Allow the gangrene free course and amputation or death is bound to follow.

Have you a secret sin?

PRAYER

Lord, help me to deal with my sin right away. Amen

WISDOM

Unconfessed sin is septic.

Exposed

*"Then the sailors said to each other, "Come, let us cast lots to find out who is responsible for this calamity." They cast lots and **the lot fell on Jonah**"*
Jonah 1:7.

REFLECTION

Jonah was exposed when the lot fell on him. The providence of God has a way of catching up with us when we are out of the will of God. Jonah was trying to evade his prophetic responsibility when seemingly nature conspired against him with a violent storm.

During the storm, he is then discovered to be fast asleep below deck, in the midst of his crisis. He is aroused to prayer, but his prayer is useless because he is in no condition to talk to God, for there is iniquity in His heart.

How terrible it is for a Christian to be found unable to make contact with God because of unconfessed sin in his life. In fact, how tragic it is when a Christian is discovered to be the very source of the problem. Imagine such a Christian being called upon to pray for a person, or a person who is on the verge of committing suicide, and all that Christian can do is to go through the treadmill of prayer to no avail.

When such Christians pray the calamity only worsens. What is your spiritual state? It is time to search our hearts for an answer. A crisis could come suddenly and expose the true spiritual condition of our hearts revealing the desperate condition of our souls before God.

PRAYER

Lord, help me to purge myself of secret sins. Amen

WISDOM

In a crisis, unconfessed sin is a curse.

Identified By Lot

"Then the sailors said to each other, "Come, let us cast lots to find out who is responsible for this calamity." They cast lots and **the lot fell on Jonah***"*
Jonah 1:7.

REFLECTION

Casting of lot to decide an issue was widely used in ancient times. *"Casting the lot settles disputes and keep strong opponents apart"* Proverbs 18:18. It was used as an appeal to deity to determine what was to be done in different and difficult situations. *"The lot is cast into the lap, but its every decision is from the Lord"* Proverbs 16:33.

There are many passages in the Old Testament that give examples of decisions arrived at by using lot. The original allotments of land to seven tribes of Israel were determined by lot (Joshua 18:7). In times of war, the Jewish tribe who should first engage the enemy was determined by lot (Judges 20:9). The matter of identifying a guilty person was done by lot (I Samuel 14:41).

In our text, the sailors determined to uncover the culprit who was responsible for this life threatening calamity. They resorted to lots and the lot fell on the guilty Jonah.

No silent prayer urgently sent up to God could avert his exposure. This was the man that God was pursuing and this was the man his fellow-travelers identified as the cause of their woes.

We cannot run away from God, can we? Things were not going Jonah's way, and neither will our way be favored with the blessings of God, if we turn our backs on our commitment to God.

PRAYER

Lord, help me to keep my commitment to you. Amen

WISDOM

Your sin will find you out.

Is Lot Valid For Today?

SCRIPTURE   January 27

*"Then the sailors said to each other, "**Come, let us cast lots to find out** who is responsible for this calamity." They cast lots and the lot fell on Jonah"*
Jonah 1:7.

REFLECTION

Jonah was uncovered by the casting of lots but is the method still valid? In this Age of Grace and the Holy Spirit should Christians use lots to determine God's will? What says the New Testament? The only mention of the method being used is by the 'church to be' (Acts 1:26).

It was the method used in that single 'transitional period', combined with prayer, to determine who would replace Judas in the apostolic band. However, the church has the full revelation of God to decide all matters of faith. Therefore the church today, by prayer, the Word and the Holy Spirit makes all important decisions.

Certainly, it seems clear God has now placed in His church the gift of discernment. Ananias, trying to 'pull a fast one' on the church did not survive to make his boast, for the Spirit through Peter exposed his evil intent. What the Church needs today are men and women in touch with the Spirit of God, gifted to discern the mind of God for our times.

When the gift of discernment is exercised no church filled with the Spirit, will be a haven for sin. No church under the control of the Spirit will need to be casting lots for election of officers, or exposing the guilty in her midst or deciding when or where to have street meetings. Every local church should be able to discern the mind of the Lord and determine what God would have them do in difficult situations.

How do you make your important decisions?

PRAYER

Lord, help me to depend on the Spirit for my decisions in life. Amen

WISDOM

Before making a decision, consult God.

Cross Examined!

*"So they asked him "**Tell us**, who is responsible for making all this trouble for us? **What** do you do? **Where** do you come from? **What** is your country? **From what** people are you?""*
Jonah 1:8.

REFLECTION

Trouble tends to worsen. This was the experience of Jonah. He was caught and now was being peppered with questions. His captors demanded straight answers. There was Jonah feeling stupid. The plans he had imagined that would get him away from the reach of God had backfired.

The fury of their questions tumbling over each other matched the fury of the storm. The questions were personal and searching. The sailors were in no mood for evasive answers. Their suspect, whom they believed to be the cause of their predicament, had better start talking the truth quickly.

The groans and the creaking of their bobbing ship demanded urgent answers. The taste of salt water was on their lips and the sting was in their eyes. The angry waves had them drenched from head to toe.

They believed that the hope of their survival was now in the hands of the man they had before them. Would he be honest with them? Would he be honest before God? Would he play the role of 'the man' or would he be evasive in this decisive moment and further threaten the lives of these terrified people?

What about you and me? Are we ready to admit guilt when we are in the wrong? Are we prepared to be honest with those whose future may depend upon our frank and honest answers?

PRAYER

Lord, help me to be courageous and honest when I am wrong. Amen

WISDOM

Blunt questions need honest answers.

Cornered!

*"So they asked him "Tell us, **who is responsible for making all this trouble for us?** What do you do? Where do you come from? What is your country? From what people are you?""*
Jonah 1:8.

REFLECTION

Running from God leads to a dead end in life. Sooner or later the adventure we thought so promising turns sour or into a nightmare. Sidelining God in our lives will come to an abrupt end. Sooner than later, and the sooner the better, we must confront ourselves, even perhaps through painful circumstances we never conceived in our minds.

Jonah experienced such painful circumstances. When he did, there was no smile on his face, he trembled, self condemned. He was now wiser but sad. Sin increases sorrow. Satan deceives to destroy. Do not play into his hands. Repent and let God use you to His glory.

The backslider tends to be persistently stubborn. Could anyone have persuaded Jonah not to take that reckless course in life? I think not! Could anyone have persuaded the prodigal son that the path he was about to embark on would lead to degradation and poverty? I am pretty certain his father counseled him, but the counsel was like water on a duck's back. Could anyone have persuaded Hosea's wife, Gomer that her wayward path would lead to shame and slavery? I think not!

Once the human mind is made up on a course of action, persuasion rarely works. Our sin and folly are sometimes our greatest 'correctors'. Jonah was now learning that hard lesson.

What about you? Are you too, like Jonah, on a ship to 'Tarshish'?

PRAYER

Lord, help me to yield to you today. Amen

WISDOM

A word to the wise is sufficient.

Confession!

*"He answered, **I am a Hebrew and I worship The LORD**, the God of heaven, who made the sea and the land"*
Jonah 1:9.

REFLECTION

The sailors asked for an honest confession and that is what they got. Jonah admitted to two important things in this verse: one, he was a Hebrew, and the other, he worshipped God.

The first mention of the word 'Hebrew' is to be found in Genesis 14:13. It speaks of Abram, the Hebrew, the father of the Hebrew people and a man of great faith in the Living God, Jehovah. Through Abram, whose name was changed to Abraham, God promised to bless multitudes. The Hebrews, who also became known as Israelites, were seen as a nation of Jehovah's favor, for God delivered Israel from cruel Egyptian bondage and made with Israel an everlasting covenant. It was to the Hebrew people that God committed the revelation of Himself and His Word.

The Hebrew people were indeed special or a 'peculiar' people, whom God had called out of darkness into His light to bear witness of Him to the entire world. The Apostle Paul, writing to the Philippians, boasts of his human pedigree when he declared that he was, *"A Hebrew of Hebrews"* Philippians 3:5.

Do you know who you are? What would be the first thing to come from your mouth as to your true identity? Would it be? "I am a Christian?" Or would it be 'I am a Jamaican' or 'American' or 'I am an accountant,' or mechanic,' 'an engineer'? Whatever you regard as most important is what your lips will utter, when you declare who you are.

PRAYER

Lord, help me to know who I am. Amen

WISDOM

The lips will confess what is uppermost on the heart.

Confession!

*"He answered, **I am a Hebrew and I worship The LORD**, the God of heaven, who made the sea and the land"*
Jonah 1:9.

REFLECTION

Jonah knew his family tree and spiritual heritage. Knowing our line of descent is important. It can work to our advantage in the grand scheme of life. Sometimes our pedigree can get us into positions of influence.

But sometimes our roots can go against us. Yes, there can be a family record that will cause us to struggle all our lives to gain credibility and acceptance. Nevertheless, with God's help, we can be overcomers.

The second part of Jonah's confession is even more important than the first. You can have pedigree and yet be lost. You can be a physical descendant of Abraham and still don't know God. In other words, despite having in our family tree spiritual giants or heroes of the Christian faith, we still can be lost. This reality is now very common in the occident, for previous generations looked more to God.

Becoming a Christian then, is more than heritage. We cannot become a Christian by mere heritage or association with Christians. To become a Christian you must have a personal experience with God. It is a spiritual encounter one and one with the Living God. This experience goes beyond any ritual. Jonah knew about this contact with God. Were he alive today he would not be talking about being a member of a church, but of a real, warm, vibrant relationship with God.

It is strange how unusual events can stir our faith and renew our conviction and our relationship with the Lord. This runaway servant of God was now coming to terms with his God. Are you?

PRAYER

Lord, help me to live out my confession of you. Amen

WISDOM

Adversity can deepen spirituality.

Worship

*"He answered, I am a Hebrew and **I worship The LORD**, the God of heaven, who made the sea and the land"*
Jonah 1:9.

REFLECTION

Some Christians associate worship with any church service held on a Sunday while others associate worship with the celebration of the Lord's Supper. Both groups identify worship with corporate activity. But worship is not necessarily only a corporate activity.

Individual worship must be considered. Even during corporate worship there ought to be individual worship and so there is invariably present those who go through the paces in corporate worship but do not enter into the spirit of the congregational exercise of worship.

Individual worship can be a wonderful experience. Worship is a matter of the heart and its intimacy is realized when contract with the covenant keeping God is established. Our individual spirits may soar on the wings of cherub and thus enter the Throne Room of Heaven permitting us to behold God's Majesty and recognize His worth and so, bow in His presence in true worship.

Jonah's declaration was about identification, not exultation. He was saying in effect, 'I acknowledge the LORD.' But that statement can be made in exultation, if indeed we soar in spirit to the divine Throne of Grace, exalting the Savior.

Furthermore, this wonderful experience can be ours despite our circumstances. We can bow our souls before God and worship in circumstances of adversity or prosperity. Do you worship sincerely when your circumstances are bad?

PRAYER

Lord, teach me to worship you in all circumstances of life. Amen

WISDOM

Worship in adversity displays pure Christianity.

Impediments To Worship

*"He answered, I am a Hebrew and **I worship The LORD**, the God of heaven, who made the sea and the land"*
Jonah 1:9.

REFLECTION

There are times in our lives when worship is a struggle or even an impossible feat. One such time is, if like Jonah, we are running away from God. Worship demands a pure heart and disobedience robs us of that. The moment the heart swerves from the path of righteousness worship is degraded.

Having a rival to God is another impediment to worship, for God's requirement of us is total. Anything or anyone that rivals the time or energy or resources we must give to God is an idol. God ordered Abraham to offer his son Isaac as a burnt offering to Him. Isaac had become, it seems, an idol in the life of Abraham and this was the only way God could get him back on the right path. God will brook no rivals.

A spouse can become an idol, so too a child. Anything can supplant God in the life of a person - a car, a house, a job – and the list goes on. Whatever inordinately consumes our affection, time, and energy or expenditure will eventually become a god. We must carefully guard our hearts against any object, or activity or person or occupation challenging or replacing God in our lives. God is a jealous God and He will not give His glory to another.

Are you experiencing true worship?

PRAYER

Lord, help me to put away the things that hinder worship. Amen

WISDOM

True worship is pure.

Impediments To Worship

*"He answered, I am a Hebrew and **I worship The LORD**, the God of heaven, who made the sea and the land"*
Jonah 1:9.

REFLECTION

Jonah's declaration of faith in God is defined by the experience of worship. God desires worship and decrees the conditions of its acceptability.

Worship is the highest human experience. There is nothing more important. Yet there are things in our lives that can hinder worship, for they put a barrier between our souls and God.

For instance, if we harbor an unforgiving spirit, or if we tell lies, worship then becomes impossible.

When greed and unjust practices stain our lives, then bowing in worship is all sham. When we treat with contempt anyone made in God's image – God will hide His face from us.

When we fail to confess known sins in our lives, God will give us no audience. No true worship can take place when our hearts condemn us. Sin must be removed before true worship can commence.

What a thrilling experience is true worship. How refreshing and uplifting to commune with God, exalting His Person, appreciating His Calvary work, magnifying His name. Earth's pleasures pale in comparison to such heavenly joy.

PRAYER

Lord, help me to remove today all barriers to true worship of you. Amen

WISDOM

To ensure honesty of heart is being smart.

Worship - An Encounter

*"He answered, I am a Hebrew and **I worship The LORD**, the God of heaven, who made the sea and the land"*
Jonah 1:9.

REFLECTION

Sincere worship is always in the presence of God. This means that the physical location can be anywhere. Worship is the innermost part of our being becoming aware of the majesty, greatness, power, glory, acts and holiness of God. Worship occurs when we are overwhelmed by the awe of God's splendor. Worship brings us to the gate of heaven and into the house of God. Worship introduces us to a dimension of spirituality that transcends anything our natural minds can conceive.

Wherever and whenever worship occurs, the experience is awesome. Jacob excitedly exclaimed after having such an encounter with God – *"Surely the Lord is in this place"* Genesis 28:16. Again he said, *"How awesome is this place!"* Genesis 28:17. The power of God's person sanctifies the place in which worship occurs.

True worship takes us beyond the 'shadows' and the 'torn curtains' of God's earthly temples right into the Holy of Holies where God sits in splendor to receive our praise. There is the Heavenly Temple above which we visit through the Holy Spirit, and are able to peer at Him who is invisible, whose dominion has no border and whose Kingdom has no end. Therefore, worship that is true always impacts the mind and leaves the dew of heaven on our brow.

When you truly worship, you can never be the same again. Have you ever truly worshipped God?

PRAYER

Lord, help me to truly worship you today. Amen

WISDOM

Worship makes 'visible' the Invisible God.

Qualities Of A Worshipper

*"He answered, I am a Hebrew and **I worship The LORD**, the God of heaven, who made the sea and the land"*
Jonah 1:9.

REFLECTION

The first qualification of a true worshipper is the experience of knowing the true God. The Apostle Paul pointed to the fact that the ancient Athenians had an altar dedicated to, "AN UNKNOWN GOD." Jesus told the Samaritans, *"You Samaritans worship **what you do not know**"* John 4:22. God does not want ignorant worshippers. He wants those who worship Him in spirit and in truth (John 4: 24).

Another important qualification for true worship is love for God. Worship is an affair of the heart. If the devotion of the heart is out of place, then worship will lack passion and the commitment that it deserves. Our love for God should have no 'ifs' or 'buts.' Worship should be experienced in confidence (Hebrews 10:19).

Worship is the product of preparation. To truly worship we must learn to sit at the 'feet' of our Lord and absorb everything He has to offer of Himself. Quiet contemplation of His person and His worth in His presence is the annex to worship. Being still in His presence is something we all have to cultivate. We must shut from our minds the flurry of human activity and attune our minds to hear from God.

Have you ever done that? To truly experience worship of quality, we must cease our feverish day-to-day, rat race scurrying and rest in the presence of God. True worship demands that we stand on holy ground. Therefore, to experience such worship, we need to take off the sandals of human activity and simply bow in worship. The experience makes an amazing difference. Try doing that today.

PRAYER

Lord, I bow in awe in your holy presence and just adore you. Amen

WISDOM

Worship harnesses our energies to focus on God alone.

Qualities Of A Worshipper

*"He answered, I am a Hebrew and **I worship The LORD**, the God of heaven, who made the sea and the land"*
Jonah 1:9.

REFLECTION

Worship is the greatest expression of our devotion to God. True worshippers of God will spend time reading the Word of God. This is necessary to protect us from false concepts of God. The Bible will inform us about God and about what is acceptable worship of God.

Therefore, we must make it our business to know all that the Bible has to say about worship of God. A superficial reading of the Word will never do. A brief time in the Word cannot meet adequately the deep need of 'knowing' the Infinite God, who desires passionately human worship.

The Word then must become the food of the soul and the fuel of the spirit. The Word must dwell in us richly. Only the Word can effectively become nutritional fortification against 'spiritual diseases' and 'viruses.' The Word builds up our spiritual 'immune system' against false doctrines and distorted concepts of God and the true worship of Him.

The Word of God sanctifies us, and this is a necessary prerequisite for experiencing true worship. Sanctification is about being separated **from** everything that defiles the mind, body and spirit. Also, sanctification is about dedication **unto** everything that is wholesome, pure, and righteous in the presence of God.

Worship involves our total being offered to God. Worship is giving our all. Have You?

PRAYER

Lord, help me to be sanctified, so that I can truly worship you. Amen

WISDOM

Knowledge of worship is still not the experience of worship.

Worship God

*"He answered, I am a Hebrew and **I worship The LORD**, the God of heaven, who made the sea and the land"*
Jonah 1:9.

REFLECTION

Saying prayers is not the same as praying. One is powerless and the other is powerful. One is rote and the other is real – real contact with the Living God.

Worship for some is sheer hollow rote and ritual devoid of any substance, and lacking in reality. On the other hand, true worship is a powerful encounter, whereby the soul is overawed by the wonder and majesty of God's presence.

Worship cannot be pumped up by human emotions or primed by the imagination for it is an experience we enter into entirely by faith and not by sight. If there is 'no presence' of God, no operation of the Spirit, no conditioning of the heart, no holiness of life, then true worship cannot be realized.

When true worship occurs, the Spirit takes us beyond the brazen altar, symbolic of our salvation; beyond the laver, symbolic of our sanctification; through the Holy Place, symbolic of our Lord's provision for His own; through to the Holy of Holies, the place of our Lord's presence – His glorious presence – and where only in His presence, can worship take place.

Have you ever encountered God in the Most Holy Place?

PRAYER

Lord, help me to prepare myself to meet you in worship in the Most Holy Place. Amen

WISDOM

The wonder of worship is the joy of the faithful.

The God Of Heaven

*"He answered, I am a Hebrew and I worship The LORD, **the God of heaven**, who made the sea and the land"*
Jonah 1:9.

REFLECTION

Who is this God that we worship? Well, Jonah supplies us with a basic answer. He is *"the God of heaven"* and as such, He is the exalted One. He is the Ruler of the universe. His sovereignty is not in the arena of dispute nor His power or ability. He is the God of heaven.

The earth is not exempt from His control and rule. Political power is in His hands and He does what He pleases in the affairs of men. He establishes rulers or removes them from office. Authority and might are in His hands and there is no power that can withstand His will.

Despite His great might and power, He is merciful and forgiving. He keeps His promises and His covenants. And He has appointed Christians to be His special servants, to magnify His name and to do His will. Part of that will is to share the knowledge of His salvation through Christ with lost humanity - lost in sin.

He loves sinners but hates sin. Sin angers the God of heaven. Therefore, He has provided the means whereby sins can be forgiven. Furthermore, to encourage us to appropriate the means, He has provided through His Son, He has sent the Holy Spirit to convict us and urge us unto salvation.

The God of heaven hears and answers prayer. He is the God of mighty deeds and wonderful works. When in difficulty, call upon Him and He will provide the guidance in your crisis. It is this God who has promised to establish an eternal kingdom of righteousness on this earth.

PRAYER

Lord, help me to listen to the Spirit. Amen

WISDOM

The God of Heaven is our Heavenly Father.

The God Of Heaven

*"He answered, I am a Hebrew and I worship The LORD, the God of heaven, **who made the sea and the land**"*
Jonah 1:9.

REFLECTION

Jonah recognized the God of heaven as the Creator. When God made the cosmos there was no existing material then, from which He could have fashioned the things that we now see. He conceived the marvelous idea of what a Universe would look like, what laws would govern it and how the entire system would relate, one part to the other. When God conceives of something He does it on a grand scale.

How does God go about building stuff? He has two methods. He either speaks it into being by the Word of power or He uses the material He has created to fashion say, a man. Then He can use, say, a rib from the man and make a woman. God does not have a power problem.

Creation is not a product of chance, but the product of the all-wise and all-powerful God. We look at a suspension bridge and we have no difficulty believing that it has a builder. We look at a huge ocean-liner or at a nuclear plant or a space craft and conclude that they were built by someone. Is it not strange that when we cast our eyes heavenward and look at the vast array of stars and galaxies we suddenly have brain damage and say they came into being by chance? Give me a break.

"For every house is built by someone, but God is the builder of everything" Hebrew 4:3. It is God, Jonah insists, that made the sea with its vast array of potential to sustain the creatures that inhabit it. God made the land too, and all its creatures and the wherewithal to sustain the lives of its creatures. Everything we see around has design and purpose. It did not happen by chance. God made them all.

PRAYER

Lord, help me to thank you daily. Amen

WISDOM

Creation makes it plain that there is a Creator.

What Have You Done?

*"This terrified them and they asked, "**What have you done?**" (They knew he was running away from the LORD, because he had already told them so")*
Jonah 1:10.

REFLECTION

How does it feel to be in the midst of people as an exposed fugitive? Jonah was awakened to his folly by his shipmates. They finally became aware that they were harboring not only a fugitive but a fugitive from a powerful and angry God, whose wrath churned the seas to fury.

Jonah had been given a mission to warn the city of Nineveh of God's impending destruction of the place and the people. But Jonah eschewed the task. His disobedience unmasked, his fellow travelers were horrified by the conduct of the prophet. They confronted him with astonishment – *"What have you done?"* Jonah 1:10. Sometimes, only when we are caught and confronted do we become aware of the magnitude of our sin against God and our crime against our fellowmen. How could Jonah just shrug off his role of witnessing like that? How could he have entertained such a dastardly thought?

Are you like Jonah? Am I like Jonah? Are we not shirking our Christian responsibility to tell our sinful 'Nineveh' of the impending wrath of God? Isn't it true that the sins of the spirit are of a more serious nature than the sins of the flesh? Isn't it true that every Christian is responsible for the blood of the people we should be telling the gospel and have not been doing so?

A backslider endangers the life and souls of others. Yet, God in grace awaits our return, so that He might abundantly pardon. Are you ready now to repent and return to God in obedience?

PRAYER

Lord, help me to fulfill the divine mandate you have given me. Amen

WISDOM

Act while you have opportunity.

Rough Seas!

*"The **sea was getting rougher and rougher**. So they asked him, "What should we do to you to make the sea calm for us?"*
Jonah 1:11.

REFLECTION

Chastening is a process to bring us closer to God. Confession of our sin is the first step in the right direction. But confession has different levels and depths of 'sincerity.' There may be the confession of convenience. For instance you got caught red-handed and you confess. Or on the other hand there is the confession of embarrassment. All the evidence gathered identifies you as the culprit and so you confess.

Confession many times proceeds only from the lips and the heart remains defiant and unaffected. We still have not yet surrendered the cherished sin. God is not fooled by our nightly confessions of our daily sins, if the heart is not sincere and transparent. We cannot curry favor God or try to 'sweet Him up'.

We have learnt to go through this accustomed path to try and persuade conscience not to make life miserable for us. It does not work if we would have power with God and authority with men. To bring us to our senses, God is going to permit our 'sea' to get rougher and rougher and those around us to get impatient with our folly and the trouble our sin has created for them.

Our sins affect others. My sin affects others and could even physically endanger them. What sin can I commit that does not affect my relationship with God and my fellowmen? If I lie, cheat, steal, be envious, etc. it impacts upon others. Unconfessed sin brings God into the equation of our lives with His chastening rod to correct us.

PRAYER

Lord, I thank you for chastening me when I stray. Amen

WISDOM

Chastening tells me that God loves me.

Life Out Of Control!

*"The sea was getting rougher and rougher. So they asked him, "**What should we do to you to make the sea calm for us?**"*
Jonah 1:11.

REFLECTION

For countless multitudes, life is like the troubled and restless sea. The prospect for calm waters and favorable winds is a distant hope. Possibly in your life the violent waves are now pounding your frail vessel. You are being swamped with water and you are not sure how much longer you can withstand the violence of this foul weather.

The economic waves follow each other in rapid succession and relentlessly pound your frail bark and you are wondering how much longer you can hold out before being swallowed by the angry sea.

You may live or work in an area where violence is out of control and you feel insecure day and night. Waves of fear and often times cold sweat bathe your body. Your every thought is controlled by fear and there is no peace within.

Maybe you are in an emotional storm. Nothing seems to be going right in your relationship with your boyfriend or girlfriend. You are getting the signal you are no longer wanted and it is creating anxious moments for you. Or maybe your husband is becoming friendly with another woman and your marriage is headed for the rocks and you are wondering how you can avoid that catastrophe. You desire desperately for the seas to become calm again so that some type of control can be regained. Discouraged soul, there is hope. Jesus who patrols the troubled sea of life can bring calm and sanity to your seemly helpless situation. Call upon Him now.

PRAYER

Lord, my life is out of control and I call upon you to help me now. Amen.

WISDOM

When you don't know what to do ask somebody who does.

43

Self Preservation

*"The sea was getting rougher and rougher. So they asked him, "**What should we do to you to make the sea calm for us?**"*
Jonah 1:11.

REFLECTION

Self preservation is the most powerful drive that exists in our breast. Nazi experiments in the last World War demonstrated that self preservation in most instances will sacrifice even the ones closest and dearest to us when it comes to the crunch.

Jonah was now face to face with this instinct. The sailors were now in a situation that stirred up this drive. Look at their question to Jonah – *What shall WE* **do to you** *to make the sea calm for US*? WE want an answer and WE want it NOW. A flash of lightening lit up the skies and the crack of thunder was ominous.

The principle enunciated by Satan was becoming operational in the lives of the sailors – *"Skin for skin... A man will give all he has for His own life"* Job2:4. Life is precious and danger brings this to the fore. Extreme danger will bring to light our true character.

Peter in extreme danger put no value to his relationship to Christ. His love for Christ evaporated into nothingness. His proud and arrogant boast of dying for Jesus melted in terror before the law of self preservation.

Do you know what you would do in that situation when 'the rubber meets the road'? If you were Jonah what would be your response to their question?

PRAYER

Lord, give me grace to behave in all situations to bring honor to you. Amen

WISDOM

Danger removes all masks of pretense.

Taking Responsibility

"Pick me up and throw me into the sea," he replied, "And it will become calm. I **know that** *it is my fault that this great storm has come upon you."*
Jonah 1:12.

REFLECTION

Taking responsibility for our fault in difficult and trying situations is never easy. It is easier to assign blame and try to absolve ourselves of our own defects. To say, 'The buck stops here,' takes courage. To make the decisive admission at the right time can save lives, jobs, friendship or a marriage.

Jonah's admission was going to involve personal injury and maybe the ultimate sacrifice of his life. To correct our faults may involve 'eating crow', or suffering a battered self esteem, or going down a notch or two in some people's opinion, or severe criticism. The opposite can be true also. You could go up a notch or two in the opinion of others for having the strength to admit you are wrong. This opens the door for forgiveness, reconciliation and healing. It could be the beginning of a new day and a new lease on life.

Jonah's decision now took into consideration the interest of others. His life of living purely for self came to an end. Living for self is never a recipe for a happy life. This is the attitude of Cain who had no love for his brother.

Coming to terms with your guilt makes you feel good on the inside in spite of the cost to you. Coming to the end of yourself gives God an opportunity to work in you.

PRAYER

Lord, teach me to care for others especially when I have caused them hurt. Amen

WISDOM

Do the right thing in a crisis no matter what the personal cost.

The Certainty Of Faith

*"Pick me up and throw me into the sea," he replied, "**And it will become calm.**
I know that it is <u>my fault</u> that this great storm has come upon you."*
Jonah 1:12.

REFLECTION

Jonah was a prophet of God in spite of the fact that he was trying to escape
from his prophetic duty. He predicted that the sea would become calm for the
crew and passengers the moment his body hit the water.

We Christians, as servants of the living God, also speak with certainty and
assurance on matters of faith. When we declare, 'Thus saith the Lord' from
the Word of God, it is not an empty formula but the powerful statements of
the God of heaven. The word of God cannot fail. Its integrity and faithfulness
is forever settled in heaven. The Word of God has power because God honors
His Word.

Elijah the Tishbite is sent by God to declare the will of God to wicked king
Ahab. He thunders with assurance of faith and the powerful backing of heaven
that there would be no rain or dew until he says so. So said, so done.

God's Word is the source of the miraculous and the supernatural. It is
through the Word, faith is generated and the power of God is revealed. God's
Word can still the tempest of the troubled heart. It is God's Word that brings
calm, peace and serenity to the anxious and the perplexed. Speak it today and
bring healing to some troubled soul.

PRAYER

Lord, I thank you for the power of Your Word when I exercise faith in it.
Amen

WISDOM

Faith in God's Word is the key that turns on the Power of God.

Death To The Old Self

*"Pick me up and throw me into the sea," he replied, "**And it will become calm.** I know that it is <u>my fault</u> that this great storm has come upon you."* Jonah 1:12.

REFLECTION

The old self that we inherited from Adam, is the source of **all our problems.** That fallen, corrupt nature that resides in us cannot please God. That nature is selfish, self centered and is hostile towards God. That nature is incapable of doing any good that is acceptable to God. No way can that nature be altered religiously to become acceptable to the Most Holy.

When we received Christ as Savior that nature was not repaired but we got a new one from God. So the Christian has two natures. One capable of pleasing God, and as for the other, that is a mission that is impossible. The nature transmitted to us through our parents is the source of our sin, rebellion, self righteousness and all the other vices imaginable. To give into this nature is the path to spiritual defeat and misery. Its short term pleasures eventually lead to slavery.

The only cure for the old self or our fallen nature is 'death.' You and I need to jettison that nature. We need to throw it into the sea to its death. That nature must be crucified and thus rendered powerless. I can say categorically that we will never experience the fullness of life and victory in Christ unless that old nature is denied. The fullness of life resides in the new nature. That nature must be daily fed the Word, nurtured to maturity by obedience to the Lordship of Christ.

You will never experience 'calm seas' until the old self has died.

PRAYER

Lord, help me to die daily to the old self and allow the new self to dominate my life. Amen

WISDOM

The new nature, if allowed to dominate your life, is the path to victory.

Human Effort Futile

*"Instead, the men **did their best** to row back to land. **But they could not,** for the sea grew even wilder than before"*
Jonah 1:13.

REFLECTION

Doing our best is never good enough unless we are doing exactly what God says. God told Jonah that calm would come if he was thrown overboard into the sea. Instead, the men decided to do their best. Divine instructions may appear not to our liking, but doing otherwise is futile. Introducing human logic and effort to try and attain our ambitions and goals, instead of simply following God is flawed thinking.

Divine instructions tend to go against the dictates of our fallen human nature. Most times, we do not comprehend what God is doing, yet in our folly we try to assist God in our human ways and so to our own detriment. What God has determined, He is able to perform and His desired end will be achieved in spite of us. His thoughts will always prevail, for they are superior and right. (See Isaiah 55:8-9)

Because God's wisdom is better than ours, ever perfect and good, we ought to forget about doing our best for salvation. God has a wonderful plan and all we have to do is exercise faith in the Divine provision. Too many people believe that they can get to heaven by doing their best. This is a 'good works' formula that is contrary to God's faith plan.

Salvation cannot be attained by human effort or merit. Salvation is a gift that God offers to us without any strings or obligations attached. *"I give unto them eternal life"* John 10:28(ASV) is what the Savior says. All you need to do is to receive the gift by faith.

PRAYER

Lord, help me to accept your instructions today no matter how they conflict with my human reason. Amen

WISDOM

To ignore a divine command and replace it with human wisdom is folly.

The Storm Intensifies

*"Instead, the men **did their best** to row back to land. But they could not, for **the sea grew even wilder than before**"*
Jonah 1:13.

REFLECTION

What an arduous task that must have been rowing against the waves and the wind! Have you ever been on the sea trying your very best to row to safety? Can you imagine how those sailors must have felt as their greatest efforts was no match against the fury and violence of the storm? The whole experience must have been like a nightmare.

Sometimes in life we do have experiences like that, when everything that we conceive and do is of no avail. We become stressed out and unhappy and even our bodies begin to respond negatively, leading us rapidly to the point of despair and hopelessness.

However, when such storms arise in our lives we must learn to appreciate that they are not designed to destroy us but to instruct us. We can learn something of this truth by observing the struggle of a butterfly to liberate itself from the cocoon. Was that fierce struggle designed to weaken or strengthen the existence of the emerging butterfly?

God quite often uses the storms of life to speak to us. However some of our storms and their growing intensity are generally of our own making. They are furious because we shut our ears to God's voice, and close our eyes to His leading as we march in the direction of self-will to our own hurt. Is there an '**Instead**' in your life? Are there things you are doing 'instead' of paying attention to the counsel of the Word? For example 'instead' of confessing your sin are you continuing in it? If so your 'Jonah' has to be cast into the sea if you would have calm.

PRAYER

Lord, help me to throw my Jonah out, now. Amen

WISDOM

To obey is better than to sacrifice.

Your Crisis And God

"Then they cried to the LORD, "O LORD, please do not let us die for taking this man's life. Do not hold us accountable for killing an innocent man, for you, O LORD have done as you pleased"
Jonah 1:14.

REFLECTION

A common pattern emerges. We need to take careful note of it if we are to live the victorious Christian life. This popular practice must be abandoned. It is that only when everything else fails we turn to God in earnest. These mariners had earlier cried to their false gods. But false gods are vain and behind them at any rate are the diabolical forces of the spiritual world of darkness.

In that ship was one true believer in the living God. His testimony regarding the great God of heaven and their common dreadful experience, awoke in them the desire for His help. Fortunately, the one true God is merciful and always await our penitence and turning to Him. Their lifeless idols proved inadequate for them in their moment of crisis.

In the days of Elijah the god Baal proved himself worthless to his worshippers when the nation was faced with a crisis. Baal's worshippers were not short of show for they shouted lustily and danced with great energy and even lanced themselves until their blood flowed. Their sincerity was intense, yet, Baal remained silent and powerless.

Your crisis may have brought you to the place where you desperately need a genuine encounter with the LORD. Your prayers up to this point in time may have had deep sincerity, but even that failed. Now for the first time you truly see your need of the Living God. Your crisis has opened that door for you to call upon Him.

PRAYER

Lord, help me to acknowledge you today in all things. Amen

WISDOM

God is our ever present help in time of trouble.

Pray In A Crisis

*"Then **they cried to the LORD**, "O LORD, please do not let us die for taking this man's life. Do not hold us accountable for killing an innocent man, for you, O LORD have done as you pleased"*
Jonah 1:14.

REFLECTION

The word "Then" suggests an important change of intention and direction. We may safely say a crucial change occurred. A new direction was chosen. Making important decisions that on the surface seem morally wrong is no easy undertaking. To seemingly go against the principles that you once thought right or best is not readily done. But the sailors did it even if reluctantly, for their consciences restrained them. Their prayer reflects much effort to ease their consciences which forbids the wanton taking of human life.

The mariners had a terrible decision to make that involved a man's life. They were thinking of throwing Jonah overboard into the perilous sea. To them no man could survive that experience. Yet they were convinced that getting rid of Jonah was the solution to their problem.

The spiritually anguished sailors did not want to go about their task carelessly, or without due consideration, so they turned to God in earnest prayer. The man Jonah had instructed them to throw him overboard if they would save their lives and he seemed to be speaking with divine authority. But how could they be certain that this man was not mentally deranged or some kind of religious freak?

When you want to know the will of God in extreme circumstances, a good avenue is prayer. When you have to make a quick and vital decision - pray. When your back is against the wall - pray. Do not make any decision without prayer. Cultivate the habit. Pray, always pray.

PRAYER

Lord, help me to pray daily. Amen

WISDOM

Pray when it hurts.

51

Killing The Innocent

*"Then **they cried to the LORD,** "O LORD, please do not let us die for taking this man's life. Do not hold us accountable for killing an innocent man, for you, O LORD have done as you pleased"*
Jonah 1:14.

REFLECTION

These pagan sailors had a strong conscience about killing an innocent man. Regrettably the matter of killing an innocent man today gets little sensitive response from the society. There is more rage and outcry when the wicked are killed.

When the innocent are robbed and gunned down in our streets, it no longer stirs our passion and our sense of justice and does not always make the headlines. Blood guilt is now spoken in a whisper. The witnesses to these dreadful events are terrified to testify in court. Human life is no longer held sacred in our society. The pulpit is no longer alarmed or horrified by these wanton deaths that daily take place in our society. We have grown to accept them as a part of life's reality.

Our hearts have become callous or indifferent to the social degradations that now ravage our land. Love for our neighbor is disappearing from our hearts and reverence for God is now on the scaffold. Conscience has been deadened and justice has fallen prey in our streets.

The plea of the blood of the innocent is heard, and the guilty will be punished. Justice shall prevail, if not in this life, then surely in the next.

How concerned are you when the innocent are targeted and then eliminated?

PRAYER

Lord, help me to let my voice be heard when murder is committed. Amen

WISDOM

When awe for God is absent, then wickedness is prevalent.

Accountability

*"Then they cried to the LORD, "O LORD, please do not let us die for taking this man's life. **Do not hold us accountable** for killing an innocent man, for you, O LORD have done as you pleased"*
Jonah 1:14.

REFLECTION

The prayer of the mariners raises some serious moral issues and one such matter relates to accountability. The context of Jonah's case is indeed, unusual. The course of action contemplated was to cast Jonah overboard, believing that the violence of the waves would finish him off. That was their human perspective.

Situations do arise to convince some persons that death is better. Take for instance a child that is mercilessly provoked by a parent, to the point of contemplating suicide, believing that to die is better than to live.

Let us look at another example. You had the responsibility of caring for an invalid. But you became derelict in the discharge of your duty which resulted in the death of the invalid. Do you think you will escape the judgment of God?

Did not king David in the Bible arrange the death of Uriah to make it look like he was a victim of war? Did not Jezebel set up Naboth and falsely accused him of blasphemy and then had him stoned to death?

No matter what our schemes are to conceal or justify our acts of deliberate wickedness against our fellowmen, we are accountable to God for all of our actions and for the damage we have inflicted on others be it emotional, mental, physical or spiritual.

PRAYER

Lord, help me not to plot the death of others by 'hands off' design. Amen

WISDOM

Sin hidden cannot be forgiven.

God Is Sovereign

"Then they cried to the LORD, "O LORD, please do not let us die for taking this man's life. Do not hold us accountable for killing an innocent man, for you, O LORD have done as you pleased"
Jonah 1:14.

REFLECTION

There is a sovereign God who is in charge of the universe. As much as multitudes would like to eliminate Him from their thinking or their everyday lives, He will never surrender to their wills or to their evil designs.

Whether we like it or not, there is One God, supreme and sovereign. He is the God of Heaven who runs things after the counsel of His own will. He does not need to consult with us to determine what His next move will be. What He has determined in an eternity past, He has continued and will continue to implement in time.

God will never be brought to a human court of justice to answer charges unjustly brought against Him by His puny creatures. Sinful man will rage against His person and disregard His laws and precepts to his own peril. He will vainly try to blot out the memory of God and the knowledge of the Most High and Holy from his mind and conscience. But God will always be and will ever reign.

Can man survive without God's air or the fish survive without God's water? Is it not insane to think we can survive without God? If God withholds the rains we perish. It is He who controls all the elements and the forces of nature and they gladly do His bidding. He exalts the base and He pulls down the mighty. He has power to take away our breath and we perish, and He is the Author of our eternal salvation.

PRAYER

Lord, help me appreciate my vulnerability to your sovereignty. Amen

WISDOM

God is answerable to no one.

God Is Sovereign

"Then they cried to the LORD, "O LORD, please do not let us die for taking this man's life. Do not hold us accountable for killing an innocent man, for you, O LORD have done as you pleased."
Jonah 1:14

REFLECTION

God works through His providence to bring to pass His gracious and wise plans. All that He allows in history will ultimately bring glory to His grace and to His justice. Take for instance the cruel and vicious crucifixion of our Lord Jesus. Both Jews and Gentiles were involved in putting the Son of God to death, but in so doing they were carrying out what God had by His council foreordained to come to pass. (Acts 4:28)

This does by no means remove the guilt of the perpetrators of this horrible crime. They did what they wanted with glee and malice. Yet it was through their wicked act God brought salvation to lost humanity. Christ's death on the cross opened the door of heaven for us. It is through the cross, forgiveness of sins was secured and death was conquered through His resurrection. God's ways are past finding out.

God is able to override the evil deeds of mankind and glorify His name. The persecution of the early church was the means the enemy used to try and suppress and eliminate Christianity. But God used that very instrument designed to destroy His church to spread and multiply believers across the Roman world and ultimately over the globe.

God is in control in spite of the storms and opposition you and I may face in this life. Don't whine, but seek His face, for out of our painful distress and trying situations, God is in the process of doing something beautiful in our lives, and generally, in His universe.

PRAYER

Lord, help me to trust you in moments of crisis. Amen

WISDOM

With God, nothing is impossible.

Time For Action

*"Then **they took Jonah and threw him overboard**, and the raging sea grew calm"*
Jonah 1:15.

REFLECTION

Having verbalized and agonized, they acted. There is a time to pray and there is a time to act. The mariners with great intensity poured out their hearts to God in the previous verse. They had instructions regarding what was next to be done. 'Jonah', the problem, was to be thrown overboard. This action was drastic but absolutely necessary. It was his life or theirs. The eternal law of survival 'kicked in' so Jonah had to go.

I must take personal responsibility for ridding my soul of that which is creating the storm in my life. Take the case of Joshua in the Bible. He was on His face before God seeking an answer for Israel's defeat before the enemy. God's response was for him to quit praying and deal with the sin in the camp. Achan the source of a nation's problem had allowed greed and lust to get the better of him. He took forbidden stuff and then buried them in his tent. But he was exposed and eliminated, and the nation became again open to blessing.

We **will never** have victory or peace of mind unless we deal with that offending matter that sticks out like a sore thumb in our lives. It is **the roadblock** between our soul and God.

If there is a cherished sin in your life it must be thrown overboard. It must be dealt with now if you would have the 'raging sea' in your life become calm. If you would see the miraculous hand of God in your experience, then that offending 'Jonah' must now be grabbed and mercilessly hurled into the turbulent sea. What use is prayer and resolve if the necessary course of action is not taken?

PRAYER

Lord, help me to cast 'Jonah' into the raging sea. Amen

WISDOM

When it is time to act, prayer will not work.

Jonah Will Never Jump!

*"Then **they took Jonah and threw him overboard,** and the raging sea grew calm"*
Jonah 1:15.

REFLECTION

We are using 'Jonah' in our study as a type of our fallen, sinful nature. This nature, inherited from Adam, makes us naturally disobedient to God, and stubbornly inclined against submitting to God's will. This nature is corrupt and no matter how hard we try to refine it, it will never be acceptable to God. You don't have to teach this nature evil for that is inborn. It is from this nature that all the problems we see around us and in us arise.

When we became Christians, God gave each of us a new nature. This is what makes us new creatures in Christ. This new nature qualifies us to be a part of God's household and thus a part of His family. When we were born-again we obtained it and it is this nature that equips us for godly and pure living. This rebirth took place when we received Jesus into our lives as personal Savior.

If you have never asked Jesus into your heart, you only have the old nature you inherited from your parents that they inherited from Adam. This old, corrupt nature we must throw overboard, for its desires are in conflict with the will of God for our lives. As long as the old nature is in control of our lives the raging sea will remain unabated. This nature will never volunteer to jump overboard. It has to be thrown overboard.

Are you prepared for your 'Jonah' to die? Then cast him overboard today.

PRAYER

Lord, help me to reject the impulse of my old nature and embrace instead, the urging of my new nature. Amen

WISDOM

Only a new nature can overthrow the old nature.

Peril Of Disodedience

*"Then **they took Jonah and threw him overboard**, and the raging sea grew calm"*
Jonah 1:15.

REFLECTION

Obedience to God's decrees always brings blessings, but disobedience leads to distress. Disobedience always has an enormous cost. We tend not to think of the cost to ourselves when we wander off the path of life. Disobedience has a deceptive charm that lures and entices us to a path of reckless disregard for the pure and wholesome. Despite its dangers, we are inclined to pursue this even at the peril of our lives.

When we break loose from the protection of God and His blessing we put ourselves on the trail of the predicted curses spoken of in the Word. This is dangerous for those curses shall come to pass in our experience, to our chagrin. For example, in the Bible we are told the story of the prodigal son who was sick of home, so headed for the 'far country,' and excitement. There he ended up cheated of everything he had – riches, virtue and spirituality.

In this story Jonah's disobedience led to degradation. Jonah is a picture of the salt-less believer, who has lost his savor. Therefore, he became like that which is good for nothing but to be trampled on. Ah, the way of the transgressor is hard says the Bible.

When we break God's laws, we must appreciate that those very laws will break us and grind us to powder. Jonah, cast overboard, was now on his way down to what seemed certain death. He must have thought of the wages of disobedience. What about you? Do you think your disobedience will go unnoticed and unpunished?

PRAYER

Lord, help me recognize that the destiny of disobedience is fixed and certain. Amen

WISDOM

Disobedience brings curses but obedience, blessings.

Calming The Troubled Waters

*"Then they took Jonah and threw him overboard, and **the raging sea grew calm"***
Jonah 1:15.

REFLECTION

This true story of Jonah is full of wonderful lessons concerning God's goodness, love, mercy and salvation. For example, we learn that calm and safety could not be restored to the mariners until Jonah was punished. Similarly, Jesus died as our Savior; for only by His death could you and I have peace with God. In our text only one man on board that ship could save the day. He had to 'die' that they might be saved.

In God's plan for the world of lost humanity only one man could save our world and reconcile us to God - Jesus. Glory to God, Jesus gave Himself to the fury of God's wrath against sin. He absorbed the full measure of the divine displeasure as His soul was made an offering for sin. On the cross He suffered the devil's worst to gain for us God's best.

There was none other worthy of bridging the gap between sinful mankind and a holy God, except Jesus. He loved us in spite of our sins and waywardness and made it possible for calm to be restored to our troubled, threatened and tormented souls. Praise everlasting be unto Jesus, our only Savior.

Are you living in the calm of forgiven sin?

PRAYER

Lord, help me to daily thank Jesus for dying for me. Amen

WISDOM

Internal turbulence ceases when obedience to Jesus increases.

Reaction To Divine Response

SCRIPTURE   February 29

*"At this **the men greatly feared the LORD**, and they offered a sacrifice to the LORD and made vows to him"*
Jonah 1:16.

REFLECTION

God always keeps His Word. With Jonah thrown into the deep, the violence of the storm came to an abrupt end. The presence, power and reverence for God could be felt aboard ship at this amazing wonder. There was a hush as awe swept over every heart at this amazing act of God. Not even the sails fluttered as they joined in giving glory to God.

What Jonah, the man of God said, came to pass in a manner that was beyond their wildest expectations. This event brings to mind another storm story of the Bible. This time we turn to the New Testament. It took place on the Sea of Galilee in the time of our Lord. In that boat were terrified disciples fearing the worst was about to happen. In their terror they appealed to Jesus to do something about the dreadful condition and He, with dignity and majesty, responded by speaking to the wind and waves. Instantly, there was complete calm.

The spiritual and emotional impact it had on His disciples was tremendous. They now saw Jesus in a different light. As a matter of fact the focus of their overwhelmed spirits shifted from the now stilled storm to the majesty of His person, authority and power. *"What kind of man is this? Even winds and waves obey him!"* Matthew 8:27.

Any person, who has experienced the merciless violence and battering of the storms of life, as well as the calm when he turned to God, can testify to God's greatness. The divine response in their crisis made them marvel at the greatness of God. Such dramatic changes will pull us into a deeper relationship to the God of miracles, wonder and awe.

PRAYER

Lord, help me to see more clearly and love you more dearly. Amen

WISDOM

God is always there in our darkest hour.

Men And Reverence For God

*"At this **the men greatly feared the LORD**, and they offered a sacrifice to the LORD and made vows to him"*
Jonah 1:16.

REFLECTION

These sailors must have been tough, adventurous characters, for sea travel then was perilous. But when God acts in power even hardened pagans are softened and begin to greatly fear the Lord. Regrettably, there are so many men who think it is 'macho' to put God on the periphery of their lives. So much so that in most churches women greatly out number men.

Perhaps the reason for this lack of men standing up for God is that Satan has targeted our men to deceive and destroy them. God has designed men to function as leaders in the home and in the church, and Satan knows that if this is not so, chaos will develop. This has certainly happened, for today it is mostly men who are involved in crime, violence, drugs, irresponsible sex and phantom fatherhood.

No society can be stable without men fulfilling their responsible leadership role before God and in the society. This is the divine design for social order. The challenge is tremendous, for it takes courage to stand for righteousness. It is much easier to indulge in the vices of our sinful nature, than to respect and care for women and the family.

For men of such quality to arise, much prayer is required. Only qualified men can truly transform society. Only men of impeccable spiritual stature, who have stood the test of time, qualify to be leaders and examples for our sons to emulate. It takes God's power to touch men and bring them to reverence and service. May God ignite our pulpits to encourage men to be attracted to the greatest man, Jesus.

PRAYER

Lord, help me to help men to fear you. Amen

WISDOM

A wise man is one who puts God First.

Of Vows

*"At this the men greatly feared the LORD, and they offered a sacrifice to the LORD **and made vows to him"***
Jonah 1:16.

REFLECTION

A vow is a solemn undertaking and should not be rashly made. Vows are promises that can be made to oneself, to another, and, of course, to God. Desperate and life-threatening situations favor persons making serious promises to God and it is usually a pledge to grateful and faithful service to Him for the rest of their lives.

How sad it is, therefore, that when the danger passes, the 'solemn' pledge evaporates with it and the promise to God becomes void. A man and woman vow in the presence of God to be faithful to each other, but as the relationship enters into foul weather that vow often goes under, never to surface again. Then there are parents who fail to honor their promises made to their children, who on being abandoned are unprepared for the harsh realities of this world.

All vows made in the presence of God are binding and He will hold us accountable for our utterances. *"Do not be **quick with your mouth**, do not be **hasty in your heart** to utter anything before God. God is in heaven and you are on earth, so **let your words be few**....When you make a vow to God do not delay in fulfilling it. **He has no pleasure in fools**; fulfill your vow. It is **better not to vow** <u>than to make a vow and not fulfill it.</u> Do not let your mouth lead you into sin"*

Ecclesiastes 5:2, 4.

God delivered you out of your trouble when in desperation you called upon Him, therefore now honor your promise to Him.

PRAYER

Lord, help me to fulfill the promise I made to you now that the danger has passed. Amen

WISDOM

A promise made is a debt to be paid.

More On Vows

*"At this the men greatly feared the LORD, and they offered a sacrifice to the LORD **and made vows to him"***
Jonah 1:16.

REFLECTION

Reverence for God validates the sincerity of our promises made to God. When the fear of God deteriorates in our lives then a breach is made in our lives, from which breach the devil can and most likely will operate and create untold mischief in our lives. Once we enter the 'gray area' of life, when our 'no' is no longer 'no' and our 'yes' is no longer 'yes', then integrity has now taken its flight from our lives.

When Christ is no longer Lord, the treacherous 'old self' becomes enthroned. Resultantly, instead of moral absolutes, compromise is reinstated. When that happens, the soul becomes the boardroom for excuses. It is then that vows are termed 'mistakes' and we may even enter a plea of temporary spiritual insanity for the breaking of the vows we made to God in the presence of the holy angels.

But whatever might be the mitigating circumstance or various excuses, with such reasoning God is not in the least impressed. That's all part of our self centeredness. Rather, God will insist that we meet His demand to honor our words pledged to Him. No person who stands in awe of God will ever think that the flimsy veil of excuses will ever prevail in the presence of God. We cannot twist and manipulate God to fit our timetable and our availability. We cannot make a pledge to God and then run off to do what we please. That's what Jonah did.

But Jonah's behavior had serious consequences – much more than he imagined would have been the case. We cannot disregard our vows and not bring great sorrow on ourselves.

PRAYER

Lord, help me to see the serious nature of the vows I make. Amen

WISDOM

Silly excuses cannot nullify the vows I make to God.

More On Vows

*"At this the men greatly feared the LORD, and they offered a sacrifice to the LORD **and made vows to him"***
Jonah 1:16.

REFLECTION

An encounter with the Divine Presence naturally awakens the desire in the heart to respond with some kind of commitment to God.

We learn from the Bible story of Jacob that when he was fleeing from his brother Esau for stealing his blessing (Genesis 27), Jacob had a craving for spiritual things. However, we learn too that he made the mistake of seeking to satisfy that craving carnally. He loved short cuts and so was prepared to cut corners to achieve even spiritual goals. It took him 20 years to have that problem corrected.

On His flight to Haran, he stopped for the night and went to sleep. That night he had a dream through which God spoke to him prophetically of his future. He awoke from his dream with the consciousness of God's presence and it was awesome. It left an indelible imprint on his soul and he consecrated the place of his meeting with God and gave it a new name – Bethel, meaning, House of God. There, **he vowed to give God <u>a tenth</u> of what God gave him.**

Here is a Biblical principle that should challenge all of us – a genuine encounter with God transforms and awakens the desire to serve Him in some **tangible way.** The flip side of that is, if you are not committed to God in some significantly "Tangible way", then it may be safely concluded that you have never had a genuine encounter with God. In effect, that means, you are suffering from poverty of the spirit.

PRAYER

Lord, help me to experience that which will make my soul respond in tangible ways. Amen

WISDOM

Poverty of the spirit is a disease of the soul.

Cheating On Our Vows

March 05

*"At this the men greatly feared the LORD, and they offered a sacrifice to the LORD **and made vows to him**"*
Jonah 1:16.

REFLECTION

Today we will zoom in on a vow cheater. What will he offer to the Lord? What is the quality of his sacrifice? The disposition of such a person is seen in Malachi 1:14 – *"Cursed is the cheat who has **an acceptable male** in his flock and vows to give it, **but then** sacrifices a blemished animal to the LORD."*

The cheater of vows is a person given to changing his mind on matters of importance, whether suddenly or not, in a degrading way. He will substitute what is promised for something inferior and of little or no value to him. He is enamored with the spirit of hypocrisy. He has an excuse for every occasion. Anancism marks all his dealings whether it be with God or with man.

This cheat is lacking in integrity, sincerity, loyalty and fidelity. Reliability is not one of his assets. Whatever he says in his devotion to God must be taken with a pinch of salt in spite of the fervor of his tone, his oratory and even his seemingly apparent sincerity. Whatever his commitments or undertakings are, he will not honor them with any seriousness.

His problems evolve from a very sick heart that is divorced from the Lord. If he is unrepentant, no way can that cheat with that attitude evolve into a dynamic and useful person. The only cure for the cheater of vows is repentance and a new heart from God.

Are you a cheat?

PRAYER

Lord, help me to honor you always, with my whole being. Amen

WISDOM

Ultimately cheaters will never win.

Rash Vows

*"At this the men greatly feared the LORD, and they offered a sacrifice to the LORD **and made vows to him"***
Jonah 1:16.

REFLECTION

Which of us have not made hasty and rash statements to God? In the passion of a moment, as we faced overwhelming odds, we vowed rashly. The wine of passion intoxicates the soul in those sacred moments and without due consideration as to the consequences, we make vows that commit us to a particular course of action, if God should see us through a certain situation. Whether in private or public, we become trapped to fulfill avowed obligations.

In the Bible we read of Jephthah who ensnared himself with such a vow. He was just about to engage in battle with the Ammonites when he said to the LORD, *"If you give the Ammonites into **my hands**, whatever comes out of the door of **my house** to **meet me** when **I** return in triumph from the Ammonites <u>will be the LORD's</u>, and **I will** <u>sacrifice it as a burnt offering</u>"* Judges 11:30-31.

When he returned from battle in triumph his only child, his daughter, met him. He was devastated, and cried in anguish, *"Oh! My daughter! You have made me miserable and wretched, because I have made a vow to the LORD **that I cannot break"*** Judges 11:35.

'Rash' vows, as long as they do not go against the spirit of the Word, are just as binding as those that are more sober. You cannot make a promise to God and then think you can worm your way out of it by saying it was a mistake. Vows must be honored be they short term, medium or those that are binding for the rest of our lives.

PRAYER

Lord, always help me to vow wisely. Amen

WISDOM

Think tomorrow when you talk today.

Honored Vow

*"At this the men greatly feared the LORD, and they offered a sacrifice to the LORD **and made vows to him"***
Jonah 1:16.

REFLECTION

These sailors made vows to God. What are vows? They are binding commitments. Vows to God are more than mere utterances of empty promises. Vows are commitments to a particular course of action. Vows are the true test of our spiritual integrity and determination.

In the Bible we read of a woman who is outstanding in keeping her vow to God. Hannah is an example of a woman of integrity who honored her promise to the Lord. She was a barren woman who asked God for a son and got one. She called him Samuel. She determined that this child she asked for would be given back to God and His service. Here is what she said, *"I prayed for this child, and the LORD has granted me what I asked of Him. **So now I give him to the LORD.** For his whole life he will be given over to the LORD"* 1 Samuel 1:27.

Hannah honored her word and what a mighty man of God Samuel became! He was a man of integrity, a prophet of stature, a judge of Israel, founder of the School of the Prophets, a man mighty in prayer, an anointer of kings, and two books of the Bible bear his name.

Her example is one all parents should emulate. Pledging her child to the LORD she dared to follow through on it, and the returns were great. Dedicating our children to the Lord demands a life of godly commitment and training of our offspring. Nurturing our young ones must not be left to chance, but rather to honoring our pledge to God.

Have you vowed to do anything for God? Then honor it.

PRAYER

Lord, help me to keep my vows to you. Amen

WISDOM

Broken vows bring curses but honored vows bring blessing.

Annulled Vow

March 08

*"At this the men greatly feared the LORD, and they offered a sacrifice to the LORD **and made vows to him**"*
Jonah 1:16.

REFLECTION

Vows always remind us of what is permanent. Therefore, the question arises, is there scope for getting out of a vow? Can a person for any reason be released from a vow made to God? This concern is worth exploring. There are at least three cases given in the Bible (Numbers 30) whereby a pledge can be annulled, all of them in relationship to a **father** or a **husband**.

The first case relates to a young woman living in her father's house making a vow to the Lord. If her father hears what she has pledged he can either make it binding by remaining silent or he can forbid her and God will release her from the obligation of her vow.

The second case is that of a woman who makes a vow to God **before** marriage. On getting married, if her husband gets wind of her vow, he can annul that pledge or make it stand by keeping silent. His silence makes the vow binding.

The third case is that of a woman who makes a vow to the Lord **after** marriage. Her vow will remain binding if her husband says nothing on hearing of it, or he may release her from it. He cannot then change his mind at a later day for the vow is now binding on his wife.

On the other hand, the vows of widows and divorced women are binding. They have no wiggle room. Therefore they must be careful what they say to God on the spur of the moment, for a pledge has permanence and serious consequences.

PRAYER

Lord, help me to vow wisely. Amen

WISDOM

God holds us responsible for our utterances, be they rash or sober.

Nazirite Vow

*"At this the men greatly feared the LORD, and they offered a sacrifice to the LORD **and made vows to him"***
Jonah 1:16.

REFLECTION

We have been examining the subject of vows broadly. Now we shall briefly examine one vow, and perhaps the best known one is the Nazirite vow. The passage that deals with this subject in its greatest details is to be found in Numbers 6. This vow could be taken by a man or a woman. This vow was not permanent, and it was voluntary. However in the Bible, there are three persons who were Nazirites for life - Samson, Samuel and John the Baptist.

The vow of the Nazirite did not pledge something to the Lord, but rather it was a separation of oneself to the Lord. During the period of the vow one would abstain from all grape related products. No razor was to be used on his hair, including his beard, until the vow was completed. He was not to go near any dead body during the period of his separation. Contact with a body would annul his separation.

Holiness in body, soul and spirit was the goal of this vow. Therefore if we would enter the spirit of this vow and transfer its principles into our lives, then Romans 12:1-2 is a good place to begin. In these verses our bodies become the object of dedication to God and the sanctification of our minds, the sure path to renewal and the discerning of the will of God for our lives. This is the only life that is pleasing to the Lord.

Are you committed in body, soul and spirit to the Lord?

PRAYER

Lord, help me to surrender all of my life to you in sacred service. Amen

WISDOM

External conformity without internal renewal is - empty ritual.

Violated Vow

"At this the men greatly feared the LORD, and they offered a sacrifice to the LORD and made vows to him"
Jonah 1:16.

REFLECTION

We continue to focus on the Nazirite Vow, with particular reference to two of the three Biblical examples. The two on whom we focus today are from the Old Testament, Samson and Samuel. Interestingly both of them came from wombs that were once barren. Both were Nazirites from birth, and both were judges of Israel. However, in terms of differences between these two Samuel fulfilled all the requirements of his calling, while Samson, a 'spiritual playboy,' had a series of violations with terrible consequences.

Samson, dedicated from the womb to serve God, swerved from the path of loyalty, fidelity and integrity to God, to indulgences in the sins of the flesh. His marriage to a pagan woman began his downward path of sorrow. He got involved with a prostitute and subsequently, with a woman called Delilah, who exploited him for gain.

He violated his vow by eating honey from a carcass of a lion, came in contact with the dead in battle and eventually lost his hair while sleeping on the lap of the teaser. Samson soon discovered that you reap only what you sow. The Bible sums up the penalty of Samson's folly in these words, *"Then the Philistines seized him, gouged out his eyes and took him to Gaza. Binding him with bronze shackles, they set him to grinding in the prison"* Judges 16:21.

We cannot violate our pledge to God and expect joy in the end. The tragedy that overtakes the violator of vows will commence with light consequences, but eventually they will become the slaves of Satan.

PRAYER

Lord, help me to see beyond the pleasures of broken vows. Amen

WISDOM

Vows violated lead to degraded lives.

Scourging

"But the LORD provided a great fish to swallow Jonah, and Jonah was inside the fish three days and three nights"
Jonah 1:17.

REFLECTION

Jonah's journey by ship came to a dramatic, judgmental end. He entered another dimension of the chastening hand of God. God can play hardball and tough love is applied that takes chastening to another level called scourging. It is an experience no believer will ever forget for it is like being swallowed by a great fish and all the nightmares that ensue.

Deviating from God's path for your life is a sure path to unhappiness and sorrows. Such a path will unrelentingly traumatize you day and night. Jonah was in the process of experiencing the displeasure of God and His chastening hand upon his life.

Jonah, by running away from God, brought him into a storm of trouble. First, he had exposure of his sin and the shame that brings, and then he was cast overboard to what seemed to be certain death, but the worst part of his experience was just ahead - something that perhaps seemed worse than death.

Sin not honestly dealt with, brings untold misery. Yet we tend to hold on to our sins as if they are prized treasure. Its toxins enter our blood stream and yet we will not give up our folly. Sin pollutes our lifeline to heaven and robs us of the joys of living.

Sin enslaves; sin is a tyrant. Sin never relaxes its hold, not even for a moment. The spirit of disobedience is controlled by demonic forces. But God has his methods of dealing with his disobedient children, so that He might bring them back on the path of righteousness.

PRAYER

Lord, help me to ever remain on the path of righteousness. Amen

WISDOM

If you listen to God's urging you will avoid God's scourging.

Scourging Is Painful

*"But the LORD provided a great fish to swallow Jonah, and **Jonah was inside the fish three days and three nights**"*
Jonah 1:17.

REFLECTION

When Jonah was thrown into the churning waters he must have considered that to be the end. The record does not indicate whether he could swim. Jonah seemed to be plummeting to certain death as his body hit the angry water. He sank quickly below the surface and to his utter astonishment and horror he saw a great fish headed in his direction. He was live bait for this monster. It was as if this great fish was waiting for him. Perhaps he tried to evade the great fish, but evidently his efforts proved futile, for it opened its huge mouth and in one gulp Jonah was swallowed whole.

As Jonah made his journey down into the belly of the great fish he must have prayed for a quick end, but that was not to be. While he lost track of time in this horrible situation, his stay down there must have seemed like an eternity. As far as recorded knowledge goes, he was the first man to survive three days and nights under water and live to tell it.

The great fish experience was God's merciful provision for his servant Jonah. God sometimes has to reach us through pain. But it was just the thing Jonah needed to bring him back in line with God's will. Such experiences purge the soul of shallowness, pretence, God-dodging and lack of commitment that is pure, sincere and genuine. Nothing enriches the prayer life more than a dreadful and painful experience. This is the avenue God has to use to get our full attention, so that He can produce in us repentance that leads to productive service. Too often, for too many, God is never truly appreciated until we stare death in the face.

PRAYER

Lord, help me to learn from the painful lessons of life the powerful principles of Christian living. Amen

WISDOM

I must resign to God's design.

Swallowed By A Great Fish?

*"But the LORD provided a great fish to swallow Jonah, and **Jonah was inside the fish three days and three nights**"*
Jonah 1:17.

REFLECTION

The story of Jonah is true but there are many people who doubt it. Of course, to believe it, you must believe in miracles. Well, do you? Can an axe head float? The answer of course is 'no', but one miraculously floated in the time of Elisha. Can a donkey talk? Of course not, but God opened the mouth of Balaam's donkey that was being harshly treated with this response, *"What have I done to you to make you beat me these three times?"* Numbers 22:25.

In the time of Jesus, it was the praise of children that prevented the very stones from crying out. Why then, should it be thought incredible that Jonah was swallowed by a great fish and supernaturally kept alive for three days? Jesus believed it was a historical event.

From my perspective, if the word of God had said that Jonah was swallowed by a minnow I would believe it. How much more credible then, that the Word speaks of Jonah being swallowed by a great fish? There seems no doubt that this particular fish was prepared for this task. The anti-supernaturalist tries to explain away the wonderful works of God. He takes issues with everything that defy a natural explanation.

A good example of this skepticism can be seen when they spoke of Jesus' amazing raising of Lazarus from the dead. The evidence was overwhelming. Persons hostile towards Jesus could not gainsay this miracle, but it did not change their attitude towards Him. When we try to divest God of the supernatural, we are only exposing our folly and the horrid spiritual darkness of our souls.

PRAYER

Lord, help me to always believe Your Word. Amen

WISDOM

The spiritual will embrace the supernatural.

Jonah A Type Of Christ

*"But the LORD provided a great fish to swallow Jonah, and **Jonah was inside the fish three days and three nights"***
Jonah 1:17.

REFLECTION

Jonah is a type of Christ in His burial and resurrection. Jesus Himself endorses this analysis, as He interacted with contentious Pharisees and teachers of the law. They were demanding a miraculous sign from Him, despite the fact that He had performed many miracles in their presence.

Jesus' response to His detractors said, *"An evil and adulterous generation seeketh after a sign; and there shall no sign be given to it but the **sign of Jonah** the prophet: for as Jonah was three days and three nights in the belly of the whale; (Greek is sea monster) so shall the Son of Man be three days and three nights in the heart of the earth"*

Matthew 12:39-40 (A.S.V.).

Jesus' reference to "the sign of Jonah" identifies Jonah's experience as linked to the greatest sign miracle in the entire Bible – the resurrection which completes the Gospel. Jesus died for our sins and by doing so He paid our ransom; He was then buried and on the third day came to life again. Those are the essentials of the Gospel.

When you accept Him as your Savior, you enter into His resurrection life. The resurrection of Christ sets Christianity apart from all other religions. The resurrection is the sign that proves beyond the shadow of a doubt that Jesus is the only authentic Savior.

Do you know Him?

PRAYER

Lord, help me to believe in miracles. Amen

WISDOM

If you can believe in the greatest miracle, Jesus' resurrection, then you can believe in the lesser miracle, Jonah's survival in the great fish.

Praying In The Great Fish

"From inside the fish Jonah prayed to the LORD his God"
Jonah 2:1.

REFLECTION

'Sincerity' expressed under pressure, sometimes proves to be hypocritical. So often commitment made in fair weather melts away into nothingness in bad weather. Because of insincerity our relationship with the Lord can become devoid of the essence of true fellowship. What is needed when this happens is an experience that will make us realize how desperate our condition is, and so bring us into genuine spiritual renewal.

Caught in such situations, our running away from God must be converted into our running toward God. There is no better place for that new direction to begin than inside the belly of the great fish that God has prepared. It is then that the multiple options we thought we had are reduced to one. When we are shut up like that, it is then we will utilize prayer to its maximum until we get deliverance.

It is in the belly of the 'great fish' that real praying begins, becoming dynamic. It is in the 'great fish' that our seeming strength and ability are lost and our weaknesses are revealed. It is when we are overwhelmed by forces greater than ourselves that we have a change of focus to Him, the Almighty God. It is when we have no room to maneuver, and there is no glimmer of light and it looks like we will be digested by our circumstances, that prayer and God become our only hope.

It is in the belly of the fish that we pray with sincerity and desperation to the LORD our God.

PRAYER

Lord, help me to pray in sincerity. Amen

WISDOM

Adverse circumstances can forever deepen our spiritual relationship.

Being Purged In The 'Fish'

SCRIPTURE   March 16

"From inside the fish Jonah prayed to the LORD his God"
Jonah 2:1.

REFLECTION

Why does God permit His children to go through the agonizing experience of being 'inside the fish.'? Perhaps a good answer is to liken agonizing experiences as a means of purifying us. In this regard we can think of gold placed in the furnace to remove its impurities. So therefore, we can say that to be placed in the furnace of God's purifying fires is the only cure for our backsliding.

The backsliding Peter comes to mind as one who had to learn this lesson. Listen to him a few hours before the arrest of our Lord Jesus – *"Even if all fall away on account of you, I never will"* Matthew 26:33. Self-confident Peter had to be placed in the "belly of the great fish" to learn to put no confidence in the flesh.

Humility is not a virtue acquired overnight. Brokenness is a process the old self despises. For the braggart the great fish experience is a necessity if he would learn that it is not by his might or power that spiritual growth is attained.

Look again at our friend Peter as he is challenged by a servant girl of being a follower of Jesus Christ. At the time Peter is in the presence of a hostile crowd that seeks his Master's blood. Does he now play the man and make good his boast? He quickly evaluates the situation and chooses self over Christ, not once, but three times in rapid succession. One penetrating glance from the eyes of the Master plunges him inside the great fish to be purged of the old self.

Have you ever found yourself ashamed to own Jesus?

PRAYER

Lord, help me to avoid the necessity of being scourged. Amen

WISDOM

Purging is necessary for growing.

The Pain Of Purging

"From inside the fish Jonah prayed to the LORD his God"
Jonah 2:1.

REFLECTION

There are certain sounds in our lives that trigger particular responses and emotions. For Peter the crowing of a rooster was his call to shame. It was followed by the all knowing look of his Master that beckoned him to seek some quiet spot to weep bitterly over his terrible failure. But perhaps His Master's speedy trial, crucifixion and burial only made his gloom greater.

Peter therefore agonized with the guilt that swamped his soul. All his other failures began to work their way out of the woodwork to add to his agony. Granted, he had had deep sleep on that fateful night when our Lord was betrayed and then arrested. Jesus had requested of the inner three that they stay awake and pray. From his denial to the unexpected resurrection of Christ, Peter had no rest in his soul. It was a time of perplexing, heart-searching and frightful flashbacks as again and again he relived his denials of his Lord. Jesus rebuking him for failure only added pain to his already battered and bruised affections.

Jonah inside the great fish, had no joy, but only gloom, and with no apparent ray of hope. In the darkness of his soul there seemed no light on the horizon. Sleep departed from his eyes and wave after wave of sorrow disturbed his hapless soul.

Are you passing through what seems to be an endless valley of guilt and shame? Does the agony of your failure seem to get worse? Then join Jonah and Peter in pouring out your soul to God in sorrow and contrition for that is your best hope of getting out of your hell.

PRAYER

Lord, help me to right myself with you. Amen

WISDOM

The haunting memories of sin can be purged from the soul by God's grace.

Prayer

*"From inside the fish **Jonah prayed** to the LORD his God"*
Jonah 2:1.

REFLECTION

Prayer is the most powerful 'tool' available to the believer. It is a spiritual 'tool' all Christians have but few have mastered. Yet, this 'tool' can be effectively used by a child. The key to effective prayer is our relationship with the Lord. The more intimate the relationship, the more effective the prayer.

Sin is the greatest hindrance to prayer. As a hindrance it is followed closely by its bedfellow, doubt. On the other hand Faith is Prayer's bosom friend. Indeed, without faith, we are merely shadow boxing. The disciples were so impressed by Jesus' prayer life that they urged Jesus to teach them to pray. The passion and petition of a man of prayer is something worth emulating. The impact of such leaves a powerful impression on the mind.

There are levels of intensity in this matter of prayer. Intensity in prayer is often fueled by need, and the greater the need, the greater the desperation, and so the greater the urgency and fervor in prayer. In short, our praying in the comfort of our bedroom is not the same as Jonah's in the belly of the great fish. His circumstances made his prayer more intense, as his life hung in the balance.

However, whether you are in a crisis or not, prayer ought to characterize your daily walk with God. The more you practice it, the better you are being equipped for any spiritual emergency. Jonah's prayer from the belly of the fish demonstrates that reliance on God in desperate times is necessary for deliverance, and that intensity in prayer is always needed, for God honors the faith of the repentant.

PRAYER

Lord, help me to pray with greater intensity. Amen

WISDOM

Crisis is the great teacher of the art of prayer.

Prayer

*"From inside the fish **Jonah prayed** to the LORD his God"*
Jonah 2:1.

REFLECTION

Prayer is a powerful means of communication. James says, *"The prayer of a righteous man is powerful and effective"* James 5:16. Notice that James is speaking about the prayers of a righteous man. For our prayers to be effective our lives must be clean and for that too, we can pray. Prayer is holding a conversation with God, as was the case of Abraham pleading on behalf of sin-sick Sodom to be spared.

Prayer is not a monologue, it is dialogue. We must listen to God, even before we speak. And when we talk to God, we must allow God to respond. In the case of Abraham a request was made and there was an immediate response and so the conversation between the two went on to its conclusion.

Prayer is talking to God – holding conversation with God. This was what Elijah on Mount Carmel did and there was an immediate and miraculous response from heaven as the fire of God fell upon the sacrifice and consumed it (I Kings 18).

Of course not all prayers have an immediate response. Take the example of barren Hannah who prayed for a child for some time before her request for a son was granted.

Also, we need to be aware of the danger of prayer being reduced to meaningless babble when our requests are not immediately granted. Importunity, conviction, zeal, faith and prevailing upon God must characterize our prayers. Once our prayer is in harmony with the Word we should **never retire from praying until the request is granted**.

PRAYER

Lord, help me to cultivate the habit of praying with persistence. Amen

WISDOM

Prayer not only changes things, but changes us as well.

Sin Is Distress

*"He said, "In **my distress** I called to the LORD, and he answered me. **From the depths of the grave,** I called for help, and you listened to my cry"*
Jonah 2:2.

REFLECTION

Sin brings death, disease, disappointment, disgrace, distress and sorrow. Such realities are the companions of death. They are dangerous and real. Spiritual peril lays bare the nakedness of our souls.

A dear saint of God once said, 'Sickness has no shame'. How true! Equally true is confession of sin that has placed you in the 'depths of the grave' of guilt, and, now aroused by an accusing conscience, knows no shame. Multitudes have openly confessed their sins at the altar of repentance.

Sin is a prison with bars that are ever closing in on its victims restricting their every freedom. It is a strait jacket that tightens its grip whenever you move. It is like an electric chair with its victim strapped in, just seconds from execution.

Concealed sin is terrible for the inner man. Sin has never elevated anyone, but rather it has cast many into an abyss of despair. The Bible speaks of sin in terms of *" a man fled from a lion only to meet a bear, as though he entered his house and rested his hand on the wall only to have a snake bite him"* Amos 5:19. The horrible consequences of sin are inescapable both in this life and in the life to come.

The distress, trauma, guilt, degradation and penalty of sin can only be treated by the Great Physician. When sin's burdens become unbearable, Jesus can still save and remove its oppression through forgiveness.

PRAYER

Lord, help me to honestly confess my sins to you. Amen

WISDOM

Sin destroys but salvation restores.

Prayer And The Omnipresent God

*"He said, "In my distress **I called to the LORD**, and he answered me. **From** the depths of the grave, **I called for help**, and you listened to my cry"* Jonah 2:2.

REFLECTION

God hears sincere prayers. Prayers are not directed to a God that is deaf, callous, limited in ability or lacking in presence. The worshippers of false gods will get no response to their prayers no matter how long or how intense and how much they dance and prance or mutilate their bodies, to get attention.

In one of the most thrilling Old Testament stories of divine assistance, Elijah, the prophet of the Living God, taunts the worshippers of the impotent false gods. *"Shout louder!"...Perhaps he is deep in thought or busy, or traveling. Maybe he is sleeping and must be awakened"...But there was no response, no one answered, no one paid attention"* I Kings 18:27, 29.

The Christian's prayer is to the living God, who is omnipresent, and who answers prayer. There is no place in this vast universe we could ever go, to escape the presence of God. The Russian cosmonauts in outer space said they saw no sign of God. Did they expect to use their physical eyes to see the invisible God? Had something gone awry and had they time to pray they would have found in an instant, the very One who is invisible.

God *"is not far from each of us. For in Him we live, and move and have our being...we are His offspring"* Acts 17:28. Jonah did not hesitate to call on Him in his terror and he got a wonderful response.

PRAYER

Lord, help me to call upon you, for I know **you are there**. Amen

WISDOM

Emergencies make believers even of infidels.

Prayer And The Omniscient God

SCRIPTURE   March 22

*"He said, "In my distress I called to the LORD, and **he answered me**. **From** the depths of the grave, I called for help, and **you listened to my cry**"*
Jonah 2:2.

REFLECTION

What if! What if God were present, but impotent? What good would it be for God to be available but useless? What if God was there but couldn't help? If so, would He not be like an infinite zombie? What if there were no more to God than 'mere' presence?

God's presence must not be underrated. He is present everywhere all the time. No other creature has that ability to be omnipresent. Satan does not have the attribute of omnipresence. He is limited to one place at any given moment in time. Therefore, he cannot tempt more than one person at a time, but he has billions of agents who assist him in his work. In one man alone he had a legion of helpers. There is one devil but many demons. So there are a lot of those evil beings around to create mayhem on earth.

God's omnipresence is not to be likened to the air around us, for that attribute is combined with other powerful attributes that make God unique, without rivals. The God we serve is intelligent and the essence of all knowledge. God's knowledge is not acquired, but is innate.

His knowledge never increases through experience. He is the source and the dispenser of all knowledge. God is omniscient; therefore, He knows my need before I even whisper them in prayer. Nothing is hidden from the omniscient God. He cannot be 'conned' so don't even try it. All things are naked before Him. He understands our problems and that of the universe and He has a solution for every problem.

PRAYER

Lord, help me to call upon you in time of need. Amen

WISDOM

Whatever our problems, God is present and competent.

Prayer And The Omnipotent God

SCRIPTURE   March 23

*"He said, "In my distress I called to the LORD, and **he answered me**. From the depths of the grave, I called for help, and **you listened to my cry**"*
Jonah 2:2.

REFLECTION

As we reflect on the God of the universe we must be impressed by His remarkable character. We have discussed that He is omnipresent and omniscient. We learn now that He is omnipotent. This means He has the capacity to perform mighty acts; therefore, He is able to deliver us.

Furthermore, we can rest assured that God will always use His unique attributes to treat us well. This is because of His other wonderful attributes. He is also the God of love, wisdom, truth, grace, mercy, goodness and faithfulness. He can be fully trusted and His desire is that we should fully trust Him.

All God's attributes blend in perfect harmony in His person. We, indeed, call upon the God who is always there, who knows our deepest thought, and understands our every tear or sigh, yet, despite our weakness, He will use His power to lift us when we are beyond ordinary help, by His extraordinary love, grace, knowledge and power.

Surely, prayer takes on fresh, dynamic and new meaning when we know the wonderful attributes of the God we have access to, through prayer. This Father knows and fulfills the highest functions of the office of "Father'. He is the God who answers our calls personally. He listens to our cries. Jonah was in trouble of his own making that brought him into grief, sorrow and pain. We do not have to bewail our backslidden state and wallow in our moral filth a moment longer. We just have to repent.

PRAYER

Lord, help me to lean upon your great power that delivers. Amen

WISDOM

As we utter, He will save us from the gutter!

God Is The Answer

*"He said, "In my distress I called to the LORD, and **he answered me**. From the depths of the grave, I called for help, and **you listened to my cry"***
Jonah 2:2.

REFLECTION

Our humanity loves fellowship. Therefore, we fear loneliness. There are times in our lives that even in a crowd or among friends there is a deep loneliness that brings an uneasiness that unsettles the soul. In such circumstances, we feel as if we are on a ledge without adequate footing, and there is not much for the hands to grip. In those moments, mental, emotional and spiritual exhaustion take their toll, and we feel like surrendering to the anxiety and depression that will lead us to do something really stupid.

But when we reach such limits of our abilities, God is there for us, ready, waiting for our call. During such times, we should not allow pride or any other false human props to hinder us from calling on the Lord. Call upon Him then, and He will help, as He always will, for He is good all the time.

Peter was walking on water, but before long his faith gave way to doubt, his doubt led to fear, and he sank. But his fear quickly led him back to faith in his Lord's ability to rescue him and when in his desperation he cried out, *"Lord, save me"* Matthew 14:30 (ASV), Jesus responded and did just that – He delivered Peter. The Bible says, *"Call to me and I will answer you and tell you great and unsearchable things you do not know"* Jeremiah 33:3.

The God we serve is never searching for an answer or solution. He is the ANSWER; He is the solution.

PRAYER

Lord, help me to trust you, even when all seems lost. Amen

WISDOM

Trust in God banishes fear.

The Fury Of God's Rebuke

SCRIPTURE March 25

"You hurled me into the deep, into the very heart of the seas, and the currents swirled about me, all your waves and breakers swept over me"
Jonah 2:3.

REFLECTION

Our relationship with God is defined by our attitude to sin. There is one of two paths to follow when we sin against God. We may choose to pass judgment on ourselves and promptly deal with our sins, or we may choose to be obstinate and then allow God to deal with us in judgment. Keeping short accounts of our sins is the path we should choose.

Should we choose to sin with impunity then we are bound to incur the displeasure of God that will be like the raging sea. Jonah chose to resist God and he is here describing in our text, in poetic language, the severity of his afflictions, as God began to judge him. He tells us of how he felt when the raging waters swept over him.

We anger God when we indulge in sin, and so we should expect to experience God's wrath. If there is complacency or an attitude of indifference in sinful indulgences we are storing up against ourselves the divine displeasure and it will surely overwhelm us and bring us into excruciating distress and absolute misery. God hates sin. All sin is the violation of God's holy laws. Sin defiles, weakens moral resolve and brings us into conflict with conscience and with God.

Sin has its own inbuilt penalties which devalue and cheapen us. Sin is a very strong and powerful force and its currents, waves and breakers will bring us to utter shame and ruin. However, sins, if properly evaluated, can bring us to our senses, and so to repentance, and back to fellowship with God, and joy in the Lord.

PRAYER

Lord, help me to surrender to you. Amen

WISDOM

Surrender leads to victory.

Satan's Role In Chasening & Scourging

March 26

*"You **hurled me** into the deep, into the very heart of the seas, and the currents swirled about me, **all your waves and** breakers swept over me"*
Jonah 2:3

REFLECTION

God is loving and good but when judging sin His hand can become heavy on us, for He hates sin. If we persist in sinning, we place ourselves into the hands of the Enemy who is cruel. Although God allows Satan and his cohorts to play a role in our discipline, God is always there for us, ready to redeem us or restore us, if we repent.

Satan played a part in the refinement of Simon Peter. God used that wicked instrument to produce a desirable product. *"Simon, Simon, Satan has asked to sift you like wheat"* Luke 22:31. To rid us of the 'husk' and separate us from the 'chaff' the Enemy plays a vital role. It's in those adverse and severe situations we truly learn to cry to God for deliverance from the power of self and the tyranny of sin.

When we fall under the cruel whip of the Enemy it makes us long for God, for His mercy and grace. The Apostle Paul told us of Hymenaeus and Alexander who were handed over to Satan so that they may be taught not to blaspheme. A person expelled from the church is delivered to Satan for some rather crucial lessons, tailored to bring such a one back to the gracious hand of God for mercy and deliverance.

Jonah's thoughts as a backslider are important: *"You **hurled me**"* and it is *"**All Your** waves and breakers swept over me."* Are you passing under the judgment waves of God? If so, God's desire is to produce Christ-likeness in you. You must purge yourself from all known sin and return to Him, right now.

PRAYER

Lord, help me to cease from sin, right now. Amen.

WISDOM

Resisting evil builds spiritual muscles.

Sin Has Inescapable Consequences

SCRIPTURE   March 27

*"**You hurled me** into the deep, into the very heart of the seas, and the currents swirled about me, **all your waves and** breakers swept over me"* Jonah 2:3. (Read II Chronicles 21)

REFLECTION

Three avenues of temptation face us constantly. There is the fallen inherent nature, which defiles us; then there is the enticing, sensual and alluring desire for worldly values, which characterize our behavior, and of course there is the Devil, always busy trying to make us obey and worship him. These can work as separate entities, or two may combine to seduce and try to destabilize us. Sometimes, all three may join forces and lead a charge against us, for the purpose of our utter destruction.

In II Chronicles 21:1 Satan led an assault against King David, using as his chief instrument human pride. When the enemy slides through a door that is left ajar he can fill the mind with conceit that drives the ego to do things that are contrary to the will and mind of God. Motive for action God will judge. When reason for our action springs from impure motives, the enemy triumphs in our lives and the decision made could even be costly in human lives as David was soon to discover.

When pride enters the arena of our decision, the wise and solid counsel of others is ignored. Of course, this is later regretted. Foolish decisions soon awaken conscience to our horrible wickedness. Then, we become face to face with the options of our judgment. We can prolong the pain by spiritual starvation and dehydration, or we may choose to have the Enemy run rough shod over us leaving us utterly ruined and devastated. Or we may choose to face the music and put ourselves into the hands of a merciful God. The pain will be sharp and acute but it will be swift, and it will produce a humble and wiser person.

PRAYER

Lord, help me to break from sin and worship you. Amen

WISDOM

God's judgment for sin is inescapable.

Jesus Is Our Substitute

"You hurled me into the deep, into the very heart of the seas, and the currents swirled about me; all your waves and breakers swept over me*"*
Jonah 2:3.

REFLECTION

Jonah's disobedience brought him into collision with God's displeasure. That always happens when we walk outside the blessings of God's will. When we pursue such a path we are certain to experience great hardships, tribulation, distress and anguish of soul. Our supreme example of someone living for God is Jesus, who did no sin. He was the spotless and undefiled Son of God who took of our nature, but never sinned. To achieve that, He lived in constant, intense communication with His Father.

During his earthly ministry he was despised and rejected of men who hated Him without justification, and eventually crucified Him at Calvary. Both Jews and Gentiles participated in His murder. The Roman judge found no fault in Him deserving the sentence of death, yet, allowed it. At Calvary, all the waves and breakers swept over Him, as he endured great humiliation at the hands of His creature, man.

But that was not all. He endured the full fury and rage of divine wrath as He became our sin offering on the cross in order to secure our eternal salvation. On the cross He willingly took our place so that we might have forgiveness of our sins and obtain eternal life. He, indeed, was 'hurled into the deep" in order that you and I may walk free. On the cross He was our substitute. There, He took our place that we might escape the judgment. But that can happen only if you give Him your heart and let Him become your personal Savior.

PRAYER

Lord, help me open my heart to you now, so that I may receive you as my personal Savior. Amen

WISDOM

Calvary is heaven's door open for us.

Banished!

*"I said, 'I **have been banished from your sight**; yet I will look again towards your holy temple'"*
Jonah 2:4.

REFLECTION

To live for God is to experience joy, but to live for self and sin is awful. To live even for a moment without the sense of God's presence is anything but delightful. Many have glibly spoken of eternal separation from God, but that is foolish. They speak of having 'wild' parties in the dungeons of darkness; they speak of going to hell as being 'no big thing'. But those who speak frivolously about such serious matters have never contemplated what banishment from the presence of God really is.

We all will at one time or another have a foretaste of hell in our experience and those are experiences we never ever want to repeat. Hell is a place of unrelieved gloom and horrible darkness, yea; it is an unending night of endless pain. It is a place of absolute loneliness and haunting memories. It is a place of regret and a conscience that bites more tenaciously than a bulldog. There will be no music, no song, no parties, and no bond of friendship and worst of all, no help from God.

It is a place that is punctuated with blood curling screams and shrieks and moans and groans and gnashing of teeth. There are laments and repenting and confessing that are met by an eerie silence from the God of Justice.

If we live in sin now we cut ourselves off from the presence of God and place ourselves in the annex of hell. Indulgence in sin is bondage to vice and leads ultimately to eternal separation from Him who is Life indeed, unless you repent. Therefore, flee from sin, now.

PRAYER

Lord, help me to awaken to the horrors of sin. Amen

WISDOM

Hell denied does not hell remove.

Banished!

"I said, 'I have been banished from your sight; yet I will look again towards your holy temple'"
Jonah 2:4.

REFLECTION

Banishment from God can either be temporary or permanent. Banishment has to do with a lack of relationship. It is a separation, a lack of communication, yea, an alienation from the Living God. Sin, in all cases, is the root cause. When we are out of touch with God then prayer is an exercise in futility. When disobedience to God characterizes the life, then the flow of blessings from God ceases and barrenness, fruitlessness and aimless wandering in a spiritual wilderness follow.

This was the case with Israel's first king, Saul. He stumbled from one act of disobedience to another, each compounding the other and hardening the conscience to the point that God ceased to communicate with him in his official capacity as king or as a private individual. We read in I Samuel 28:7, *"When Saul saw the Philistine army, he was afraid; terror filled his heart. He inquired of the LORD, **but the LORD did not answer him** by dreams or Urim or prophet."* So what this wicked king resorted to was to consult a witch for spiritual counsel and guidance. Of course, he ended his miserable life by falling on his own sword in battle.

If we play Russian roulette with our souls in this life our end will be catastrophic. We cannot live in contempt of God's Word in this life and expect our end to be anything but miserable banishment from God's presence. If you are living in reckless disregard to God you had better change your ways before it is eternally too late.

PRAYER

Lord, help me to live as a good steward of your blessings in the here and now. Amen

WISDOM

God's way is best, by any test.

Banished!

*"I said, 'I **have been banished from your sight**; yet I will look again towards your holy temple'"*
Jonah 2:4.

REFLECTION

The God of heaven established His presence on earth in unique ways. Firstly He came to reside in the Tabernacle in the wilderness, and then in the Temple in Jerusalem. His manifested presence dwelt in the Holy of Holies between the two cherubim on top of the mercy seat that was the cover for the Ark that contained the Ten Commandments.

It was from this place that God spoke and the Bible identifies it as His Throne. It was here that atonement was made for sin once a year. The manifested presence of God departed the Temple during the reign of Zedekiah, shortly before the destruction of the Temple in 586 BC (Ezek. 11:22-23). According to the Bible that glory shall return to the Temple, yet to be rebuilt, during the millennial reign of Christ (Ezek. 43:1-7).

The prayer of Solomon tends to have heightened the value and importance of the Temple in the life of the Israelites. As a matter of fact the entire land of Israel was regarded as sacred and even today we call it the Holy Land. We can appreciate David's concern when he said, *"Now do not let my blood fall to the ground far from the presence of the LORD"* I Samuel 26:20.

Jonah's great concern of being banished from his sight has some geographical implications, even though he knew that God's presence was not to be limited to an earthly Tabernacle. But, of course, that was no ordinary place. To Him it was holy ground. Tell me, does God's presence mean something to you? Do you cherish Him?

PRAYER

Lord, help me to recognize always your holy presence. Amen

WISDOM

Holiness with God is closeness with God.

Looking To God!

*"I said, 'I have been banished from your sight; yet **I will look again towards your holy temple**'"*
Jonah 2:4.

REFLECTION

When should we turn to God for help? The correct answer is immediately or constantly. But, regrettably, the false idea exists, and even believers often adopt it, that we turn to God when all else fails. This wrong idea can be fatal. When the waters overwhelm us it might be too late. Having our faith jerked into action by a crisis we cannot handle with our meager resources is frightening and forbidding. Why wait until we have been 'swallowed alive by the great fish' of circumstances?

Strange how a crisis suddenly makes us conscious of our spiritual need as was Jonah's case. Strange how a crisis causes our spiritual compass, which was gone awry, to be suddenly reoriented to Him who is our True North! Jonah said, *"I will look again towards your holy temple."* He neglected God when the circumstances were favorable, but cries out in desperation when the angry waves engulfed him.

Jonah, however, is so much like us. We cry to God when we are in the deep but once we are delivered, we drift from His way, His house and His service.

How is it with you? Are you always grateful to God? Do you always look to Him? What now hinders your fellowship with God?

PRAYER

Lord, help me to be true to you today and always. Amen

WISDOM

Adversity can advance spirituality.

Looking To God!

*"I said, 'I have been banished from your sight; yet **I will look again towards your holy temple'"***
Jonah 2:4.

REFLECTION

Does prayer work? Do you think that it would have made any significant difference in those critical situations of your life, if you had prayed? It is reported in the medical field that patients who prayed or had others pray for them have had a higher rate of recovery in contrast to others lacking in prayer. Prayer has been attributed to the miraculous recovery of the sick in many cases, and this has baffled medical science.

Of course there is no 'magic' to prayer. God does not use magic for healing, or deliverance from seemingly impossible circumstances, of needs being met that defy chance, or the outpouring of unusual favor, or the reversal of dreadful and harmful decisions, etc. It is God who is responsible for these amazing results. When we trust God for the impossible, He is more than able to perform it. Our focus is not on the words we utter, or even with the intensity of our petitions, but rather on the ability of God to act in power in a decisive manner. This is the secret of the effectiveness of prayer.

Jonah under the waves was more focused on God than a man that is trapped in a burning building, who is looking to the firemen to rescue him from certain death. The firemen, in spite of their courageous efforts might fail, but the ability of God to deliver is certain. Prayer is much more than an appeal to God for help. It is an encounter with God, an experience of intimacy, of drawing near to someone dear.

How is your prayer life?

PRAYER

Lord, help me to give thanks daily for your many blessings. Amen

WISDOM

Desperation removes the phony and uncovers the authentic God.

Jesus Banished For Us!

"I said, 'I have been banished from your sight; yet I will look again towards your holy temple'"
Jonah 2:4.

REFLECTION

Almost two thousand years ago an event occurred that forever changed the course of history. It was indeed a strange day for in the middle of the day a great darkness came over the whole land until about three in the afternoon. There was a cry from the cross that echoed from that hill that is heard even today, for those who have ears to hear –*"My God, My God, why hast thou forsaken me"* Matthew 27:46 (A.S.V.).

Jesus, the Son of God, went to the cross and paid the price for our sins. In doing so, He experienced the horror of being banished from the presence of God because of our sins. The spiritual darkness did not merely hover over his head but it descended and wholly enveloped Him. In those moments, all the dreadful venom of our sins was absorbed in His person. He was bearing our hell in a very personal way.

We can never know the full measure of His suffering but we know that as He suffered on the cross the full fury of God's wrath was unleashed on Him. On the cross He was banished from the very presence of God. He gave His life for us that we can enter into the joy of Salvation and enjoy now and forever a beautiful relationship with God.

Why should you allow anything to come between your soul and the Savior? He drank the bitter cup of judgment for you, so that you can drink from the cup of salvation. He was banished from the presence of God in order that you may draw near to God. He took your judgment of hell that you can have the joy of heaven. Should you not give Him your all as of today?

PRAYER

Lord, help me to appreciate more the cost of my salvation. Amen

WISDOM

Recognizing His suffering brings great blessing.

Engulfed By Problems?

*"The engulfing waters threatened me, **the deep surrounded me**; seaweed was wrapped around my head"*
Jonah 2:5.

REFLECTION

Most people will never know what it is like to be in the belly of a fish. But at least we can imagine. Jonah's graphic descriptions help. While there, Jonah must have become conscious that every moment of his life was dependent upon the mercy, providence and power of God. Here was a man trapped in the belly of a great fish, fighting for survival in the midst of the sea. If there was ever a man whose predicament seemed dismally hopeless, that man was Jonah.

Reflect carefully on his situation. He was about to be digested by a great fish and the terror of that alone must have overwhelmed his soul. Everything seemed to have conspired against him and so his spirit sank to its lowest depth. There was an eerie feeling of loneliness and abandonment.

This was the ideal time for self pity to 'kick' in and thus add to his misery. It was the right time it seemed, to become irrational and confused. Apart from gastric slime all over him, seaweed on his head and elsewhere entangled him. His reality was harsh and so denial did not help at this time. What was happening was real.

Are you in a similar reality? Is there a feeling of being trapped in an environment that is inhospitable even seemingly impossible for survival? Are you in a situation where there is no room to maneuver and you are about to give up and resign yourself to a dreadful end? Ah! Have faith. Jonah was delivered and you too, can be. Don't give up, for God sees your trouble and will deliver you out of it.

PRAYER

Lord, help me in my difficult situation to find hope in you. Amen

WISDOM

Despair is the mother of hope, not death.

Sin Sinks!

*"To the roots of the mountain **I sank down**; the earth beneath **barred me** in forever"*
Jonah 2:6.

REFLECTION

Jonah was running from God and this only brought him into distress on a scale that he never thought possible. Running from God puts us on a downward path that will produce nothing but sorrow. Departure from God is to disconnect from Life. Let no one deceive you, for you can never ever achieve a life of fulfillment, satisfaction, blessedness and contentment outside of the will of God.

When we begin a "journey to Joppa" we will quickly sink to the very depths of the deep and into a life of disappointment and despair. The first step in the wrong direction in life will only entangle us in a mire of sin and its horrible consequences. The more we struggle in it, the more enslave we become. No person who makes disobedience their goal in life will ever come out whole. Sin is a destructive force that puts the total man out of commission. Sin, like the law of gravity, pulls down, and it will bring us to the undesirable dregs of life.

If we want a wretched life, then live in sin. As leprosy causes the flesh to rot, so sin degrades those who live in it. Sin will never take us to the mountain top in exciting and exhilarating experiences with God. Sin will always lead to the valley of frustration and painful anguish. Sin takes us into the arena of God's displeasure and curse.

You can choose to remain in sin or escape its hold through Christ. What will you do?

PRAYER

Lord, help me to look away from sin and unto you. Amen

WISDOM

The path of sin has no high ground.

Sin Has Penalties!

"To the roots of the mountain I sank down; the earth beneath barred me in forever"
Jonah 2:6.

REFLECTION

When a Christian sins, and fails to deal expeditiously with that offense against God, it is just a matter of time before the hand of God will move into noticeable action in that life. No believer, no matter how clever he or she tries to cover his or her track, will ever get away with it. Judgment begins in the house of God.

If we are members of His household, God will not tolerate our misconduct. His hand of chastening will overtake us, and should we be so foolish as to ignore His discipline, He will resort to sterner measures that will be excruciating and could even end in an untimely death.

Should we as Christians begin to live carelessly and have no regard for the violation of God's holy laws, we are setting up ourselves for the judgment of God, which can be very sudden. God's judgment was lethal for the sons of Aaron, Nadab and Abihu, as they offered up unauthorized fire before the Lord. They were consumed in a moment. Ananias and Saphira thought they could pull the wool over the eyes of the Apostles, but were instantly struck dead. God judges sin.

Jonah tried to escape his assigned responsibility but God confronted him with an experience close to death. *"It is a fearful thing to fall into the hands of the living God"* Hebrews 10:31 (K.J.V), even in this Day of Grace. God has saved us for a purpose and if we are trying to frustrate the counsel of God for our lives we have nothing to gain from such action but pain and sorrow. *"Shall we continue in sin, that grace may abound? God forbid"* Romans 6:1-2 (K.J.V.).

PRAYER

Lord, help me to recognize and do your will always. Amen

WISDOM

God knows your sin.

Profile Of A Backslider

*"To the roots of the mountain **I sank down**; the earth beneath **barred me** in forever"*
Jonah 2:6. (Read Psalm 32:3)

REFLECTION

In Psalm 32 we get into the mind of a man who had committed two horrendous sins. He went to bed with another man's wife and when he discovered she was pregnant, he tried to cover it with guile. When that too failed, he used the sword of Ammon, the enemy, to commit what he thought was the perfect murder.

Somehow, when we sin, we think we can exclude God and conscience as witnesses. We try to con ourselves into believing that we can somehow 'blindfold' God with an excuse and then proceed to live like normal, upright persons with no stain of sin on our hands. When Christians sin they always leave some evidence of their deeds. While they may try and cover their tracks with pretence, hypocrisy and even denial, yet, they cannot silence the nagging, accusing, disturbing, annoying voice of conscience which, when aroused, will not keep silent.

We may not confess that sin to anyone. We may even try to buy the silence of witnesses for we don't want decent people in our neighborhood to think that we are 'that kind of person.' But trying to buy off conscience is quite another story, for when conscience is aroused, it is like an army of mighty warriors with battering rams intent on destroying the fortification of lies we try to erect and hide behind. The pounding of conscience is relentless. Under its battering life takes a turn for the worst. *"When I kept silent, my bones wasted away through my groaning all the day long"* Psalm 32:3 (A.S.V.). Concealed sin may be likened unto putting live coals of fire in the bosom.

PRAYER

Lord, help me to be honest with you in all areas of my life. Amen

WISDOM

Concealed sin generates more sin.

Profile Of A Backslider

*"When I kept silent, **my bones wasted away through my groaning all day long**"*
Psalm 32:3

REFLECTION

Sincere believers are always ashamed of the evil they have committed. That is why invariably, we make much effort to hide the dirt under the rug, out of sight of prying eyes. We don't want our 'little' misadventure, or our 'little' secret to become a scandal. Therefore we learn to conceal our sins and to guard our secrets with the care of security agents at Fort Knox, depository of U. S. gold.

What better way to keep a secret but to keep silent? If I don't talk who will know? The only problem with sin is that it is somewhat like pregnancy which means that while it can be concealed for a time, it will soon be evident to all when the 'belly' begins to show.

The most difficult part of keeping a sinful act a secret is dealing with the matter internally. To use a medical analogy for making moral application, leaving 'internal bleeding' unattended will prove detrimental or even fatal. Guilt affects our health and saps our vitality. Guilt is like a cancer eating away at our vital organs. Therefore while we may have the outward appearance of health for a season, there is no inward soundness but rather decay and rottenness.

Concealed sin cannot produce a contented mind, for sin is a very disruptive force. Life becomes listless and the whole person becomes sour and disoriented. Concealed sin brings unrelieved pain and sorrow to the total personality. Concealed sin destroys. If you choose to hide it, you will prove the truth of all this meditation has been saying.

PRAYER

Lord, help me to confess my sin and experience joy in the Holy Spirit. Amen

WISDOM

Sin brings persistent pain that can be relieved only by confession.

Profile Of A Backslider

*"For day and night your hand was heavy upon me; **my strength was sapped** as in the heat of summer"*
Psalm 32:4.

REFLECTION

When we go astray from the Lord, life becomes vexing and unpleasant. Then, God Himself takes the battle to us and blocks all blessings on our lives. He contends with us and life becomes gloomy and filled with sadness. The grieved Holy Spirit within makes us conscious day and night, of our unconfessed sin, and our wayward behavior. The sweet peace of God is now absent from the life and we become cranky, contentious, bitter and at times aggressive.

When we are in such a condition of unrepentance, sourness develops in our life for there is the absence of joy. Therefore life becomes a drag day and night. We dread being alone, for it is then that the heaviness of spirit is at its worst and the affliction of the soul is intensified. We even become vulnerable to drug abuse. In this terrible state, sin disrupts fellowship and communion with God. Prayer then becomes a vain exercise and this only adds to our anxiety and frustration.

For the unrepentant sinner, there is no buoyancy, energy, purpose, drive or enthusiasm, but only a sense of numbness and deadness. Depression becomes our fellow-traveler and we curse the day we were born. All our days are overcast with dark clouds and not a ray of light breaks through. When sin is in our lives true happiness goes on vacation. A change for the better will come only when we put sin on vacation. Are you willing to do that?

PRAYER

Lord, help me to return to you today. Amen

WISDOM

God's chastening changes backsliders.

Profile Of A Backslider

*"For day and night your hand was heavy upon me; **my strength was sapped** as in the heat of summer"*
Psalm 32:4

REFLECTION

God not only disciplines Christians but sometimes increases that discipline. This happens when a sinning Christian behaves like a stubborn horse or mule. Also to use a medical analogy, spiritual dehydration is guaranteed to all those who hold unto cherished sins. Spiritual dehydration is a manifestation of the displeasure of God with our behavior and manner of life. When the moisture, sweetness and nutrition of the fruit of the Spirit are denied our spirit, then it is sapped dry and left parched.

A body without moisture cannot survive. When the blast of God's wrath penetrates our souls and we become debilitated, disoriented and 'dried out', it is time to recognize the heavy hand of God on our lives, beckoning us to turn from our sin and return to the Lord. God's discipline will make us weak, sickly, or even take us to an early grave.

God desires us to be like trees planted by streams of water (Psalm 1). In that location we will never be lacking in moisture or nutrition. His desire for the Christian is to have streams of living water flowing out of his being. Christ wants us to enjoy the *"well of water springing up unto eternal life"* John 4:14.

As for the harmful 'heat of the sun' God can provide us with protection from its harm. He will provide the shelter we need from its lethal rays. If you deal honestly with your sins in His presence, He will restore the vital moisture for your 'dried out' soul from His own reservoir.

PRAYER

Lord, help me to act now in returning to you. Amen.

WISDOM

God's affliction is instruction.

God Of The Impossible

*"To the roots of the mountain I sank down; the earth beneath barred me in forever. **But you brought** my life up from the pit, O LORD my God"*
Jonah 2:6.

REFLECTION

Jonah's troubles were beyond the help of ordinary means. Here was a man trapped in the midst of the sea in the belly of a great fish. No man could survive that ordeal in a fish and live to testify about it. His experience is as close as you could get to an out of the body experience.

But it was from the unique and lowly position that Jonah's faith soared up to God. How strange yet sure are the ways of God. Ever so often it is when we are eyeball-to-eyeball with the impossible, that the God of the impossible becomes a living reality. It is in that circumstance, when we are hemmed in on every side by forces hostile to us, with the devil ready to launch his final assault on our juggler, that God appears and gives us the victory. It is in those extreme, heart-wrenching and desperate emergencies that the God of hope makes His appearance and does the extraordinary.

Again and again, the saints of God testify, that their most enduring and sweetest memories are when God turns up in the nick of time and rescues them from dire trouble. It is those experiences we now treasure and would never trade place with anyone. It is when God delivers our lives from the pit that songs of rejoicing are born. It is by those experiences that the cornerstone of our faith is reinforced and our boast in our God, who is mighty to deliver, becomes a reality.

Never give up on God when faced with the impossible for He is more than able to rescue us out of every human predicament conceivable.

PRAYER

Lord, help me to have confidence in you in all circumstances. Amen

WISDOM

Dreadful circumstances draw us near to a firmer faith in God.

Sign Of Jonah

*"To the roots of the mountain I sank down; the earth beneath barred me in forever. **But you brought my life up** from the pit, O LORD my God"*
Jonah 2:6.

REFLECTION

Sin brings us into endless troubles and finally into death and judgment. Jonah's disobedience brought on the tempest of God's displeasure, his being cast into the sea and then being entombed three days in the belly of a great fish, and, finally his deliverance from the jaws of death.

Jonah was a type of another who did not sin, yet suffered and died on a cross as our substitute. Jonah being cast into the 'water of death' saved a ship and its crew. Jesus, on the other hand, dying on a cross, saved the world.

"For as Jonah was three days and three nights in the belly of the whale (sea monster); so shall the Son of Man be three days and three nights in the heart of the earth" Matthew 12:40 (A.S.V).

God did not abandon Jonah in the belly of the great fish and neither did God abandon Jesus in the tomb. And after Jesus died, God by the miracle of His resurrection, disarmed death and opened the door to eternal life for all those who will trust Jesus as Savior.

Jesus is the Only Answer to man's victory over sin, disease and death. He is the Only Door to eternal life. Because He lives you also can live. So, why not invite Jesus into your heart as your personal Savior, even now.

PRAYER

Lord, help me without delay to invite you into my heart to be my personal Savior. Amen

WISDOM

Deliverance is here!

Remember God?

*"**When my life was ebbing away,** <u>I remembered you,</u> LORD, and my prayer rose to you to your holy temple"*
Jonah 2:7.

REFLECTION

Don't wait for the extreme to happen in your life to bring God to the forefront. When we fix our minds on the fleeting things of this life, the threat of death is a grand reminder to us as to what is really valuable in life. When catastrophe intrudes our comfort zone, and life spins out of control, it is then that God is brought to mind in a forceful way.

When there is money in the bank, job security, harmony in the home, good health and good prospects, we tend to forget God. When life looks rosy and we greet the day with this song, "O what a beautiful morning, O what a beautiful day, I have a beautiful feeling everything is going my way" beware the ugly, the unexpected. Soon the unthinkable can stare us in the face. Our relationship with God that was on low throttle or even in hibernation needs to be revived. The ugly unexpected jolts us to the reality that our only hope of survival in this world of sin is dependence on God's grace and mercy.

Therefore we need constantly to remind ourselves that God is not a God of convenience to be utilized at our pleasure. Jonah at this point in his life was going through the refining mill of God's scourging and it was having telling effects on his entire life. God was now emerging on center stage in his life and prayer was no longer a formality, but rather an urgent exercise of the soul. Confession had become deep, repentance genuine, and sincerity was at its premium in reaching out to God, in his desperation. When circumstances whip us, it is a gentle and at times a cruel reminder to us of the important role God ought to play in our lives.

PRAYER

Lord, help me to give you the priority you deserve in my life. Amen

WISDOM

Don't wait for a calamity in your life to call upon God.

Sin Tarnishes The Memory Of God

*"When my life was ebbing away, **I remembered you**, **LORD**, and my prayer rose to you to your holy temple"*
Jonah 2:7.

REFLECTION

Jonah, deluged by sin, remembered the Lord. When sin enters and takes up residence in our souls the memory of God is greatly diminished. When sin sits on the throne of our lives the holy nature of God becomes distorted and diluted. When sin guards the entrance to our wills, it destroys the fortifications of righteousness in our souls and tears down everything that is decent, just, pure, and worthy of God.

Sin desecrates the inner sanctuary of our lives and introduces vile and evil practices that violate the Ten Commandments of God. The secret springs of our lives become polluted and poisoned. Our hands become defiled with evil activities and our bodies become instruments of immoral sex and illicit drug abuse. Greed rules the nest and corruption and vice become our common practice.

Sin may be likened to shutters that exclude the light of God from the life and imprisons us into a dark, filthy, slimy, despicable, proud and arrogant life style that defiles, enslaves, restricts, brings shame, riddles the conscience with guilt, drives self esteem into a pit of despair and leaves the self with endless unresolved conflicts. Sin destroys completely.

A new day dawned for Jonah when he prayed and was delivered. It is only when the backslider turns his or her battered mind, body and spirit to God that the desire for God increases. When prayer is made for God to intervene, He will, for He is gracious, kind, gentle, loving and forgiving toward the repentant. Why not turn to God today?

PRAYER

Lord, help me to avoid sinning. Amen

WISDOM

Tragedy has a way of putting God on the front burners of our lives.

Godly Sorrow And Prayer

*"When my life was ebbing away, I remembered you, LORD, and **my prayer rose to you to your holy temple**"*
Jonah 2:7.

REFLECTION

Jonah was a backslider who was coming to the end of his sliding with a humble, broken and contrite spirit. He had passed through the school of God's severe discipline and he had no plans to repeat that course for it had almost taken his life. The final lesson in this course taught him what godly sorrow is and he was now exercising it with sincerity of heart, intensity of spirit and an urgency and passion he had never before experienced.

Please note the difference between sorrow and godly sorrow. Godly sorrow is that which brings us to the place of repentance. It is a place where we turn from disobedience with urgency. It is the place where sin is renounced, condemned and forsaken. Jonah was not now at God's altar putting on a show of repentance. The scourging he had endured had cleansed him from a life of pretence and a false sense of spirituality. This prayer came from the depths of his heart and like a sweet aroma it rose up to delight the heart of God.

David said, *"I **acknowledged** my sin unto thee, and mine iniquity **did I not hide**"* Psalm 32:5 (A.S.V.). It took David just about nine months of chastening to come to the place where he admitted his sin and then turned from it with revulsion and abhorrence.

How long is it taking you? Don't you think it is about time you repent of your wickedness so that your prayers may rise to God in His holy temple?

PRAYER

Lord, help me to pray from a heart cleansed of sin. Amen

WISDOM

Prayer rises to God only when our hearts are cleansed.

Dealing With Sin

*"When my life was ebbing away, I remembered you, LORD, and **my prayer rose to you to your holy temple**"*
Jonah 2:7.

REFLECTION

Jonah's prayerful honesty impresses. Dealing honestly with our sins in our prayer is most important. The Psalmist said, *"I will confess my transgressions to the LORD"* Psalm 32:5. General confession will never prove adequate. Our sins must be identified and owned by us in the presence of God. If we lied, we must confess the lie, if we smeared someone, we must admit to it, if we lusted, we must be prepared to bare our soul to God in all honesty.

There is a blessedness attached to honest confession of sin in our lives. Confession must pass the stage of excuse, rationalization and justification and be owned and acknowledged as wicked acts against God. If there is no genuine confession of our sins then it stands to reason that there is no genuine forgiveness. When sins are forgiven the inner man is cleansed and a great burden is lifted. I recently heard a man excitedly exclaim, "I feel like a ton has come off my soul. I feel light." This man had experienced the cancellation of the debt he owned God. That made him a very happy man, and that too, can happen to you.

Sin is a crushing weight on body, soul and spirit and when it is removed there is just cause for a person to rejoice and shout with gladness. This said gentleman cried with hot tears bathing his face, "Mama, I am a new man." Forgiveness of sin is the very foundation of a spiritual awakening, a new and healthy relationship with the Lord, a renewal of the soul and the foundation for transformed human relationships.

PRAYER

Lord, help me to have a fresh start. Amen

WISDOM

Confession delayed means mercy denied.

107

God Is Holy

*"When my life was ebbing away, I remembered you, LORD, and my prayer rose to you **to your holy temple**"*
Jonah 2:7.

REFLECTION

We, like Isaiah of the Bible, live in a world where sin and evil dominate every aspect of life. It is difficult to conceive in our minds of a being that is separate and apart from sin; of a being that is absolutely holy, righteous, just. Such a being, therefore is to be reverenced by us, for such is the divine being our souls must recognize as God. No sinner could even for a second endure the full glare of the awesome majesty and splendor of God, who dwells in unapproachable light.

God hates our sins with a perfect hatred and He cannot compromise, condone or excuse it. Sin is against the very nature of God and is abhorrent to His being. Therefore, for God, sin must be judged with the greatest severity. For prayer to be effective we must appreciate the One to whom our prayer is addressed. There is one attribute that permeates the nature of God and affects all His actions, it is His holiness.

Jonah spoke of God's holy temple because Jonah knew that's where a holy God lives. We as believers are to be holy for God our Father is holy. If we confess ourselves to be children of God, then we must ensure pure hearts, clean hands, and walk in the truth. Holiness must characterize our lives. When we sin it must be dealt with instantly and not allowed to fester in our hearts for sin and prayer cannot mix. For prayer to reach the ear of God our lives must be right in His sight.

God has made abundant provision for our cleansing through the blood of Christ on the cross. Avail yourself of that cleansing blood when defiled by sin. When you do it will make a difference in your prayer.

PRAYER

Lord, help me to always walk in holiness of life. Amen

WISDOM

Power in prayer is bound up in holiness of life.

Idolatry!

*"Those who cling to **worthless idols** forfeit the grace that could be theirs"*
Jonah 2:8.

REFLECTION

Jonah was confronted by the idolatry of pagans and was challenged. In our world idolatry is alive and well. Idolatry is not peculiar to pagan nations but can be found in countries where Christianity is the official religion. An idol is any object that is worshipped in the place of God. The Apostle Paul in addressing the Athenians on Mars' Hill stated, *"We ought not to think that the Godhead is like unto gold or silver or stone, graven by art and device of man"* Acts 17:29.

Notice that Jonah assesses idols to be worthless rather than worshipful. He is right. An idol is the ultimate insult to God. To exchange *"The glory of the incorruptible God for the likeness of an image of corruptible man, and of birds and four-footed beasts, and creeping things"* (Romans 1:23) (A.S.V.) demonstrates the depravity of the human heart. An idol is lifeless and hence has no power. Behind those lifeless forms is an evil power and the worship that is offered to idols is in fact worship that is offered to the Devil and his demons.

We must recognize demonic reality. Demonic presence is real and evil, and hence, idolatry draws us away from the worship of God into a system that is diabolical. Idols are not an aid to worship but a distraction from the worship of the living God so be wary of idols.

Now there are attitudes that smack of idolatry. **Stubbornness** the Bible tells us is *"as idolatry"* I Samuel 15:23 (A.S.V). Another attitude is **greed** (Ephesians 5:5). The best way to guard against all such things that war against the soul is to make Christ the Lord of our lives.

PRAYER

Lord, help me to be wholly devoted to you. Amen

WISDOM

To guard against idolatry we must worship God wholeheartedly.

Miss Grace!

"Those who cling to worthless idols ***forfeit the grace*** *that could be theirs"* Jonah 2:8.

REFLECTION

Jonah's message makes us focus now on consequences. He warns that when the heart and its affection are misguided, God and all His benefits will be missed. When we hold fast to that which is false then the things of eternal value go unnoticed. The heart can easily become the shrine for idolatry and a haven for vile and unwholesome desires, therefore, we must guard our hearts diligently and devotedly.

To break out of the cocoon of selfish ambition, pride, abuse of sex, greed, self-righteousness, anger, and superstition is no easy undertaking. We have a nature that sides with darkness and that has little desire for the things of God. We would in our unregenerate state cling to that which is false and destructive and that damns our souls to hell, rather than cry out to God for grace and mercy.

Jonah recognizes that there are those who would rather *"cling to worthless idols."* This is because the prophet knew that the heart of man is a very dark place of deceit and wickedness, without natural desire for truth. In spiritual matters, mankind, and history bears this out, will go for the lie rather than the truth.

How then, can sinful hearts find God? There is only one way. The Lord must open our eyes by His Spirit removing the scales from them. God's grace is now in operation, ready to do just that. You have, therefore, the opportunity right now to receive the gift of eternal life through Christ our Savior. Why cheat your soul of eternal life and a glorious tomorrow, when your sins can be forgiven today?

PRAYER

Lord, help me right now to receive Jesus into my heart as Savior. Amen

WISDOM

God's time is now.

God's Grace

*"Those who cling to worthless idols forfeit **the grace** that could be theirs"*
Jonah 2:8.

REFLECTION

God's grace is truly amazing, and Jonah came to acknowledge that. Under the Old Testament economy one could approach God through the sacrifice of certain animals as prescribed by the law. It was a merciful provision of God whereby the sinner could approach God, but even that in itself was inadequate. The book of Hebrews informs us that the blood of bulls and goats could not remove sin.

Rivers of animal blood flowed for centuries but its effects were only short term. All that blood was pointing to the future to that perfect person, the Lord Jesus Christ, who was to become our High Priest and also the offering for our sins. In time He became incarnate. He was identified by John as God's Lamb who would once and for all take away the sin of the world (John 1:29).

Speaking of Christ the Bible declares, *"But he, when he had offered one sacrifice for our sins for ever, sat down on the right hand of God"* Hebrews 10:12 (A.S.V.). Christ's death on the cross introduced to all mankind God's wonderful plan of salvation. It is through Him the wonderful grace of God became a living reality. There is no need ever to repeat His sacrifice, hence, there is no more need of animal sacrifices, for the precious blood of Christ shed has opened the door of salvation once and for all.

The work of salvation is an accomplished reality and it is yours at no cost. It is free but it is not cheap. Why not embrace it now?

PRAYER

Lord, help me to receive your grace. Amen

WISDOM

God's grace is amazing.

God's Grace

*"Those who cling to worthless idols forfeit **the grace** that could be theirs"*
Jonah 2:8.

REFLECTION

Jonah made a profound statement when he spoke of grace. In the New Testament the Apostle Paul was fascinated by this subject. In writing to the Corinthians he said, *"For ye know the grace of our Lord Jesus Christ, that, though he was rich, yet for your sakes he became poor, that ye through his poverty might become rich"* II Corinthians 8:9 (A.S.V.). Grace took the Son of God from His exalted and glorious throne to the place of the cursed and the damned. Jesus gave up the constant worship and adoration of angels to be born in a manger. He gave up the outward manifestations of divine splendor to be made lower than an angel, yea, to be made a man. He came to earth to serve and to give His life as a ransom for humanity – all because of grace.

Because of grace the Scriptures explain, Jesus became nothing to make us something. While He sojourned here on earth He did not associate Himself with the rich, the famous and the powerful, but with the poor and lowly – mostly with fishermen, tax collectors, sinners and the outcast of society. Grace is like that; it bends low to lift high.

Of course, grace cost, but He paid it all, so that we pay nothing. He was despised, maligned, hounded and persecuted. He was betrayed by one of His own for a paltry sum of money. Even one member of the inner circle denied Him. Justice was denied Him both by the religious and civil authorities. He was crucified as a common criminal. All that He suffered was for one purpose - to bring us the grace of God, that we might obtain salvation. Jonah rejoiced in the truth of God's redeeming grace.

PRAYER

Lord, help me to lay hold daily on your grace. Amen

WISDOM

Grace opens our eyes to appreciate Christ the Savior

Saved By Grace

*"Those who cling to worthless idols forfeit **the grace** that could be theirs"* Jonah 2:8.

REFLECTION

The Apostle Paul in explaining salvation emphasizes the significance of grace. He says *"For **by grace have ye been saved** through faith; and that not of yourselves, **it is the gift of God;** not by works, that no man should glory"* Ephesians 2:8-9 (A.S.V). Jonah too, recognized this truth even though he lived in the Old Testament times. It is crucial to understand the role of grace in salvation. God's plan of salvation excludes all human effort, and that, for a good reason. Fallen human nature is morally and spiritually brittle and defective and so to attain salvation by our feeble works is destined to failure.

The Apostle Paul provides us with a clear picture of the hopeless human condition. *"For we also once were **foolish, disobedient, deceived,** serving divers lusts and pleasures, living **in malice** and envy, hateful, hating one another"* Titus 3:3 (A.S.V). No good acceptable to God can be found in our fallen human nature (Romans 8:5-8).

Any good performed by our fallen nature is at best defective. God's goodness has no defect and, hence, this takes us to a level that is unattainable by the 'flesh'. The Scripture states categorically, *"There is none that doeth good, no, not as much as one"* Romans 3:12 (A.S.V).

God's provision for our salvation is therefore not based on human attainment, but rather on divine grace. Salvation is a gift to be received by faith. This removes all ground for boasting and hence God gets all the glory. Have you as yet accepted God's gift of salvation?

PRAYER

Lord, help me to make you my Savior today. Amen

WISDOM

God's Word informs but God's grace transforms.

Grace Produces Inward Changes

*"Those who cling to worthless idols forfeit **the grace** that could be theirs"*
Jonah 2:8.

REFLECTION

Jonah's experience was a thrilling example of how God's grace triumphed in a city of evil inhabitants. The grace of God produces wonderful changes even in unlikely settings. These changes are not the result of human effort, but rather the transforming work of the Spirit resulting in spiritual birth in the heart of whoever believes. Spiritual birth provides a new nature, the miraculous work of the Holy Spirit. But despite the greatness of that miracle the old nature is not destroyed.

Let us for a moment consider this doctrine of the believer having two natures by taking a close look at Saul of Tarsus. On his way to persecute the Christians in Damascus, he met the Lord Jesus and his entire world went into a spin. His heart was changed by a miracle of God. After his conversion, he began preaching Christ. Before, Paul, who hated Christ so intensely became passionately in love with Christ. Before, Paul thought Christianity was an evil to be stamped out. After, Paul became its apologist and chief missionary.

Grace reached the inner core of Saul's being where wickedness reigned and in an instant, an infusion of grace brought a change of heart, purity of thought and purposefulness of action. The desire to pursue a path of good was generated by the Spirit of grace. These changes were not superficial, but permanent.

Yet Paul, throughout his Christian life described the doing of good as a constant struggle against sinful desires. But by God's grace all sin can be overcome. How is your struggle against internal evil?

PRAYER

Lord, help me today to lean upon your grace. Amen

WISDOM

Grace is God's work from start to finish.

Grace Working Throuh Us

"But by the grace of God I am what I am, and his grace to me was not without effect. No, I worked harder than all of them – yet not I, but the grace of God that was with me"
I Corinthians 15:10.

REFLECTION

Grace puts God at the centre of our lives. When grace is elsewhere, sin is there. Christian maturity does not spring from the energy of self but from the grace that was introduced into our lives when Christ became our Savior. We are not born with this grace which connects us to God. Only the believer has within God's resource of grace. It is this grace, flowing in us and through us, that brings us the rich dynamics of God's blessings.

Understanding God's grace is important for living by God's grace. Our native might, power, intellect and wisdom all work contrary to God's grace. The self, the enemy of grace, fosters jealousy, strife and misery. Such works of the flesh bring no glory to God. When grace reigns in our hearts a new dimension of spiritual values, gifts or abilities are demonstrated, wholly energized by the Spirit of God. Apart from God's grace we can do nothing. All our natural talents and gifts are given to us by God. To pretend that this is not so is to deceive ourselves.

The marvel of God's grace is that it works within us such wonders. It brings us into a sphere where supernatural abilities become operational in our lives. If we are to be strong in the Lord and live in His might, we must allow the grace of God to work in our members, to the praise of His glory. By means of grace, God becomes a partner in our sphere of ministry, providing us with the riches and the power to succeed in authentic Christian living. It is through God's grace we become great achievers.

PRAYER

Lord, help me by your grace to live for your glory. Amen

WISDOM

For grace to be effective in us the body must be surrendered to Christ.

Grace Rejected

"How much more severely do you think a man deserves to be punished who has **trampled** *the* <u>Son of God</u> *under foot, who has treated* **as an unholy thing** <u>the blood of the covenant</u> *that sanctified him, and who has* **insulted** <u>the Spirit of grace</u>?*
Hebrews 10:29.

REFLECTION

Sin causes us to resist grace, and blinds us to its consequences. If we reject the offer of God's grace we shall suffer the consequences, for all eternity. The nature of sin is to harden the heart and hence to make us indifferent and callous to the things of God. When the convicting work of the Spirit is constantly resisted we only display our contempt for what Christ did on the cross for us.

This is a powerful verse. It makes explicit God's thoughts about grace. We learn that every time we reject the grace of God, we are trampling on the Son of God and His sacrifice. We learn too, that when God reaches out to us by His grace and we display an attitude of rejection or a lack of appreciation of what He did for us on the cross, we hurt God deeply and personally.

Sin is the only thing that keeps anyone from accepting Christ as Savior. When Christ is rejected, then sin is accepted, and the Devil rejoices.

When the Spirit bids you come and you say, "No," in your heart, He is insulted. If you reject the Savior and die in your sins, you will have to endure in your person the eternal consequences of that decision. This means there will be no avenue of escape from eternal darkness, where light never shines. God's appeal goes out to you today. Why not invite the Savior now into your heart?

PRAYER

Lord, help me to surrender daily to your grace. Amen

WISDOM

Grace rejected means God insulted.

Song Of Thanksgiving

*"But I, with **a song of thanksgiving**, will sacrifice to you. What I have vowed I will make good. Salvation comes from the LORD"*
Jonah 2:9.

REFLECTION

Songs of thanksgiving to God emanate from redeemed hearts. Those who practice idolatry by bowing down before a lifeless piece of wood, stone or metal skillfully crafted by human hands or those who masquerade as Christians, yet worship the idols of their hearts, know nothing about songs of thanksgiving or what is true sacrifice to God.

Songs of thanksgiving are more than words uttered by the lips. Such singing transcends mere vocal expressions. Many persons get excited externally and will sing and dance with vigor, yet their hearts are far away from the Lord.

Songs of thanksgiving must not be confused with shouts. Israel shouted when the Ark was brought back into their camp. The ark at that time had become nothing more than a magic box, a religious charm. In the ark were the Ten Commandments, and those who shouted that day had already willfully spurned those laws in their hearts. Their delusion came to a sorrowful end when they were soundly defeated by their enemy, the Philistines (I Samuel 4:5-11).

Songs of thanksgiving can only come from the heart when there is a meaningful relationship with God. When we walk closely with God songs of thanksgiving will burst forth from the heart, even as we are about our normal, ordinary business. There is always a cause, a focus, a reality why the heart overflows with thanksgiving to God. Is there a song in your heart?

PRAYER

Lord, help me sing with sincerity Songs of Thanksgiving for Your salvation. Amen

WISDOM

If truly redeemed, we will be thankful to Him.

Give Thanks!

*"But I, with **a song of thanksgiving**, will sacrifice to you. What I have vowed I will make good. Salvation comes from the LORD"*
Jonah 2:9.

REFLECTION

Thankfulness is a good thing. Regrettably, we human beings are fundamentally selfish and so are not very thankful. This is because sin's roots are embedded in our sin nature. Jesus cleansed ten lepers and only one returned to give Him thanks (Luke 17:6). Under the Old Testament law provision was made in the sacrifices for an offering of thanksgiving (Leviticus 7:11, 12, 13).

The redeemed of the Lord ought always to be thankful. God blessed Israel but this privileged nation was not always thankful. During the first 40 years of Israel's history, after their mighty deliverance out of Egyptian bondage, there is not much thanksgiving recorded in that time frame. That journey in the wilderness was a diary of complaints, murmuring and grumblings in spite of the presence and power of God in their midst.

Now what happened to them was recorded for our learning (I Corinthians 10:11). We will discover, if we take a good look at ourselves, that we are no different than Israel was in the wilderness. Focus on the negatives in life generates an ungrateful heart and a complaining disposition. The Psalmist calls us to take a different view toward life when he says' *"O **give thanks** unto Jehovah; for **he is good**; for his **loving kindness endureth** for ever"* Psalm 107:1 (A.S.V.).

A change in attitude puts the life in a new direction where we begin to see genuine reasons to be thankful and this makes us pleasant, happy and fulfilled. Instead of grumbling today, why not give thanks to God?

PRAYER

Lord, help me to live always thanking you. Amen

WISDOM

Only the grateful can be thankful.

Sacrifice To God

*"But I, with **a song of thanksgiving**, will sacrifice to you. What I have vowed I will make good. Salvation comes from the LORD"*
Jonah 2:9.

REFLECTION

A heart that is thankful is a heart that can truly worship. Such a person has discovered the value of God in his life and thus will make time for Him in his daily life. To have God on the periphery of our lives is foolish. However, for Him to be central, we must spend time with Him daily and offer to Him regularly, even profusely, our sacrifice of praise.

Our time spent with the Lord must be planned, methodical, and of course, meaningful. It is the most important part of our day and we should not allow anything to rival or cheat us of our encounter with God. It is there the fire of our love for Him is stoked. It is there our expressions of appreciation for His grace and favor are remembered and nurtured. It is there too, we build our relationship with the Lord and hence come to know Him intimately.

Enoch walked with God and Abraham was the friend of God because they honored God daily in their lives. It is in those encounters that vows are made and honored. When the heart drifts from God, vows are taken lightly and oft times broken. But the moment the soul is restored, as was the case with Jonah, those promises made to God are renewed and honored.

Promises made to God cannot be discarded or ignored, taken lightly, or forgotten. They must be honored for God holds us to our word. A heart in the right place makes all the difference in a relationship.

PRAYER

Lord, help me to delight to do your will from a grateful heart. Amen

WISDOM

Commitment of heart leads to performance that delights the heart of God.

Salvation Is Of God

*"But I, with a song of thanksgiving, will sacrifice to you. What I have vowed I will make good. **Salvation comes from the LORD**"*
Jonah 2:9.

REFLECTION

The Lord is unique and so He is the Lord, even our Savior. But there are many pretenders and so false saviors. The Bible warns that such a time would come, when false claimants would arise and would deceive multitudes with their pernicious lies. The truth must be told - a sinner cannot be our Savior, for he too, stands in need of salvation.

Salvation has to come from another source other than ourselves. Our text provides the answer to the deepest need of the human heart - deliverance from sin. *"Salvation comes from the LORD."* Indeed, God is the author of our salvation. Fallen man does not have the spiritual acumen to rise above his sin. His nature and his habits are bound by the law of sin and death. We are slaves to sin and that is the stark reality. There is a tyrant in us that drives us to do wrong, in spite of our best intentions or efforts.

Only God through Christ can deliver us from sin. This He does by giving us a new nature. Salvation can only come when the issue of sin is resolved and Jesus did just that. God's salvation comes from a rebirth. God's salvation comes through Christ having taken our place on a cross and dying for our sins.

Thank God, His remedy for sin is now available. The door of salvation is open and our sins can be forgiven. New life is now available to us in Christ. Will you accept Christ today as your personal Savior?

PRAYER

Lord, help me to receive you into my heart as my personal Savior. Amen

WISDOM

Salvation is instant and permanent.

Deliverance Is Precious

*"And the LORD commanded the fish, **and it vomited Jonah onto dry land"***
Jonah 2:10.

REFLECTION

God has power over His creation. If man has the ability to make birds, reptiles, animals and creatures of the sea obey them, how much more God? God spoke, and thereby made from nothing the earth, the sun, moon and the stars. Everything we see above, around, beneath and beyond us owes its origin to God.

The prophet Job draws our attention to God's amazing control over His creation (Job 38-41). Job informs us about God's control over all entities. He is the one who establishes their laws. All things perform according to their determined courses. Justice, wrath, truth, life, death are the prerogative of deity. He is sovereign and does what He pleases and is answerable to no creature, visible or invisible, for what He does.

God will never relinquish His power or give or share His glory with any other. Therefore, it was at the behest of God that a great fish swallowed Jonah. It was in the great fish that Jonah was taught precious lessons in obedience. It was in the great fish he truly learnt to pray. It was there he mastered the true meaning of life, his mission, of being thankful, and, of course learned to honor his vows.

The great fish swallowed him in one gulp for him to learn his painful lessons and ejected him, a transformed, humbled man with a mission for God. Coming out of distress can be just as dramatic as getting into it. Rebellion against God brings us into the school of scourging, but obedience brings us into peace, joy, safety and joyous walking with the Lord.

PRAYER

Lord, help me to submit to you. Amen

WISDOM

Bitter lessons can make us better persons.

Divine Hand In Our Affairs

*"And the **LORD** commanded the fish, and it vomited Jonah onto dry land"*
Jonah 2:10.

REFLECTION

Evidence is a powerful tool. It vindicates truth. It gives assurance to reality. Jonah's 'nightmare' was over. His feet on the shore were enough to convince him that his harrowing experience in the great fish was past. It was like the children of Israel, under Moses, seeing the dead bodies of the Egyptian oppressors washing ashore on the Red Sea.

That power that had once held them in terrifying bondage was now in scattered, lifeless form. The military might of Egypt was overwhelmed by the power of God and Israel was now free. The terrifying darkness and repulsive slime inside the great fish gave way to brilliant, warm sunshine and wonderful fresh air.

You may have passed through a terrible ordeal in life when you had despaired of even living to tell the story. Then, suddenly God intervened to make a glorious difference.

When God steps in, sorrow is turned to singing; pain to pleasure. Do you remember how Abraham, about to slay his son Isaac, experienced God's miraculous intervention? We are told of God's provision of *"a ram caught in the thicket"* Genesis 22: 13(A.S.V.) to take Isaac's place. Like Jonah your great fish has vomited you up on a safe place and now you have a new zest for life and mission for God. He is the One who orders the events in the course of our lives, and when we are swallowed up, He delivers; when we are vomited up, He lifts us up!

PRAYER

Lord, help me to understand better how all things work for my good. Amen

WISDOM

Circumstances that swallow us up will one day vomit us out, and then God will lift us up!

God Of The Second Chance

*"And **the word** of the LORD **came** to Jonah **a second time**"*
Jonah 3:1.

REFLECTION

Jonah running from his divine task did not annul the need for that message to be delivered. What God determines He will see to it that it is done in the very way He has chosen. God will pursue with vigor and purpose, even with the chastening and scourging of His servant, to bring him to the point of obedience to the divine command.

God does not give up on us. He is the God of the second chance. So let us not think of running off on a path that will take us out of the will of God. We cannot hide ourselves in sin. There is no place we can go that will get God off our track. He will not simply take our case off His file. God loves more than we realize. We have not yet begun to understand God's love for us. He will use our very disobedience as the scourge to bring us back in line with His will.

We will then discover that God's will is always best. The path of disobedience always leads us into a horrible pit of sorrow, pain, depression, and guilt. But such experiences can be beneficial, if they cause us to hasten back to God to be delivered.

Jonah, thankfully, learnt His lesson and once again came to the place in his life where the voice of God could be heard. The task God has for you is unique to you and no one else can effectively fulfill what God has especially created you for. You are important to God and so are the people of 'Nineveh' who need to hear the message of God from your lips.

PRAYER

Lord, help me, on my second chance, to submit to your will. Amen

WISDOM

God's will prevails ultimately.

Tell God's Message

*"**Go** to the great city of Nineveh and **proclaim** to it the message I give you"* Jonah 3:2.

REFLECTION

Jonah now had his order to go to the wicked Gentile city of Nineveh and there proclaim the message he had from God. The church too, has a mandate to proclaim God's message to a sinful world. The church's mandate, note, is not to one city, but rather to the entire world which includes people of all the nations, tribes and tongues.

God is depending on the church, as He depended on Jonah, to proclaim His message. The task is formidable for the opposition is great. However, God has made available to us supernatural ability for the task.

God has made available to us a message that renews and transforms. It is offering eternal life to all who believe. It brings people out of darkness into marvelous light; a message that brings liberty to those who are in bondage and in the shadow of death.

The church's message is centered in the person of Christ. He was God taking on human nature. He loved us and demonstrated it by taking our place on a cross so that we might be reconciled to God. He died, was buried and on the third day rose from the dead and is now seated at the right hand of God, as our Savior and our Great High Priest.

"And in none other is there salvation: for neither is there any other name under heaven, that is given among men, wherein we must be saved" Acts 4:12 (A.S.V). Are you sharing this message with the lost and if you are lost why not receive this message today?

PRAYER

Lord, help me to both understand and apply your message. Amen

WISDOM

By the message proclaimed, the lost are reclaimed.

Obedience -The Key

"Jonah obeyed the word of the LORD and went to Nineveh. Now Nineveh was a very important city – a visit required three days"
Jonah 3:3.

REFLECTION

The fact that Jonah obeyed is crucial. Obedience to God is the key to a successful spiritual life. Yet, it is the greatest area of daily struggle for most Christians. Without obedience there can be no victory in our lives, no filling of the Holy Spirit, no fruit of the Spirit, yea, no power in our lives. If there is no obedience to God then know for sure that there will be no growth or maturing in the Christian faith.

Jonah did not always find it easy to obey God. He had to learn obedience in the 'school of hard knocks'. For purpose and fulfillment in life God must be obeyed. His will is best. For the Christian there can be no substitute for obedience. There is no way we can get by it or around that issue. Jesus says if we love Him then we must obey His commands. We cannot say we love God and then ignore the command of God as revealed in His Word.

A successful prayer life is the key to obedience. Joshua discovered this truth. Obeying God keeps us spiritual fit for faithful service. Obedience makes us to prosper in body, soul and spirit.

Also obedience to God makes our lives a blessing to others, as Jonah was soon to discover. The spirit of obedience will overcome the spirit of self-indulgence, and prevail in meaningful Christian activity and service for the Lord. Jonah obeyed God, and that principle ought to be the pattern for our lives.

PRAYER

Lord, help me to be more obedient to you. Amen

WISDOM

Let obedience to God be the consuming passion of your life.

God's Message And The City

*"Jonah obeyed the word of the LORD and went to Nineveh. Now **Nineveh was a very important city** – a visit required three days"*
Jonah 3:3

REFLECTION

Jonah's mission was historic. He was the first Hebrew prophet sent to a pagan city to proclaim the Word of the Lord. God's mercy extends far beyond the borders of Israel and this was but a foretaste of things to come. Nineveh at that time was the capital city of the Assyrian Empire; a world power of that day with a large army skilled in warfare and notorious for their brutality.

Important cities were the seat of government, commerce, industry, education, culture, law, justice, security, religion, and, of course sin in all its diverse manifestations. It was to this important centre that Jonah the prophet was sent with God's Word.

Cities play a very important role in the New Testament. Cities are great population centers and it was to these centers Paul, the Apostle, declared the gospel of Jesus Christ. Not only are cities great population centers, but they attract people, for whatever reason, from all over the world. Because of this fact, cities afford golden opportunities for spreading the gospel to multitudes, even to visitors from strange cultures. Take for example the Jews from Rome (Acts 2:10) who on hearing the gospel proclaimed in Jerusalem, returned to Rome with that message and quite likely established the church in Rome.

Are you sharing this Good News in the home, in the office, or in the market place?

PRAYER

Lord, help me to see the city as a great place to share this gospel. Amen

WISDOM

Cities need Christ.

The Launch

"On the first day, Jonah started into the city. He proclaimed: "Forty more days and Nineveh will be overturned"
Jonah 3:4.

REFLECTION

Launching any project is most important. Contemplating and initiating, while necessary are not sufficient. The world is full of contemplators and dreamers who never seem to get out of bed. Jonah had to travel over 500 miles just to get to his destination and then the real work would begin. Being on site is vital.

The first day in kinder prep, high school, college, on the job or on a mission for God, can impact on us negatively. Pioneering always has challenges to be faced with grit and determination. The first day is normally full of expectation, excitement and, of course, anxiety.

Jonah had a very solemn and sobering message for the inhabitants of Nineveh. In little over a month the city would be destroyed. This was a heathen city given over to idolatry, sorcery, violence and shedding of innocent blood. This was not an ordinary city, but extraordinary. Who would dare even contemplate subduing the military might of Assyria?

There was the rush of blood as Jonah opens his mouth to declare God's judgment on that city. Just as God opened the heart of Lydia to receive the message of God, so He prepares that wicked city to receive the message of judgment pronounced against it.

If God sends you on a mission, He is already at work in the hearts and minds of those you are commissioned to reach. So why not open your mouth and tell them about the grace of our Lord Jesus Christ?

PRAYER

Lord, help me to start the work you have given to me. Amen

WISDOM

Everything that needs an ending has a beginning.

The Power Of The Word

"The Ninevites believed God. They declared a fast, and all of them, from the greatest to the least, put on sackcloth"
Jonah 3:5.

REFLECTION

The message of Jonah had an extraordinary effect on the people of Nineveh. This word from God pricked their consciences, invaded their hearts and awakened faith in the One and Only true God. They were suddenly aware of the gravity of their spiritual need and the imminent danger that now confronted them. Time, which we often take for granted, was now running out on them for the judgment of God was now on the very threshold of their city and none would be spared.

The message of God is a great equalizer. It is not partial. It does not respect gender, age, social status or the status of gods we worship. The message of God drives terror into the heart of all evil doers. It rips off the mask of the self-righteous and uncovers the nakedness, poverty, blindness and folly of the human heart. All who have held God in contempt all their lives must answer for all their deeds.

The sinful inhabitants of Nineveh came to see that the gleaming sword of His wrath was ready to exact vengeance in an instance upon the careless, the wayward, the rebellious and the procrastinator.

Nineveh was face to face with the day of reckoning and they were terrified. Their only hope of being spared was to cast themselves wholly on the mercy of God - and that they did.

What about you who have been hearing the message of God from a child? Why have you not heeded God's warning? This is an opportune time to repent and trust God as your Savior.

PRAYER

Lord, help me to trust you today. Amen

WISDOM

Divine wrath awakens faith!

The Power Of Holy Living

May 08

"Watch your life and doctrine. Persevere in them, because if you do so, you will save both yourself and your hearers"
I Timothy 4:16.

REFLECTION

A preacher might have a good theological preparation, strong in voice, eloquent speech, yet be ineffective. This happens when a preacher is out of touch with his congregation, failing to connect with his audience. Jonah, God's prophet, had a message from God and he delivered that message in such a way he had the ear of every man, woman and child in Nineveh.

For preaching to touch the heart of hearers and get a positive response the Word must be delivered as a burden from God. In order for preaching to have authenticity with authority it must be delivered through the preacher in the power of the Holy Spirit. Bearing witness to God must have passion. We must be convinced that what we declare is God's truth. The message must first have its solemn impact upon us before we can convince and persuade others.

No true servant of God can afford to live carelessly. No believer can afford to be unsanctified in private or public life. The Apostle Paul exhorts us – *"Watch your life."* We cannot allow the appetites of our sinful nature and its practices to take a hold on our lives. Sin must be resisted in all its forms. If we are careless in doctrine, our lives will follow in that train. What we believe must be carefully scrutinized and all errors rejected. Clean spiritual lives and orthodox beliefs are necessary if we would have a powerful testimony for the Lord.

What is your life telling the world? What's your message to lost humanity?

PRAYER

Lord, help me to live each day for you. Amen

WISDOM

Our life is a display of who we serve.

Responsible Living

*"Watch your life and doctrine. **Persevere in them**, because if you do so, you will save both yourself and your hearers"*
I Timothy 4:16.

REFLECTION

What we believe and what we live must match. Our lives give power to what we believe. Non Christians see Christians as living books for them to read the Gospel. Our conduct will either win or repel them.

Our lives should never give to our 'hearers' an 'uncertain sound' or a note that is off key. We cannot afford to dabble in any kind of inconsistent behavior like listening to or telling off-color jokes, using coarse language, or be tempted to make or lose 'a quick buck' by dubious means.

Christians are God's lights in this world, and so we cannot afford to 'turn off' when it is convenient to us. If we do so, we will endanger many precious souls who look up to us. To regain a lost testimony is no easy undertaking. So let us not entertain the thought of taking a 'vacation' from Christian living. To maintain our Christian walk demands discipline in all areas of our lives.

God's assurance to us is that if we walk in the Spirit we will not fulfill the lust of the flesh. We will never let down our guard as long as we are Spirit-filled. The Word studied and stored in the heart keeps us fresh and relevant, making us instruments of God's salvation to those outside of Christ.

Put Christ on show in your life. Be like fine flour devoid of lumps. People will come to Christ because your life honors Him. Maintain your stand for the Lord to the praise of His glory.

PRAYER

Lord, help me to walk pleasing to you. Amen

WISDOM

Your life is a beacon of hope to others.

Know The Truth

"Watch your life and doctrine. Persevere in them, because if you do so, you will save both yourself and your hearers"
I Timothy 4:16.

REFLECTION

The Apostle Paul warns against not only a bad life but bad doctrine. It is like yeast placed in dough. Therefore, once inserted, its manifestation will soon become evident to all. People who contend that doctrines are not important are deceived. Such an idea has its origin in demons. All truth is doctrine-based, and that point needs to be emphasized. The Bible tells us to contend for the faith.

How should doctrine be taught? It must be taught by God's gifted and wise servants. The Bible says the servant of God must not quarrel about the truth. Christians teaching God's Word are encouraged to be wise as serpents and harmless as doves. God recognizes that error can be deadly. We must expose doctrines that are false and promote the truth.

We must not be gullible. Many teachings sound good, but when carefully examined in the light of God's Word, the ideas are found defective. Error mixed with truth is still error and hence dangerous.

Perverse minds will try to twist and manipulate truth to promote damnable false teachings. Biblical truth must be carefully extracted from its context and not become a pretext that is violently isolated from its context and then made to say what the false teacher wants it to say.

False teaching defiles the conscience, but God's truth upholds its integrity. To discern God's truth requires spiritual enlightenment which is a product of the Spirit.

PRAYER

Lord, help me to discern truth from error. Amen

WISDOM

The light of truth dispels the darkness of error.

Judgment Contemplated

"When the news reached the king of Nineveh, he rose from his throne, took off his royal robes, covered himself with sackcloth and sat down in the dust"
Jonah 3:6.

REFLECTION

As Jonah proclaimed the Living Word, the Spirit began convicting that great city of its great wickedness. The dreadful nature of sin began to take form and shape in their inner consciousness and the horror of their wickedness against a holy and righteous God seized their souls. For the first time they truly realized that they were standing at the edge of a fiery abyss about to join the damned who had rejected God, who had stifled conscience, who had resisted the Spirit and trampled the truth and who were forever lost in that place of eternal mourning, regret, eternal repentance and unanswered prayer.

It is a place away from the presence of God, the holy angels and the redeemed. It is a place away from joy, peace, contentment and satisfaction. It is a place of sorrow and endless woe. Hell is a horrible place for people whose sins were never forgiven.

Any person contemplating the dreadful judgment of a Holy God and the horrible destiny of the non Christian ought to act immediately as the king of Nineveh did. He humbled himself before God and looked to God to have mercy on His soul.

Your soul is your most precious possession; therefore treat its destiny as a matter of great urgency.

PRAYER

Lord, I cast myself upon you to have mercy on my soul. Save me now by your grace. Amen

WISDOM

There is no comfort or companionship in hell.

Effects Of Bad News

May 12

"When the news reached the king of Nineveh, he rose from his throne, took off his royal robes, covered himself with sackcloth and sat down in the dust" Jonah 3:6.

REFLECTION

Bad news can have a telling effect on our minds, moods and our bodies. Take for instance the case of David when he heard about the tragic death of his son Absalom. He was shaken; he wept, mourned and cried aloud. Nabal had a heart attack when his wife told him about what David was going to do and of her quick action to save the household.

When news reached the ears of Jacob that his brother Esau was coming to meet him with 400 armed men it produced in him great fear and distress. Bad news can be devastating for a nation as it was in the case of the Amorite kings. When they heard how the Lord had dried up the Jordon River to allow Israel to cross, the Bible states, *"That their hearts melted, neither was there spirit in them any more, because of the children of Israel"* Joshua 5:1 (A.S.V.)

The King of Nineveh on hearing the bad news that Nineveh was to be destroyed, quickly evaluated the situation amidst his fear and came to a rational conclusion and acted on that decision. If there was to be even a glimmer of hope for him and his city he must instantly disrobe himself of pride, arrogance, haughtiness and must robe himself in the garment of repentance, sorrow, brokenness, contrition and this he did by example.

How do you handle bad news? Does it drive you to despair or to God? Sometimes bad news is the mantle that covers a new and glorious start.

PRAYER

Lord, give me the grace to handle what appears on the surface to be bad news. Amen

WISDOM

Bad news helps us to seriously reflect on what is important in life.

God And Current Events

"Therefore this is what I will do to you, Israel, and because I will do this to you, prepare to meet your God, O Israel"
Amos 4:12.

REFLECTION

In every generation the voice of God thunders dire warnings to careless and reckless people to turn from their sins. But people are not interested and they turn a deaf ear as ancient Israel did and continue in their course and habits of sin until the cup of their iniquity is full. God is very patient with us sinners and affords us many opportunities to turn from our vile ways.

Amos in his book tells us in the fourth chapter of some of the warning signs God gives us that should make us consider the divine displeasure with our life styles.

The first one he mentions is 'empty stomach' or 'cleanness of teeth' and of course this speaks of starvation. When there is an inadequate supply of food and our street become filled with beggars, it is a sign of God's displeasure. The second sign is inadequate water. When the land becomes filled with sin, God causes nature to be unfavorable to us. The third warning affects our crops – they become diseased and insects invade our fields and of course this will court economic disaster and hardships. The fourth warning is outbreaks of plagues of all sorts.

The fifth warning is an increased in untimely deaths – murders, 'wars' and overflowing morgues. The sixth is large scale disasters that affect entire communities. The seventh is the final visitation of God in judgment upon the unrepentant and this, indeed, is the most fearful.

Are you prepared to meet God should your life come to a sudden end?

PRAYER

Lord, teach me the brevity of life and help me to serve you. Amen

WISDOM

God uses nature to speak to us, but are we listening to its voice?

Prepared To Meet God?

"Therefore this is what I will do to you, Israel, and because I will do this to you,
prepare to meet your God, *O Israel"*
Amos 4:12.

REFLECTION

Making preparation is a matter we are all familiar with. It touches just about every aspect of life and success or failure is to a large degree related to the degree of our preparation. For instance we prepare ourselves academically, socially, financially and of course we have contingency plans in place if there is a disaster. We make plans for good health, marriage, for having children, for owing a house, a car and even make arrangement with the funeral home as how our remains will be disposed of at death.

We plan parties, functions, recreations, vacations and business ventures and the list goes on. We prepare ourselves as individuals, as families, as communities and as a nation for all manner of things. Yet very low on our agenda is our preparation to meet God.

The rich fool in the parable of our Lord made abundant preparation only for this life and none for the life to come and died suddenly. The Ninevites had no time to reflect on the Living God and now His judgment was at their door. Belshazzar the king, in the midst of his partying, was weighed in God's scale and was found wanting and died in his sins that very night. Proud Nebuchadnezzar made his great boast and the judgment of God fell on him and he was insane for seven years.

It is not wise to put God on the bench of life; He must be on your field of play.

What place does God have in your life? Are you prepared to meet Him?

PRAYER

Lord, I give you my all and desire you to be Lord of my life. Amen

WISDOM

God must be central to all of our human activities if we desire true success.

Meet God Through Christ

*"Therefore this is what I will do to you, Israel, and because I will do this to you, **prepare to meet your God**, O Israel"*
Amos 4:12.

REFLECTION

Man is a religious being, yet in his fallen state there is no inclination to serve the living and true God in a way that is acceptable. The appetite for true spiritual values is not natural to his nature. There is a predisposition to embrace false religions as is evident in our world. Religions on a whole are ritualistic, laced with superstitions and their knowledge and doctrines of the true God are at best, defective.

Behind false religions are demonic forces and their mission is to keep the devotees in the dark. Christ is the only way back to God and if he is not central to your belief you are yet groping in the dark. His sacrifice and His sacrifice alone opened the door to God and forgiveness of sins.

Let no one deceive you with high sounding words for your salvation is to be found only in Christ for there is no *"other name under heaven, that is given among men, wherein we must be saved"* Acts 4:12 (A.S.V.).

If you would have a personal relationship with the Father or the Creator or by whatever name you may call Him, you must come through God the Son who identified Himself with us by taking on the nature of man.

If you would prepare yourself to meet your God, then you must own Jesus Christ as your personal Savior. There is no other option of getting into the Kingdom of God.

PRAYER

Lord, I now open my heart by faith and accept Jesus as my personal Savior. Amen

WISDOM

Jesus is the only way back to God and He will take you just as you are.

136

Power Of Contrition

"Then he issued a proclamation in Nineveh: "By the decree of the king and his nobles: Do not let any man or beast, herd or flock, taste anything; do not let them eat or drink"
Jonah 3:7.

REFLECTION

Jonah's message to the Ninevites was terrifying. It held out no hope. The payday for their sin was at the very door. They had provoked the God of heaven and He was about to respond in judgment. They were a desperate people and their situation demanded action from the heart and their leaders rose to the occasion and acted quickly and prudently.

Was there any means to avert divine wrath from being executed or stay the hand of God from carrying out His stated purpose against this wicked city? The leaders of Nineveh elected to humble themselves before the glorious God of heaven. God will not despise the contrite in heart. Those who search for Him with their whole heart will find Him.

There was no Abraham interceding for them as it was in the case of Sodom. There were no Samuels or Daniels pleading with God to save their city. There were not ten righteous persons in that city to avert certain disaster.

But the threat of disaster brings with it the hope of salvation. Hezekiah, the king, was told he was going to die and he immediately turned to God in desperate prayer, was healed and lived fifteen more years. The Ninevites in their most desperate hour turned to God in fasting and prayer and repentance and were heard.

Is your situation perilous? Humble yourself before God and lay hold of Him with all your heart. Who knows, He may yet spare you.

PRAYER

Lord, I stand broken before you; heal my backsliding. Amen

WISDOM

No one knows the depths of God's mercy.

Dealing With Sin

*"But let man and beast be covered with **sackcloth**. Let everyone **call** urgently on God. Let them **give up** their evil ways and their violence"*
Jonah 3:8.

REFLECTION

There are three important spiritual principles in our text that people of any age should contemplate in their turning to the Lord. The first is that our sins should bring us to the place of mourning, sorrow and shame. Our sins, every one of them, are hateful to God, be it stealing, lying, fornication, hate, an unforgiving spirit, murder, pride, etc. Such a life style must be confessed appropriately with deep emotions as wrong.

Our sorrow must go beyond the mere outward show or symbol of being covered with sackcloth. We must manifest a spirit that answers to that outward sign. When the heinous nature of our sin is discovered and we are face-to-face with their consequences, then the depth of our mourning must be intense and our calling on God to have mercy on us will break forth with an intensity we never knew we had within us.

Some years ago I witnessed a lady pouring out her soul before God with such intensity that great beads of sweat sprang from her forehead and ran down her face like a river. Her tears mingled with her sweat as she cried from the depths of her being for deliverance from her terrible plague of sin and suddenly there was calm in her soul for God heard her cry.

The third thing in our text, if we would have God act on our behalf, is our sin must be renounced immediately. Sin is not to be phased out as a gradual process, but must be brought to an abrupt end. How are you treating your sins?

PRAYER

Lord, help me to renounce sin in my life. Amen

WISDOM

Sin blocks blessing.

Giving Up Evil?

*"But let man and beast be covered with sackcloth. Let everyone call urgently on God. Let them **give up their evil ways and their violence**"*
Jonah 3:8.

REFLECTION

To break the cycle of sin in our lives is no easy matter. A person addicted to hard drugs, or theft, or prostitution, or pornography, or anger or worry, or whatever vice to which the affections of the heart is chained will testify of the grave and great struggle to get victory over these dreadful drives or impulses or tendencies, as we might call them.

For the Ninevites, they would either have to give them up or be destroyed and that is an important spiritual principle. The vices with which we are infatuated are destructive forces that drain the very life from our bodies. 'Vice and violence' are twins. They always hang out together. You dare rebuke a person's vice and his twin, violence, will attack you with vengeance or justification.

The matter of self control is important. However, the ability to say, 'No' to evil and, 'Yes' to good, is easier said than done. It is always the same tired excuse, "The next time I will do better." The siren cry of evil seems to drown out the voice of conscience and we end up doing the very thing we detest, and despise ourselves for doing.

When the fallen nature is in charge of the life, our course of action is predictable and our failure rate will be 100%. Sin weakens resolve and holds captive the will, the citadel of the soul.

Is sin your master or have you **died** to it?

PRAYER

Lord, help me daily to have victory in you. Amen

WISDOM

The will in God's keep will keep us from the desires of the flesh.

Association And Inspiration

*"Therefore, since we are **surrounded** by such a great cloud of witnesses, let us **throw off everything that hinders** and the sin that so easily **entangles**, and let us run with **perseverance** the race marked out for us"*
Hebrews 12:1.

REFLECTION

If we would have victory in our lives we should draw inspiration from successful people who were over comers in spite of the odds. The greatest persons who have ever adorned this world are in our camp and they are the great champions of our faith.

They were once in this race on earth and they achieved their goal with excellence of spirit. They were not daunted by the great obstacles that stood in their way. Their faith was grounded in a great, big, wonderful God who cannot fail and their lives validated that.

Should you associate with those who have a record of failure, you too will fail, but drawing on the strength of successful people gives you the drive to go on. The heroes of our faith laid aside all hindrances to achieve their goal of pleasing God. We too are in this race of life and only the winner gets the prize; therefore, run to win.

The strict discipline that characterizes the athlete that competes in the games must be ours as well. An overweight person has to be rid of all flab to gain the crown. This translates in the Christian life of ridding ourselves of harmful attitudes, dispositions, and cherished sins in our lives that entangle and make sanctification such an uphill climb.

Are you a serious competitor in this race of life?

PRAYER

Lord, help me to cast aside all things that impede spiritual growth. Amen

WISDOM

Without focus you get a blur.

Stay The Fixed Course

"Therefore, since we are surrounded by such a great cloud of witnesses, let us throw off everything that hinders and the sin that so easily entangles, and <u>let us run with perseverance the race marked out for us</u>"
Hebrews 12:1.

REFLECTION

The race of life is not a sprint and then it is over. It is a marathon, an obstacle race, which demands that we have a plan to endure to the end. The course is fixed, so there is no need to be running aimlessly. It would serve us well to get familiar with what to expect on this journey of life, and what better book to inform us than the Bible, for there the instructions to life are clear.

It is one thing to know where the instructions are, but it is quite another thing to read, assimilate and then implement them in our lives. Take for instance Psalm 1. It tells us to avoid the counsel of the wicked, keep away from the path of sinners and don't embrace the philosophy and life style of mockers. It then counsels us to read and meditate on God's Word on a daily basis for from that exercise our success in the race of life will have staying power and wonderful rewards.

There is no wiser counsel to be obtained anywhere than the counsel of the Word. It is from the Word we obtain wisdom, discretion, prudence and insight to deal with all the moral and spiritual problems that this life hurls at us. The Word gives us direction, the right type of spiritual nutrition, energy and rhythm to persevere to the very end in this race of life.

Is the Word your trainer? Are you listening to its instructions?

PRAYER

Lord, help me to run well the course marked out for me. Amen

WISDOM

The Word marks the course for us to follow.

The Eyes!

"Let us fix our eyes on Jesus, the author and perfector of our faith, who for the joy set before him endured the cross, scorning its shame, and sat down at the right hand of the throne of God"
Hebrews 12:2.

REFLECTION

Our eyes can tell our story. We can flirt with the eyes, lust, seduce, be intrigued, open ourselves to be bribed and pursue worthless things. We can be wise in our own eyes, be humble, or pure. The eyes reflect our emotions be it joy, sorrow, heaviness, reflection, seriousness, levity or depression.

The eye tells us a great deal about our physical well being or its lack. One of the first places a physician looks is in our eyes. The eye is not only a window into our health but also into our very souls. The eye reflects in so many ways our spiritual condition.

We can covenant with our eyes not to make it the vehicle of sin. We can avoid feasting them on filthy books and magazines, movies and places of questionable amusements. These sources of evil fuel the imagination only to build walls of separation between our souls and God. The physical eyes are interlocked with the spiritual eyes. Therefore we should allow the spiritual to have the control over the physical. If we do that we would be saved from much sorrow.

The Bible speaks of the opening of the eyes in revelation or illumination; of eyes that see the King of Glory; of eyes that see the world as a field to be harvested for the Kingdom; of eyes fixed on the unseen God and of conduct that is right in the eyes of men and of God.

What are your eyes saying about you?

PRAYER

Lord, help me to use my eyes to glorify you at all times. Amen

WISDOM

Our eyes betray who we really are.

Focus Makes The Difference

"Let us fix our eyes on Jesus, the author and perfector of our faith, who for the joy set before him endured the cross, scorning its shame, and sat down at the right hand of the throne of God"
Hebrews 12:2.

REFLECTION

The matter of fixing our eyes on Jesus is a matter of choice. If we would know Him as Mary did, then our eyes must look steadfastly into His eyes and that will bring us to His feet to drink deeply of His person. It is then we will discover that He is altogether lovely and without spot or blemish. The more we stare at Him is the more we will uncover His beauty. It is then we will desire to confess that we belong to Jesus and crave always to be in His presence.

As Moses' relationship with God blossomed, he requested of God to manifest to him His glory, and God did. Fixing our eyes on our Lord Jesus will transform us forever. It is going to introduce into our lives experiences we never thought possible in this life. Fixing our gaze on our Lord puts us in the place whereby the Spirit of God is able to unfold the glory, majesty, splendor and worth of our Lord Jesus.

John, on the Isle of Patmos, saw the risen, exalted Christ and was overawed by His presence and power and fell like a dead man at His feet. It is only as we see His glory are we then prepared for mission. It is only as we see Him high and lofty can we truly hear His voice speaking to us. It is only when our focus is sharp, clear and three- dimensional that we see Him as the Author and Finisher of our faith.

It is when we see Him as the author of our faith, we begin to grasp what He endured, for our sakes, to bring us to God.

PRAYER

Lord, help me to see the wonders of my glorious Savior. Amen

WISDOM

Focus reveals what is hidden from a casual or cursory glance.

Endurance & Then Enthronement

*"Let us fix our eyes on Jesus, the author and perfector of our faith, who for the joy set before him **endured the cross, scorning its shame,** and **sat down** at the right hand of the throne of God"*
Hebrews 12:2.

REFLECTION

Having a certain and fixed goal in life will make hardships, trials, and various challenges, conquerable. The vexations, the pains, the shame, and the agony recede into nothingness as set goals loom larger and with more luster and brilliance.

Jesus was motivated by the joy of His fixed goal and did not flinch when the path to achievement struck Him with great violence. He did not call upon twelve legions of angels to rescue Him from the Cross. To obtain the prize, He had to endure the dreadful agony of the cross. The path to the exalted throne would not be deterred by shameful exposure. He also scorned the shame that he endured at the hands of vile sinners and being rejected of God in order to bring us salvation.

Jesus did not merely enter the human family by His incarnation, for that was necessary if salvation was to be made a possibility. Being here, He did not malinger, try to sidestep or use any other devious means to escape the tremendous responsibility of saving a lost world. He willingly gave up His precious life for us, under the most testing circumstances that this life could ever offer.

Today, the glorified Christ is enthroned in Heaven, where our praises ascend. Meanwhile let us endure as good soldiers all hardships, for we shall be crowned if we abide faithful in Him.

Are your eyes fixed on Jesus?

PRAYER

Lord, help me to fix my eyes on Jesus. Amen

WISDOM

Christ must be Lord of all or not Lord at all.

Facing Judgment And Eternity

May 24

"Who Knows? God may yet relent and with compassion turn from his fierce anger so that we will not perish"
Jonah 3:9.

REFLECTION

As Jonah proceeds on his mission, he reaches the point that the great city of Nineveh is targeted for the judgment of God. The cup of iniquity is now full. They have been weighed in the divine balance and found wanting. The stench of their wickedness has reached high heaven.

Jonah is God's instrument to announce to them their impending judgment. God's message moves them in a most powerful manner and they urgently go into fasting, prayer, mourning and repentance. At this late stage the Ninevites are hoping that God will relent and have compassion on them and deliver them from the destruction prophesied.

Then, suddenly, they repent. The entire city humbles itself before God and cries as one man from the depths of his being, to be spared. We at times do not know the value and preciousness of life until we are face-to-face with what appears to be certain death. Maybe you are in the last stage of a terminal disease and you have wasted your life in senseless living. Now you are on the very edge of eternity, and you want God to forgive you and heal you.

Or, you are now faced with a crisis of desperation and you are going under in troubled waters. The God you have always ignored is now your only hope and in anguish of spirit you find yourself calling on Him to have mercy on you. It is amazing how tragedy makes us view God in a completely different light. Why wait for catastrophe to make it right with God? The time to turn to God is now.

PRAYER

Lord, help me to repent, today. Amen

WISDOM

Nineveh's lesson is that repentance pays.

God's Compassion Towards Us

*"**Who Knows?** God may yet relent and with compassion turn from his fierce anger so that we will not perish"*
Jonah 3:9.

REFLECTION

God is compassionate, merciful and loving, and for that we must be eternally grateful. If God were not like that all of us would perish in our sins. God's compassion to sinful, erring human beings is new every morning. His patience and longsuffering toward our folly is bountiful. But God does not delight in bringing affliction or grief to the sons and daughters of Adam. That fact is clear from this Nineveh story.

God's mercy is truly great for we are all incurably sick, morally. There is no person who can boast in God's presence of his or her own goodness or righteousness. We can never please God with our fallen nature and that is a very hard lesson to learn. As fallen creatures, all we can do is to cast ourselves on the mercy of God and pray to be spared from our just due of eternal punishment.

It is the compassion of God through Christ that shields us from the fierce and just anger of God who is angry with the wicked everyday. But to those who please Him, He demonstrates His love to a thousand generations.

The Ninevites knew what they were up against. They knew that they deserved the punishment. However, God's justice system requires repentance if His wrath is to be stayed. Thank God, the Ninevites repented.

How about you? Your sins, too, are an offense to God. Maybe your visitation is nigh at hand. Why not turn to Him and live?

PRAYER

Lord, help me to love righteousness. Amen

WISDOM

Turning from sin and turning to Christ will secure my salvation.

Judgment Stayed

*"When God saw what they did and how they turned from their evil way, he had compassion and **did not bring upon them the destruction he had threatened"***
Jonah 3:10.

REFLECTION

God gave the inhabitants of the city of Nineveh forty days to repent or be destroyed. The citizens acted quickly, in unison, and with sincerity, faith, brokenness and with pleadings to God, to have mercy on them and spare them. God did. When our attitude to sin and God is altered, then God's attitude toward us will fall within the range of His compassion and mercy.

Had they stubbornly refused to heed the warning of God and carried on in their wicked ways then Nineveh would have been destroyed by the fury of God's judgment. However, the inhabitants of this heathen city suddenly demonstrated reverence for God and His word. God saw the intent of their hearts and spared them.

Had the Ninevites attempted to fake their repentance they would have perished. We can pretend with tears and wailing, but if the heart is unaffected and our sins are left intact, we can be assured that the judgment of God will remove us from among the living prematurely.

We cannot deceive God for He does not look on the coarseness of the sackcloth we wear, or the thickness of ashes we might use to cover ourselves. Rather, God looks in our hearts and sees through our motives. If our sins remain untouched, God will certainly cut down our 'tree' in His sore displeasure. Then it will be too late for repentance.

Therefore seek God today.

PRAYER

Lord, help me to repent today. Amen

WISDOM

While we have opportunity to call on God let us do so.

Threat! Heed Or Ignore?

*"When God saw what they did and how they turned from their evil way, he had compassion and did not bring upon them the destruction **he had threatened**"* Jonah 3:10.

REFLECTION

God sometimes has to threaten us to change us. A serious threat that has dire consequences, when impressed upon the mind, can bring about wonderful changes in our lives. For instance, the threat of being thrown out of school can cause some students to upgrade their academic performance. The threat of losing your job can produce remarkable improvement in your productivity and work ethics. The threat of being fired if you are tardy one more time can bring about wonderful changes in punctuality and time use.

Even vile king Ahab, in the days of Elijah the prophet, when he heard of the terrible disasters that would overtake him and his descendants, humbled himself before God (I Kings 21:20-29).

The Bible gives warning of the terrible things that will overtake the individual, the family, the community, the parish, the county or the nation, or, for that matter, the world, if sin is not renounced. We cannot violate God's laws and ever hope to get away with it. We cannot hide from God. For some who have despised His Word, the hand-writing is already on the wall for them. Judgment is near and ahead will be many years of bitter reaping and weeping.

If you decide to 'hang tough' in your sins, then God's threat will come through and consume you, and there will be no remedy for your healing, in time or in eternity. It pays to take heed to God's warnings. Will you?

PRAYER

Lord, help me to pay close attention to your warnings in my life. Amen

WISDOM

God's threats are real.

Displeasure Leads To Anger

"But Jonah was greatly displeased and became angry"
Jonah 4:1.

REFLECTION

Why did Jonah become so displeased? He even "became angry". But about what? His prediction had not come to pass. Forty days had passed and the city Nineveh was still standing fully populated. The inhabitants had sought the face of God and obtained His mercy and pardon.

Jonah wanted to have seen all those wicked people dead, for in his judgment they were deserving of it. Jonah had no love in his heart for these cruel people and in his judgment the only good Ninevite was a dead one. Jonah could not drag himself to rejoice with the Ninevites over their repentance and salvation. The more he thought about it, the more annoyed he became with God.

Jonah was acting in the spirit of the Prodigal's elder brother in Jesus' parable. He was most annoyed that his father was having a party for his younger, wayward brother, who had returned. He did not have one good thing to say of his despicable brother who came back home, tattered and broken, and repentant.

Jonah is like us, in our natural thinking, evil is always in the forefront. What displeases us makes us detached, cold and critical. Cain's anger came to the fore when his offering was rejected by God and His brother Abel's accepted. His anger led him to murder. Take the case of selfish Nabal when he learnt what his wife Abigail did for David. The Bible says Nabal could not endure it: *"His heart died within him, and he became as a stone"* I Samuel 25:37 (A.S.V.).

Are you angry when God forgives the wicked?

PRAYER

Lord, help me to rejoice when you show mercy to the wicked. Amen

WISDOM

God's ways are not our ways.

Unpleasant Mission?

May 29

"He prayed to the LORD, "O LORD, is this not what I said when I was still at home? That is why I was so quick to flee to Tarshish. I knew that you are a gracious and compassionate God, slow to anger and abounding in love, a God who relents from sending calamity"
Jonah 4:2.

REFLECTION

There is a wicked streak in all of us. When that streak comes to the fore, we might even want God to bash in the teeth of those we hate. There are times we do not want God to relent, but would rather want God to rain fire and brimstone out of heaven upon the wicked and the ungodly. We sometimes wish evil would befall those who have fastened their teeth into our flesh and have showed no pity.

We have no desire to become the bearers of the gospel of the grace of God to such people and we would make endless excuses to hinder the gospel from reaching them through us. Such was the passionate feeling Jonah carried toward that evil empire. He allowed his prejudice and resentment to get the better of him. He just could not bring himself to side with God on this matter. You somehow get the feeling from the text that he thought God was making a mistake in sparing these people.

The early church feared Saul of Tarsus and there were many who would have loved to see his name on a tombstone. Yet, it pleased the Lord to save him and to make him a chosen instrument to take this gospel to the Gentiles.

Is there someone in your life you secretly wish dead? Why not overcome that evil desire and make it your mission to bring the saving gospel to that soul? God is gracious.

PRAYER

Lord, help me to love sinners. Amen

WISDOM

There are things we do not want to do that God wants done.

Tell Of The Gracious God

"He prayed to the LORD, "O LORD, is this not what I said when I was still at home? That is why I was so quick to flee to Tarshish. I knew that you are a **gracious** *and* **compassionate** *God,* **slow to anger** *and* **abounding in love,** *a God who* **relents from sending calamity"**
Jonah 4:2.

REFLECTION

Jonah's prayer exposes us to the tender side of God's nature. Jonah had first-hand experience of those very virtues mentioned in our text. What sinner saved by grace cannot but testify to the goodness, mercy, grace, patience and love of God towards him?

God cares very much about the ungodly and desires their salvation from the power of sin. If these virtues were not daily shown to us, our vices would swiftly take us to deserving destruction. The Bible clearly teaches that God's kindness, tolerance and patience is a path that ought to lead us to repentance (Romans 2:4).

We humans however, are spiritually blind, deaf and dead. That's why we display little or no consciousness of our desperate need of God. We do not truly know the peril of our own soul until someone else who has experienced the grace of God, tells us about Him. The Christian is the one who has this wonderful knowledge and is under orders to share this Good News with those lost in sin.

The Christian's mission is to tell them of Jesus, who is their only way back to God. We can selfishly avoid our mission and flee to our 'Tarshish' as was the intent of Jonah, or we can willingly and lovingly tell them of the God who loves them and desires their salvation. What are you doing with this good-news?

PRAYER

Lord, help me to share this Gospel with the lost. Amen

WISDOM

The soul winner is wise.

Foolish Prayer

"Now, O LORD, take away my life, for it is better for me to die than live"
Jonah 4:3.

REFLECTION

Have you ever asked God to take your life? Anger and discouragement can lead you to do that. In that state of mind you cannot see any other solution. Your burning desire is for the immediate 'satisfaction' of death at the hands of God. It is a foolish thought, inspired by the devil.

Discouraged, Elijah, after his great victory at Carmel, becomes frightened by Jezebel's threat to take his life. He runs for his life. Then we hear him praying to God to take his life! He had had enough! (I Kings 19:4) Trying circumstances in life even cause great men of faith to become depressed and suicidal.

Here is the great prophet in a moment of weakness praying, *"It is enough; now, O Jehovah, **take away my life**; for I am not better than my fathers"*   I Kings 19:4 (A.S.V). Here is a servant of God wallowing in self pity and wringing his hands in despair, desiring death over mission. Frustrated, he wants to immediately hand in his resignation to God and depart this life. His anxiety, distress and anger entertain no hope and see no tomorrow. Like a spoilt child he complains and even chides God.

Are you having one of those bleak and ugly days? On such days you want to throw in the towel and then die. Don't let your emotions triumph over your faith. Dark clouds usually pass and the sun usually shines again in your life.

Will you stand fast in those dark days and hold unto your God?

PRAYER

Lord, help me to see you always as my hope. Amen

WISDOM

Despair is the training ground for HOPE.

Are You Angry?

*"But the Lord replied, "**Have you any right to be angry?**"*
Jonah 4:4.

REFLECTION

Anger is an emotion that is not far from the surface of our lives. It is expressed everyday in varying degrees from the mild to the violent. Anger is so well integrated in our conduct that many a time we are not even aware of our obnoxious attitudes and detestable behavior.

Sometimes we don't even have to say a word, for our faces betray the vile conditions of our hearts and give ample warning to those who would seek to speak to us, for them to either put off the task or be prepared for battle.

Anger can become so ingrained in our personality that it removes all the milk of human kindness from the heart. Anger can make us behave like snapping, snarling and barking dogs. The greater the pressure, the less human our conduct and our demeanor become. When anger becomes a mere defense mechanism, it dehumanizes us and makes us into persons to be avoided at all cost.

At the centre of our anger and rage are deep psychological problems. Those who suffer from low self-esteem and inferiority complexes can compensate these deficiencies by putting their anger on show. At the root of anger is selfishness. We fear to know we are wrong. Therefore we insulate ourselves with wrathful anger.

Are we born with anger? Yes. It is part of our Adamic nature that was corrupted in Eden. But God has given Christians the Holy Spirit, who can control anger. Before you pick up the phone, before you respond to an accusation, or a request – ask yourself *"Have I a right to be angry?"*

PRAYER

Lord, help me to control my anger. Amen

WISDOM

When anger increases God consciousness decreases.

Any Right To Be Angry?

*"But the Lord replied, "**Have you any right to be angry?**"*
Jonah 4:4.

REFLECTION

Jealousy generates anger. This is forcefully illustrated in the life of Jacob and his twelve sons. Jacob favors his son Joseph and showers him with gifts, especially the gift of a beautiful multicolored coat, to the chagrin of his brothers. Parents should learn a lesson from Jacob's mistakes and attempt to love all their children equally. Failure to do that is but to foster unnecessary tension among siblings.

Consider this Scripture in the light of what is being said – *"And his brethren saw that their father loved him more than all his brethren; and they hated him and could not speak peaceably unto him"* Genesis 37:4 (A.S.V). The offshoots of jealousy will fall into formation and ugly actions will follow. Jealousy begets anger, anger hate, and hate leads to broken relationships that will seek opportunity to settle scores.

This 'golden' opportunity comes when Jacob sends his favorite son Joseph to check on his brothers in the field and bring back a report. Anger unites the brothers and it becomes the source of a conspiracy to destroy Joseph by fair means or foul. Favoritism is the root cause of deep hurts among children. Even in adulthood some persons are unable to shake off the effects and thus continue to live with a chip on their shoulder, and with anger in their hearts.

The brothers conspire to murder Joseph, but seeing that they could profit by selling him as a slave to the Midianites, sell him instead. Anger will not be satisfied until it has exacted its price.

What is now fueling your anger? How will you bring it under control?

PRAYER

Lord, help me to deal with the root causes of my anger. Amen

WISDOM

Unattended anger is a destructive force.

Any Right To Be Angry?

*"But the Lord replied, "**Have you any right to be angry?**"*
Jonah 4:4.

REFLECTION

Ahab, the king of Israel in the time of Elijah the prophet desired to either exchange or buy a vineyard belonging to Naboth but was refused. This incident instantly made the king lapse into an icy, gloomy, resentful silence that ignited the low burning fire of anger in his heart against this man Naboth. He immediately left his presence with his face downcast and headed for home and the bedroom. He slammed the door behind him as if to break it loose from its hinges and fell into the bed to do some serious sulking. In this terrible, depressed mood, he lost his appetite for food and for social contact.

Ahab foolishly allowed himself to be overwhelmed by self-pity, because of Naboth's stubborn refusal to exchange or sell his vineyard. He gave in to his hurt and wounded feelings so much that they began to fester and contaminate his mental and spiritual life. He was so affected that as long as Naboth was alive he could only harbor ill will and bitterness toward him. How tragic!

This is exactly what the demon of unforgiveness was waiting for and so he quickly knocked on the door of Ahab's heart and was instantly admitted as a companion to further fortify Ahab's miserable condition. Eventually he reached that point that he could only see one thing and that was a dead Naboth. Worse followed when his wife Jezebel quickly arranged for the 'happiness' of her wicked husband, and became an accomplice in Naboth's murder.

How important it is for sober counsel to break demonic influenced thoughts!

PRAYER

Lord, help me to conquer anger. Amen

WISDOM

God is opposed to selfish anger.

Any Right To Be Angry?

"But the Lord replied, "Have you any right to be angry?"
Jonah 4:4.

REFLECTION

The humble are less prone to sinful anger. Therefore, seek daily to cultivate humility. If you do not, you are likely to be overtaken by haughtiness and the haughtiness of the proud will ensnare and entrap you in anger. This principle is documented in the Bible for us in the action of a great king in Judea, Uzziah. He was wonderfully blessed of God, but he allowed haughtiness to conquer his heart.

Here was Uzziah the politician, now wanting to be priest. Only persons specially qualified in Israel could be priests. In God's design for worship in Israel priests could come only from the tribe of Levi and through the line of Aaron. Uzziah, the king, was from the tribe of Judah. But his vanity led to arrogance which pushed him to intrude into the holy office and functions of the priest. So with censer in hand he ventured into the temple to burn incense.

The prophet Azariah courageously rebuked him for his intrusion. Regrettably, the king, in response got into a tantrum and railed at the 80 priests. But God was no silent bystander in this contest and His judgment instantly fell on Uzziah. There was a sudden and dramatic change in his body and attitude when leprosy broke out on his forehead. He was now in no mood to contend with the priests, but rather, to flee from the temple.

What lesson can we learn from this episode? To rudely intrude into areas you are not called of God to function, and to ignore prophetic counsel is bad for your 'health' in more ways than one. Unwarranted anger will always prove humiliating, and is likely, more than anything else, to invite the judgment of God.

PRAYER

Lord, help me to control my anger. Amen

WISDOM

Anger self-destructs.

Any Right To Be Angry?

SCRIPTURE   June 05

*"But the Lord replied, "**Have you any right to be angry?**"*
Jonah 4:4.

REFLECTION

Anger can be stirred to boiling when we see our own faults mirrored in others. What we fail to detect in ourselves we harshly denounce and condemn in others without mercy or compassion. This practice is perhaps best illustrated in the story Nathan the prophet told David the king. The story is about a pet lamb, the only possession of a poor man that was ruthlessly taken away from him by a very wealthy and powerful man to provide a meal for his guest.

This rich man possessed large flocks of sheep and herds of cattle from which he could have provided for his visitor. He had nothing but disdain and contempt for the poor man and so slaughtered his lamb that was like a daughter to him. The king on hearing the story was stirred to the depths of his being by the act of the rich man. The Scriptures states, "And *David's anger was greatly kindled against the man; and he said to Nathan, As Jehovah liveth, the man that hath done this **is worthy to die**"* II Samuels 12:5-6 (A.S.V).

I can see Nathan fixing his eyes on David and solemnly declaring, *"**Thou art the man**"* II Samuels 12:7 (A.S.V). The application of the story to David was that the king had defiled another man's wife and had her husband murdered by the sword of the Ammonites. The application of that truth thrust a sword right through David's heart. If there was ever a time that anger cooled instantly and was replaced by guilt, remorse and repentance was that day in the king's palace.

Sin in me is just as ugly as it is in others, but let me first direct my anger to myself before I denounce the sin of others.

PRAYER

Lord, help me to be angry with my own sins. Amen

WISDOM

Sinful anger is never of the Spirit.

/

Any Right To Be Angry?

SCRIPTURE   June 06

"But the Lord replied, "Have you any right to be angry?"
Jonah 4:4.

REFLECTION

We could multiply illustrations from the Bible concerning the improper use of anger by both good and bad men. Proverbs is rich in instructions on the subject of both good and bad anger. Here are a few such verses:

"It is better to dwell in a desert land, than with a contentious and fretful woman" Proverbs 21:9 (A.S.V.). *"And the contentions of a wife are a continual dropping"* Proverbs 19:13 (A.S.V). *An angry man stirreths up strife, and a wrathful man aboundeth in transgressions"* Proverbs 29:22 (A.S.V.). *"A fool uttereth all his anger"* Proverbs 29:11 (A.S.V.).

Many husbands have to cope with wives who never 'let up' even for a day. They needle and rub the wrong way constantly. Such harried men are terrified to go home. They fear to face a nagging and complaining wife who would drive any normal human being crazy. Such a wife is not at peace with herself nor does she have the peace of God. On the other hand there are husbands whose anger terrify their entire households and create multitudes of psychological and mental problems for others.

Moses, under great provocation, lost his 'cool' and blew his opportunity to enter the Promised Land. Anger can ruin family relationships, destroy friendships, create tensions in businesses, conflicts in communities, wars among nations and, of course, ruin our relationship with God.

Is your anger in the fireplace or has it set your house on fire?

PRAYER

Lord, help me to regulate my anger and direct it aright. Amen

WISDOM

Unsupervised anger is like a fire out of control.

Any Right To Be Angry?

SCRIPTURE   June 07

*"But the Lord replied, "**Have you any right to be angry?**"*
Jonah 4:4.

REFLECTION

Chronic anger, whether manifested as an outburst of rage, or, repressed is not good for our health. Anger properly managed enhances our health, but, unbridled anger can cut us off in the midst of our years.

Anger releases adrenaline and other hormones into the bloodstream that cause the blood pressure, pulse and respiratory rates to rise sharply. If these are sustained, the experts tell us, we are setting up ourselves for depression, heart attack, stroke, diabetes and other serious illnesses. Poorly managed anger creates anxiety, and makes us feel weary. The experts tell us that those who allow anger to control them are more prone to get hooked on alcohol, drugs, smoking and eating disorders and this is particularly true of teenagers.

When parents exhibit unbridled anger in the home, then children are but to pattern their example. Anger as a life style is not cool. It robs us of laughter and joy and makes us into coarse and unpleasant beings to be avoided. Chronic anger does not help our immune system but makes us more likely to be sickly.

The Bible states, *"He that is slow to anger is better than the mighty; and he that ruleth his spirit, than he that taketh a city"* Proverbs 16:32 (A.S.V.). People who are given to anger do not love; for love is not easily angered, nor is it rude.

If you are angry constantly, you lack self-mastery which is a fruit of the Spirit.

PRAYER

Lord, help me to master my emotions, by dependence on Your Holy Spirit. Amen

WISDOM

Think deeply before you express yourself angrily.

A Right To Be Angry

*"But the Lord replied, "**Have you any right to be angry?**"*
Jonah 4:4

REFLECTION

An area of anger that is cause for concern is the fury of our driving on our roads. If there is an example in the Bible of what today is called '**road rage**' it would be seen in the driving of Jehu in II Kings 9:20 (A.S.V.) – *"The driving is like the driving of Jehu son of Nimshi; for he driveth furiously."*

Driving is like a life and death struggle on our congested roads. Once we enter our vehicles and venture into our snarled roads our emotional fuse becomes extremely short and this is dangerous. It is on the road that our selfishness, mean spiritedness, lack of common sense and carelessness often come to the fore. Blind fury races ahead of our speedometer and our vehicles become lethal weapons.

Driving does heighten tension. So, some bad-ride, bore, and overtake as though their lives depended on such behavior. The abused respond with cursing, swearing, name calling, and the desire to 'even the score'. Driving, if allowed, brings out aggression in us. Even the gentle, when behind the wheel of a powerful vehicle, can become a demon on the road.

Too many drivers put their patience on vacation or suspend it temporarily. But when that happens unpleasant things are bound to happen, sooner than later. Anger can put sanity on hold, and, like Jehu, drive like a mad person. Anger impairs sound judgment and rage makes poor drivers. Consequently, angry drivers imperil all other road users.

Are you in control when around the wheel?

PRAYER

Lord, help me when driving to have regard for other road users. Amen

WISDOM

Impatience fuels anger.

A Right To Be Angry

June 09

"But the Lord replied, "Have you any right to be angry?"
Jonah 4:4

REFLECTION

If we would learn the proper use of anger then we ought to study the life of Christ, the perfect God-man. If we would demonstrate the proper attitude to anger then we must cultivate Christ's likeness in our being.

Christ did not allow His emotions to dictate His expressions. Christ had His emotions under the control of His will. Christ, our perfect example was God centered, rational, and controlled by the teachings of the Word of God and under the governance of the Holy Spirit. An expression of His anger was just, based on righteous principles, and glorified God. Therefore, He was justified when he lambasted hypocrisy, chastened corrupt religious leaders and those who opposed the mercy of God extended to the afflicted because of religious scruples.

Here is an example in the life of Christ that His anger came to the fore. In Mark chapter 3 Jesus enters a place of worship, where a man in the congregation has a shriveled hand. The members of the congregation are focused on what Jesus would do to this man. Would he dare heal on the Sabbath? Jesus has the man stand before them and directs a question that goes to the very core of the matter, but their response is one of stony, sinful silence. The Scriptures state, *"He looked around at them **in anger** ... **deeply distressed** at their <u>stubborn hearts</u>"* Mark 3:5 and then proceeded to heal the man.

It is right to be angry with those who stand in the way, with flimsy excuses that mask the wickedness of their hearts, to hinder good being done to the unfortunate. Show your displeasure by speaking up and oppose injustice wherever it is.

PRAYER

Lord, help me to funnel my anger to lift up the down trodden. Amen

WISDOM

Answer the silent protesters of injustice with righteous anger.

A Right To Be Angry

*"But the Lord replied, "**Have you any right to be angry?**"*
Jonah 4:4

REFLECTION

Anger is a dynamic force. If properly used anger can honor God. It is possible to get angry for a right cause, in a wrong way. If our fallen nature gets a hold of our anger, that anger will become sinful, but if our new nature does, our anger will not be sinful.

In the time of Christ, the Temple of God had become a haven for undesirable practices. Therefore, when Jesus saw this He became very angry. His motivation for anger was proper. The place of worship and prayer had become the place of commerce. Good anger will lead to good, forceful and at times severe action.

Our Lord made a whip of cords and used it against the abusers of God's House. He was not exactly gentle with the money changers for He scattered their coins and overturned their tables. As for those who sold doves that were used for sacrifices to God, He drove them out and fervently and solemnly spoke what was uppermost on His mind, *"How dare you turn my Father's House into a market!"* John 2:16

If there was more righteous anger in our pulpits, then there would be less unrighteous anger in our churches, our homes and in the wider society. When righteous indignation is heard in the House of God, followed by holy action of godly pastors, elders and deacons, the congregation will take note and so will the community. If there is righteous anger at sinful practices, sinners will pay attention to God.

How about expressing today, righteous anger against things you have for too long been silent about. It is only when we see the evil and speak against it that our anger will become righteous and fervent.

PRAYER

Lord, help me to use my anger forcefully and wisely. Amen

WISDOM

Anger can be the key 'tool of spiritual engineering.'

A Right To Be Angry

*"But the Lord replied, "**Have you any right to be angry?**"*
Jonah 4:4

REFLECTION

We live in a critical, skeptical and unbelieving world. Proof of this fact abounds in the way so many love to argue about religious matters and do so just to score points. In the Bible we read of nine dispirited disciples engaged in a serious dispute with the Jewish religionists of that day. The disciples were unable to cast out a demon to their shame and the religious critics were taking them to task for their failure.

The disciples of Christ had an encounter with a demon possessed lad that the teachers of the law, the opponents of our Lord, could not themselves exorcise. Yet, they were quite content to argue even though they could not help. Jesus suddenly appears on the scene among the disputants and determined the cause of their confusion. Jesus with pathos and anger addressed the crowd with these words, *"O unbelieving generation...**how long** shall I stay with you? **How long** shall I put up with you?* Mark 9:19.

Jesus had been ministering, performing miracles and wonders in their midst for about three years and it was like He was not getting through to them. The lessons of faith, relevant to prayer to an all- powerful God to do the impossible were bouncing off the hard shell of unbelief that they seemed content to dwell within. He was always looking for a breakthrough, only to be disappointed again and again in the unbecoming attitudes of his hearers. Time was running out and the denseness of their spiritual development was cause for concern.

How is it with you? Is the Lord pleased with your spiritual progress and practices?

PRAYER

Lord, help me to be less critical and more practical. Amen

WISDOM

God is disappointed when we fail to grow.

A Right To Be Angry

*"But the Lord replied, "**Have you any right to be angry?**" Jonah 4:4*
REFLECTION

Anger knows no boundary. Some persons even become angry with the Lord! But such is wrong. We must be careful not to allow anger to degenerate into grudge, resentment or root of bitterness. Such is clearly reprehensible and indefensible. If we are endlessly fighting over the same matter then it clearly demonstrates a lack of understanding, maturity, wisdom and resolve.

Being spiritually mature does not eliminate emotions such as anger and lust. Disagreement among friends over important **matters of mission** can become the source of heated conflicts that can impede 'spiritual partnership.' Such was the case with Paul and Barnabas who were about to embark upon a very important mission for the Lord. Mark, who accompanied them on the first mission, deserted them, and returned home.

Subsequently Barnabas wanted Mark to come along with them on their second mission but Paul was not prepared to take him. Tempers flared as each **spoke his mind** on the matter. Paul had his way - and so did Barnabas – for the result was that they had two separate missions.

But this did not mean that Paul and Barnabas had become enemies. They kept in touch and years later, after Barnabas had made a great servant of the Lord out of Mark, Paul once again worked with him. Just to reiterate, disagreements and conflicts must never be allowed to become the source of perpetual hurt feelings, or of nursing grudges or the cause of cultivating roots of bitterness. Anger builds tension and is also the source of releasing it.

PRAYER

Lord, help me to be angry without sinning. Amen

WISDOM

Anger that destroys fellowship is sinful.

Being Mean Spirited

June 13

*"Jonah went out and sat down at a place east of the city. There he made himself
a shelter, sat in its shade and waited to see what would happen to the city"*
Jonah 4:5.

REFLECTION

Have you ever been mean spirited? Have you ever, after discerning the will
of God in a given matter, wished to do otherwise? Jonah's message of doom
for Nineveh was not looking good. The city earmarked for destruction was
experiencing salvation. The city given over to idolatry was now turning to the
living God. The city of violence was now becoming peaceful.

Jonah's expectation for Nineveh was destruction – thunder, fire – doom!
But his expectations for that city flopped and he was not prepared to accept
that. As far as he was concerned, God had let him down in that instance. His
credentials as a prophet were now in question for his prediction against that
city was not materializing.

Jonah positioned himself at a safe place, east of the city, to see what would
happen. Have you ever conned yourself into believing something you know
will never happen, will happen? Have you ever desired a dreadful misfortune
to befall an evil and a cruel man, and, instead, the mercy of God overtakes and
transforms him? Have you ever looked on someone you thought was beyond
the reach of God's grace and deserved the torments of hell, yet, God changed
him, miraculously?

Jonah could not come to terms with the scope and extent of God's
forgiveness. In your heart do you still desire evil to befall some old sinner?
Forgiveness is sometimes not easy to dispense, but necessary.

PRAYER

Lord, help me to forgive, as you do. Amen

WISDOM

Forgiving is self transforming.

God's Provision

*"Then the LORD **God provided** a vine and made it grow up over Jonah to give shade for his head to ease his discomfort and Jonah was very happy about the vine""*
Jonah 4:6

REFLECTION

Even when we are against God, He is for us. Even when we are out of sorts with ourselves, with God and the world, God abides faithful and true and concerns Himself with our well being. When we are discouraged, angry and despondent and feel like giving up, God draws near to us in wonderful ways and seeks to commune and comfort.

Discouraged Elijah had an angel baking bread for him over hot coals. Paul in the midst of a violent storm on the high seas felt all was lost, but was visited by an angel and was wonderfully strengthened. Fretful Jonah had a miracle vine that provided shelter for his head and eased his discomfort.

Sometimes things we think insignificant can make a remarkable difference to our day. A traveler weary with the heat of the sun rejoices at the sight of a tree where he can rest for awhile. Sometimes God's mercies come in small, insignificant things. Yet, those little mercies cheer our spirits. When your spirit is cast down and burdened, God may send someone with just a cheerful smile, or a word of cheer, or a telephone call, or an e-mail, or a powerful thought that elevates your thinking and lifts your spirit. God's methods of daily care are myriad.

Today take time out **to see and count** the wonderful provisions of God's mercies and miracles towards you, and for each, bless His holy name.

PRAYER

Lord, help me to discern daily your mercies in my life. Amen

WISDOM

God's provision supersedes our observation.

Suffering Reverses?

SCRIPTURE

"But at dawn the next day God provided a worm, which chewed the vine so that it withered"
Jonah 4:7.

REFLECTION

The experience of life is full of object lessons and parables and Jonah was now in God's school being taught an important one. Jonah rejoiced in the shade of the vine, but his rejoicing was short lived, for God commanded a worm to destroy the plant.

Some lessons in life have to be taught the hard way. Some may learn the lessons of life by precept followed by willing obedience. But, for others, they have to experience the sorrow and pain of life before they come to terms with obedience. To root out selfishness and self-seeking and to gain a true perspective of life, God has to sometimes provide 'the worm' to destroy that thing that provides 'the shade' in which we trust and find pleasure. What better way can God get our attention than by taking away our creature comforts? It is the best way to refocus us as to what is really important in life.

Are you passing through a rough patch in life? Is there a worm chewing at the very foundation of your creature comfort? All your gains have become reverses. What seemed so promising a short while aback is now tumbling out of control. Is there a cause! It might be wise to take an inventory of your spiritual life.

Has your relation with God been chewed up by the worm of business or pleasure? Are the concerns of God and His kingdom withered in your heart? What is God now trying to tell you through your reverses? Think!

PRAYER

Lord, help me to 'let go' of whatever negates you. Amen

WISDOM

God can use even worms to do His will.

Give In Or Get Going?

*"When the sun rose, God provided a scorching east wind, and the sun blazed on Jonah's head so that he grew faint. He wanted to die, and said, "**It would be better for me to die than to live**"*
Jonah 4:8.

REFLECTION

Emotions affect us in many ways. Events and physical discomforts can marshal an array of emotions that can put us out of sorts with ourselves and God. Circumstances influence our emotions; emotions affect desires and influence us many times in making foolish decisions. Emotions are like the mercury in a thermometer. It rises and falls with our change of 'temperature.'

Disgruntled persons are usually governed by their feelings and are quick to express their dissatisfactions. The 'scorching east wind' and 'the blazing sun' experiences are certainly going to upset them and the desire to surrender to the feelings of the moment runs very high. They have no fighting spirit, no stability to endure and overcome, no guts to face the problems of life squarely.

Worse they would rather be lying dead on a cold slab in a morgue. They are obsessed with death and not life. They don't want solutions for their minds are shut down and reason is cast aside. They curve in on themselves and in anger wallow in self pity.

Are you quickly discouraged by the blast of 'the scorching east wind' and the 'blazing sun' experiences? Do you hastily conclude that you cannot carry on any longer? Your 'tests' are designed to empower, not to lead to despair. Therefore, learn to rule your emotions and don't allow your emotions to rule you.

PRAYER

Lord, help me not to wilt under adverse circumstances. Amen

WISDOM

When you are experiencing testing try to discover the lesson God is teaching.

Angry Enough To Die?

*"But God said to Jonah, "Do you have a right to be angry about the vine?" "I do,"
he said. "**I am angry enough to die**"*
Jonah 4:9.

REFLECTION

When emotions run high, reason runs low. When pouting takes over, our value system takes a beating. In those moments that we elevate the trivial, we depreciate the spiritual. In those silly moments we don't even hold dear our very lives. In those moments of agitation not even God can reach us.

Jonah's thinking had become negative, morbid and embroiled with insignificant loss. He was now a 'sour puss'. He was in no mood to listen to anyone, get counsel or be pacified. His entire life was in the orbit of mean-spiritedness and was intent on expressing the full measure of his displeasure to whosoever would be bold enough to interfere – be it God, man or animal.

Jonah was vexed in a bad way. He became as cross as he was ignorant. O, how the little events of life show us up for what we are! We amaze people with our agitated response, sarcasm, our crestfallen countenance, our coldness and hostility.

We have learnt by harsh experience that when Mr. Sourpuss, or Miss Saucy or Mrs. Porcupine is around they are best avoided, for they have become very unsociable and inhospitable. Each is like a 10-ton truck speeding downhill, out of control.

How do you respond to things or persons that could ignite your fuse? Do you engage reason or do you open the cage of anger?

PRAYER

Lord, help me to show self control. Amen

WISDOM

When you flare up you dive down!

169

Misplaced Concerns?

"But the LORD said, "You have been concerned about this vine, though you did not tend it or make it grow. It sprang up overnight and died overnight"
Jonah 4:10.

REFLECTION

We have all experienced misplaced concerns. We have all created a storm in a teapot over such matters while demonstrating little or no concern for those things that really matter. Nowhere is this more evident than when it comes to matters that concern our spiritual well- being. We will sacrifice the eternal destiny of our souls for some carnal concern of the moment.

Jonah was angry enough to want to die over a mere vine that suddenly perished. He did not plant it, nor in any way tend it. It only provided temporary shade for him from the blazing sun. His sudden loss made him a very angry man. Is it not amazing how small and at times foolish things pull the anger trigger and create unnecessary stress on our hearts that could suddenly send us to an early grave?

Are you a defensive listener? Do you make mountains out of small matters? When the mind exaggerates small things and puts them on a pedestal, we need to stop, take stock and reeducate ourselves as to what is of value.

When small things provoke unhealthy responses we have lost our way and the mind stands in need of retooling and a new focus on God's values.

PRAYER

Lord, help me to focus always on your values. Amen

WISDOM

Emotional responses are blind to spiritual responsibilities.

Are God's Concerns Mine?

"But Nineveh has more than a hundred and twenty thousand people who cannot tell their right hand from their left, and many cattle as well. Should I not be concerned about this great city?"
Jonah 4:11.

REFLECTION

Jonah was concerned and angry at the sudden withering of a vine that he did not plant nor nurture. Yet, he had no concern or compassion for the immortal souls of an entire city. He would lose no sleep if all the Ninevites were damned to hell. After all, they were a very wicked people who were known to indulge in every vice imaginable. As far as Jonah was concerned, their cup of iniquity was full to the brim. Therefore, they should not be spared.

He would justify his selfish attitude by reasoning that the world would be a better place without drug addicts, fornicators, sodomites, murders, abusive parents, idolaters and warmongers. O, they deserve the fire and brimstone that Sodom received centuries earlier. Make them an example to others by giving them death and destruction until they and their property are but a smoldering heap of rubble. Vex them in your sore displeasure, O, LORD.

Jonah's selfishness, bigotry, and lack of compassion for the Ninevites had now sunk to the lowest depth. His contempt for them was boundless and in his heart he had no sympathy, not even a wee bit of mercy. His mind was closed to their spiritual need and he would not side with God's concern for such scum.

Have you ever harbored the Jonah spirit of utter contempt for others and secretly or openly desire their destruction? That spirit is very much 'alive and well' in our midst and must be treated as a matter of urgency.

PRAYER

Lord, help me to be merciful in my daily dealings. Amen

WISDOM

Confession must replace contempt.

God Loves Me

"But Nineveh has more than a hundred and twenty thousand people who cannot tell their right hand from their left, and many cattle as well. Should I not be concerned about this great city?"
Jonah 4:11.

REFLECTION

God loves the world. God's great concern for all humanity is beautifully expressed in His Word, *"For God so loved the world, that he gave his only begotten Son, that whosoever believeth on him should not perish, but have eternal life"* John 3:16 (A.S.V.). God's love is not merely for the mass of humanity. His love includes all, individually. God's love is personal. God loves you just as much as he loves me. God's love is not partial.

God's practical love is demonstrated in the giving of His only Son, Jesus, to die for our sins. Jesus, by His death on the cross made it possible that you and I can become children of God, through a second birth. Receiving Jesus in your heart by faith makes you a child of God.

Sin comes between us and God. But Christ's death as our substitute on the cross opened the door of salvation for us. Nineveh was to be destroyed, but Jonah's message of doom stirred their hearts to repentance and they turned away from their sins and cast themselves on the mercy of God, and, God pardoned them.

God hates your sin, but He loves you. Therefore, God desires to save you, if you will but call upon Him for mercy. Jesus pardoned the thief on the cross and he obtained salvation – the gift of eternal life.

God right now offers you eternal life as a gift. Take it, and you will be blessed.

PRAYER

Lord, help me to receive your love. Amen

WISDOM

God's love is universal and individual.

Concern For The City

*"But Nineveh has more than a hundred and twenty thousand people who cannot tell their right hand from their left, and many cattle as well. **Should I not be concerned about this great city?"***
Jonah 4:11.

REFLECTION

God seems to have great concern for great cities. God's concern for the great cities and their teeming millions across our world has not abated. Jesus' commission to his disciples is to reach the world with the gospel of the grace of God. The cities of the world have not changed over the centuries, for wherever people congregate sin is never lacking. The great cities are in spiritual darkness and need the light of the gospel. The great cities are corrupt and need the light and salt of the Word.

God's concern for a lost world involves every believer. Jonah did not want to go. He did not share God's concern. He was not desirous of seeing the lost come to the knowledge of God. The Church of Jesus Christ is full to the brim with people just like Jonah. We don't care for the children of the lost. We don't care for the parents of the lost children. We don't care for the governments of the lost cities.

Our hearts have become callous. No flame of love burns in our souls to share the salvation of God with others. But if the world is to be reached for God, it must be reached through us. God has no alternative plan. We need to meditate on the question that was posed to Jonah: *"Should I not be concerned about this great city?"* Jonah 4:11. Should I not be concerned about the millions who are rushing into eternity without hope? If we agree with God's concern, then we cannot idly sit back and say nothing to them about the well-being of their souls. Now is the time to demonstrate concern for the lost!

PRAYER

Lord, help me to do my part in reaching the great cities. Amen

WISDOM

See the city with pity.

Focused!

*"Do not say, 'Four months more and then the harvest'? I tell you, **open your eyes** and **look at** the fields. They are ripe for harvest"*
John 4:35.

REFLECTION

We all procrastinate. We all put off for another time things we should attend now. Don't we all like to put off matters that we don't regard as urgent for 'sometime' in the future? We make all types of excuses as to why it cannot be done now. However, we are dealing with the eternal souls of men and women and they cannot be treated as we would a field of grain, for souls are simply not grain. Jesus told his disciples that the souls of men are now ready to receive God's truth into their hearts.

Jesus addressed two important matters that we today need to grasp if we would be effective workers in God's field. The first is the need to **open our eyes**. If our spiritual eyes are closed, then we will be groping in the dark. If, on the other hand, we are in a spiritual slumber, then we need to be awakened to the challenge that surrounds us. Opened eyes bring us into this new awareness.

But we must not only have our eyes opened but we must be focused on the object. Jesus tells us what we should be looking at. Direction in life is important. He wants us to **look at the fields**. You will note that the word fields is plural. Our spheres of involvement are in the fields. Our Lord tells us elsewhere that the field is the world.

I would like to suggest some areas where we need to put the gospel sickle to work right away. Let us start with our homes, communities, schools, colleges, places of work and places of recreation. Wherever we are, we should share Christ and the power of the gospel, by our lives and by our lips. Are your eyes open? **Do you see the fields?**

PRAYER

Lord, help me to be a good harvester of souls. Amen

WISDOM

Opened and focused eyes will lead to Christian involvement.

Redeemed!

*"Who gave himself for us to redeem us from **all wickedness** and to **purify** for himself a people that are his very own, **eager to do what is good"***
Titus 2:14.

REFLECTION

The grace of God produces wonderful changes in the heart of a person who receives Jesus as Savior. These changes are not the result of human effort, but the result of the transforming work of the Spirit. The New Birth is the work of the Spirit, who produces a new nature, thereby making the saved person a new creation.

However, the old nature is not removed even though a new one comes in along side it. The believer then, has two natures. Consider for a moment Saul of Tarsus, a persecutor of the Early Church. He was on a mission to do havoc in the Damascus church. On his way to Damascus he met Jesus and this encounter changed his entire life, purpose and mission. His heart was transformed by a miracle of God. This man, who had been hostile and opposed to Christ, became a specially anointed minister of Christ. This man, who hated Christ, was now passionately in love with Christ. This man, who thought Christianity was an evil to be stamped out, became its chief advocate and apostle.

Ah! Grace reaches the inner core of our being. Grace transforms our inner man. Grace goes to where wickedness reigns and overthrows it and brings about purity of thought, inspires new action, generates new desires. Grace makes us to pursue the good path made possible through the wonderful operation of the Holy Spirit. These grace changes are not superficial, but are permanent.

Have you experienced the redeeming work of the Savior in your heart?

PRAYER

Lord, help me to appreciate more your salvation. Amen

WISDOM

Salvation works!

Distress For The City

*"While Paul was waiting for them at Athens, **he was greatly distressed to see that the city was full of idols"***
Acts 17:16.

REFLECTION

Being in transition does not mean we have to mark time. Notice that while Paul was waiting for his friends to join him in Athens, he did not put his Christianity into limbo. He had his spiritual eyes open and immediately saw the deep need of the city. Their spiritual darkness led him immediately to a course of gospel action.

Paul's customary course of action was to first visit the Jewish synagogue. The members of the synagogue ought to have the knowledge of God and so he would first bring them the good news of the gospel concerning Jesus Christ, who was the fulfillment of their messianic hope. This reality was predicted in the Holy Scriptures. If they came on board, then the task of effectively reaching the city would be enhanced. The next likely group that could render assistance would be those who had embraced the Jewish faith – the proselytes.

Paul went next to the marketplace and used every opportunity to share Christ with the ordinary people. He did not wait for people to come to him; he went to where the people were. He did not shy away from the intellectuals but met them head-on, with success, for some embraced Jesus. A man with a vision and passion like Paul can accomplish in short order what the church has failed to do in years.

Our great cities with their vices have not changed over the centuries. We, too, need to enter the public arena with the transforming message of the gospel. When we do that, we, too, will see amazing changes in our cities.

PRAYER

Lord, help me to become involved in reaching my city. Amen

WISDOM

Vision will lead to action.

Christ Makes The Difference

"Philip went down to a city in Samaria and proclaimed the Christ there...So there was great joy in that city"
Acts 8:5 & 8.

REFLECTION

When true servants of Christ declare the gospel message, wonderful things are bound to happen. The gospel is much more than the mere mouthing of some human philosophy or moral code. The proclaimed Word is used by the Spirit of God to produce LIFE or a REBIRTH in the hearts of those who receive it. The message of the gospel is able to overcome all resistance in the human heart and enthrone The Christ there. Through the gospel, both Satan and sin are defeated and the soul is liberated.

The supernatural message Philip proclaimed liberated those who were possessed by demons. Amazing miracles accompanied the Word and lives and life-styles were immediately altered by the message of the cross and the resurrected Christ. The impact on that city was astounding. That city exploded with great joy and new life.

The gospel impacts on all areas of the human experience. It reorients our mental health, family life, buries superstitions, gives purpose and direction, roots out corruption, breaks the power of addictive drugs, fills the heart with love, joy and peace and puts God on center stage in our lives.

Philip was excited about Jesus and that made the difference in the life of a city. No change will take place if the Christian is silent, but when the Word is shared it brings life and joy to others.

Will you share Jesus today with someone?

PRAYER

Lord, help me to share the dynamics of my faith daily. Amen

WISDOM

Christ is the answer, whatever the moral need.

Guidance For Service

"During the night Paul had a vision of a man of Macedonia standing and begging him, "Come over to Macedonia and help us""
Acts 16:9.

REFLECTION

When our lives are right with God we will have visions for service. There are areas where the work is more urgent and the need greater. Those who desire to serve God will get His guidance, as Paul and his companions did. On the other hand, there are areas of mission that the Spirit in His wisdom would not have us undertake at a particular time, but opens other doors that He crowns with great success.

God is Lord of the harvest and He knows the areas of greatest need. It is to a Cornelius hungry for the Word, that the Apostle Peter is sent. It is at Philippi, a district of Macedonia, that Lydia, whose heart the Lord opened, is converted through the preaching of Paul. Philip is sent to the Ethiopian eunuch, who was earnestly seeking after God, and is powerfully converted. Jonah is sent to Nineveh and a city is saved from divine judgment.

God works in the hearts of His messengers and He also works in the hearts of those who will receive His message. God has so arranged it that these two groups will meet at the right time. At times we are awed at God's timing, as we see the invisible hand of God at work. God had to haul and pull Jonah to accomplish his mission. Submissive Paul was guided by a vision to the place of his service.

What about you? Have you obeyed the nudge of the Holy Spirit to that area of service that he has laid on your heart recently? 'Walking in the Spirit' will expose you in the direction God wants you to serve. Say like Samuel, *"Speak; for your servant heareth"* I Samuel 3:10(A.S.V.).

PRAYER

Lord, help me to be obedient to your call for my life. Amen

WISDOM

God meets the needy.

Tell It Now!

"The Lord's message rang out from you not only in Macedonia and Achaia – your faith in God has become known everywhere. Therefore we do not need to say anything about it"
I Thessalonians 1:8.

REFLECTION

Our faith in Christ is not merely a private matter, it is something that is worth sharing and this is what the Christians in Thessalonica did. It is an impossible task to keep a believer who has been cleansed from sin, filled with the Holy Spirit, from sharing his faith with others. The leper Jesus cleansed and made whole could not hold his peace but *"began to publish it much, and to spread abroad the matter"* Mark 1:45 (A.S.V).

As Christians we should not merely share Christ out of a begrudging spirit of compulsion but from a heart that is overflowing with gratitude to God. Has not Christ removed the spiritual darkness that once enshrouded our minds? Yes, indeed, he has removed the spiritual heaviness that weighed down our spirits. God has given us *"a crown of beauty instead of ashes, the oil of gladness instead of mourning, and a garment of praise instead of a spirit of despair"* Isaiah 61:3.

We have been delivered from the horrible pit of sin and released from the prison and poison of enslaving habits. Those upon whom God has showered His grace and brought into marvelous light, are now seated in the "heavenly places" in Christ Jesus. Such persons cannot help but ring out the good-news to both friend and foe. The curse has been removed and we have entered into the freedom of the Spirit. Can we help but share this Good News with the lost?

Are you sharing the Good News? What's your plan of sharing it today?

PRAYER

Lord, help me to share this Good News daily from the joy of my heart. Amen

WISDOM

We can only share what's there!

Connecting To God's Power

"But you will receive power when the Holy Spirit comes on you; and you will be my witnesses in Jerusalem, and in all Judea and Samaria, and to the ends of the earth"
Acts 1:8.

REFLECTION

The Holy Spirit makes possible dynamic witnessing. Every Christian has the Holy Spirit but not every Christian is allowing the Holy Spirit full control of his life. A life yielded to the Holy Spirit will be marked by zeal for the Lord and His work. A life yielded to the Holy Spirit will find doing God's will a delight. As eating food nourishes the body and makes it strong, so those who depend on the Spirit are invigorated and sustained by the Holy Spirit.

The Spirit of God empowers and equips believers for action. Every person controlled by the Spirit will have a powerful sense of mission and an overwhelming desire to share the gospel. The amazing success of the early disciples of the Church can only be attributed to yieldedness to the Holy Spirit. All preaching, teaching, signs and wonders were the powerful manifestations of the Spirit through committed human channels of divine grace.

Modern technology can never replace or be a substitute for the power of God's Holy Spirit. The air waves will only be effective to the degree that those who use it are themselves anointed by the Holy Spirit. Our Jerusalem, or Judea, and Samaria and the ends of the earth will not be reached, much more conquered, apart from the work of the Holy Spirit in us.

Has the Holy Spirit ignited your life? Is He working in your life?

PRAYER

Lord, help me to make myself available, right now to the Power of Your Spirit for service. Amen

WISDOM

The wise seek the Spirit; fools ignore Him.

Christ Saves The Lost

"For the Son of Man came to seek and to save what was lost"
Luke 19:10.

REFLECTION

Jesus came on a mission that no other man could do, and that was to rescue and restore man to God. In spite of that fact, there are millions who think that they can save themselves by their own goodness. If you honestly think that your heart is 'good' then you need to judge it against the perfect standard of God's Word. If you dare to do that, the Word of God will show you that your moral heart is incapable of standing up to the scrutiny of the all-seeing eyes of God.

Should you honestly compare yourself with God's moral perfections you will agree with the conclusion of the Apostle Paul that all men are sinners. If we are all sinners, then we are all alienated from God due to a corrupt nature. Any effort on our part to try and regain lost ground through our defective nature will end in failure.

We cannot save ourselves. Such efforts could be compared to a bird trying to fly without wings, or a fish trying to swim without fins. Therefore it became necessary for the spotless Son of God to enter our world so that lost humanity might be saved. Our inherent, wicked sin nature made it impossible for us to attain that condition of perfect righteousness that God demands.

Christ dealt with the issue of sin once and for all by giving His life as our substitute on the cross. **He took away our sins** by His death, so that we can **now receive the gift of righteousness and eternal life**. This is the salvation that Christ secured for us. Do you have it?

PRAYER

Lord, help me now to surrender my life to Christ today and receive the gift of salvation. Amen

WISDOM

Salvation is a gift, not a reward.

We Are Sent- Let's Go

"Again Jesus said, "Peace be with you! As the Father has sent me, I am sending you"
John 20:21.

REFLECTION

God's peace is peculiar and qualifies us peculiarly. Only those who have the peace of God in their hearts are qualified to go into this troubled world with the gospel. Jesus equips us before He sends us. Men and women of the world do not have the **peace of God** in their heart, nor are they at **peace with God**. Men and women of the world are like the troubled and restless sea, for they can only cast up mire and mud (Isaiah 57:20). God's peace transforms lives gloriously.

God's peace is deep and restful. Some may rest in a false sense of peace, but that is easily disturbed. Jesus **gives** us His deep sweet peace and **sends** us into the world as sheep among wolves. We are **all sent** by our Savior into the very camp of the enemy. Jesus came into our hostile world with the Spirit's anointing. He came armed with the ability to cast out demons, heal the sick, and raise the dead and to preach the Glad Tidings or Good News to those who live in darkness and in the shadow of death, that they might have light.

Jesus came to do the Father's will and that He accomplished with joy. Jesus is not asking us to do something that He has not done. He, our Lord and teacher, set us an example, and this we ought to pattern. It is God's will that we share what we have come to know in Christ Jesus, so that others too will share in the joy of God's amazing salvation.

Are you responding to the command of your Lord?

PRAYER

Lord, help me to appreciate more your peace and your commission to go tell. Amen

WISDOM

The unsaved cannot come to the knowledge of God unless we tell them.

The Matchless Christ

*"That which was from the beginning, which we have **heard**, which we have **seen** with our eyes, which we have **looked at** and our hands have **touched** – this we proclaim concerning the Word of life."*
I John 1:1.

REFLECTION

If we push back time as far as we can, we would reach the beginning of creation. This is when time began. Creation has it origin not in an impersonal 'Big Bang' but in the God who is eternal, all-wise and all- powerful who said in the beginning, 'Let there be' and there was. It is at His command that something came out of nothing. The result, the grand creation that now is. God is the creator of all things, be they visible or invisible, tangible or intangible, animate or inanimate. All things were created by Him and for His pleasure.

Should we examine the history of Christ it would take us beyond the incarnation, beyond the creation of man, beyond the creation of the universe for He is the author of what is, for *"without him was not anything made that hath been made"* John 1:3b (A.S.V.). Jesus, the Son of God, has no beginning. He is the eternal great 'I AM'. Let it be clearly stated that He is not a creature or a product of the universe. He is God, blessed is He forever. Time and space boggle our finite minds, concerning these verities.

If we try and comprehend the incomprehensible it would simply blow our minds. Job said, *"Therefore have I uttered that which I understood not, things too wonderful for me, which I knew not"* Job 42:3b (A.S.V.). This person Jesus, entered, time and was the seed of a woman. He was truly flesh of our flesh. He was no phantom, or a spiritual illusion, or a fabrication but indeed, He is God, who truly partook of our humanity. Hallelujah!

PRAYER

Lord, help me to understand all I can, concerning you. Amen

WISDOM

Time is but a pause in God's eternity.

Reality Check

*"That which was from the beginning, which we have **heard**, which we have **seen** with our eyes, which we have **looked at** and our hands have **touched** – this we proclaim concerning the Word of life."*
I John 1:1.

REFLECTION

The Christian faith is historical, not mythical. It is not based upon a myth or fable but upon a real historical person. The records of the four gospels present the historical Jesus. The four accounts reveal His authentic claims, verified by His powerful miracles, His death, burial and His astonishing resurrection from among the dead. The historical records of the gospels are not based on accretions but on eye-witness testimonies of this amazing life who is, indeed, God, but who took on human nature and became a man.

John, the Apostle, the author of this epistle, is here giving an eye- witness account of his experience with Jesus. It could not be more personal. It says, *"we have heard"*, *"we have seen"*, *"we have looked upon"* and it concludes, *"our hands have touched"*. This person of whom John speaks is indeed unique. John identifies Him as the **Word of Life**. He is the very source of Life. Jesus Himself said, *"The words that I have spoken to you are spirit and they are life"* John 6:63. Peter confesses to Jesus, *"You have the words of eternal life"* John 6:68.

If you have had an encounter with Jesus and have experienced the reality of a transformed life, you cannot but join with John in proclaiming the Word of Life. No one who has met Jesus can be content with being a spectator in the stands, but must become a participant in the arena of life.

Where are you? What is your participation in Gospel proclamation?

PRAYER

Lord, help me to share with the wider world who you are. Amen

WISDOM

Faith links us to Christ.

Who Is Jesus?

"The life appeared; we have seen it and testify to it, and we proclaim to you the eternal life, which was with the Father and has appeared to us."
I John 1:2.

REFLECTION

To examine the life of Christ is to experience deep mystery. What we will instantly discover is that Jesus was more than a mere man, for He was God incarnate. Eternity and time merged in His person. He who is the eternal Son of the Father came to us in the fullness of time and was born of a virgin. He who is ageless, became a baby, grew in stature and became a mature man, who, at the age of thirty, embarked on His public ministry (Luke 3:23). About three-and-a-half years later, He gave His life on a cross to save us from our sins.

The woman at the well at first saw Him as an ordinary Jew. The Apostle Peter having his first revelation of His divine person, exclaimed, *"Depart from me; for I am a sinful man, O Lord"* Luke 5:8 (A.S.V.). To the people of Nazareth, He was the *carpenter's son*, but the disciples who witnessed Him calm the turbulent and violent sea said, He is the *"Son of the living God"* John 6:69 (K.J.V.).

Judas, His betrayer, when he could have exposed Jesus if He were a fraud, admits with stricken conscience and with a terrible sense of guilt, that he had betrayed *innocent blood* (Matthew 27:3). The temple guards who went to arrest Jesus were struck with awe by His authority and failed to accost Him.

Do you know this Jesus of whom John spoke? Can you, too, testify, with John, of this amazing person? Have you allowed Him to change your life?

PRAYER

Lord, help me to recognize more and more your extraordinary nature. Amen

WISDOM

Christianity is extraordinary.

Christian Fellowship

SCRIPTURE   July 04

*"We proclaim to you what we have **seen** and **heard**, <u>so that</u> you also may have* ***fellowship with us***. *And our fellowship is with the Father and with his Son, Christ Jesus"*
I John 1:3.

REFLECTION

Christ is the center and circumference of Christianity. Remove Him from it and instantly it becomes worthless. He is its essence and Savior. Christianity is a relationship, a partnership, yea, a participation in Christ. The first bearers of the Christian message were literal eye-witnesses of the incarnate Christ. They were attracted to Him by His person, His message, His powerful miracles, His authority and His claim to be the Son of God.

All the doubts of His disciples surfaced when Jesus died the death of a common criminal. But those doubts were immediately dispelled (except for Thomas) by His physical resurrection from the dead. No man who had seen and heard what they had could now be restrained from proclaiming this precious good-news to all and sundry. This gospel created a fellowship among those who received the message.

We are told in the Book of Acts of the response to the first message delivered by Peter on the Day of Pentecost. It was accepted by about three thousand persons and they were all baptized. We read, *"And they continued steadfastly in the **apostles' doctrine and fellowship**, and in the **breaking of bread** and in **prayers"** Acts 2:42(K.J.V.). Fellowship is not merely horizontal, that is, with each other, but is also vertical, which means that there is a fellowship, a spiritual participation and union, with the Father and with the Son, and with the Holy Spirit.

Is your Christian fellowship both horizontal and vertical?

PRAYER

Lord, help me to enjoy the full scope of Christian fellowship. Amen

WISDOM

It is wisdom to embrace Jesus and the fellowship of His people.

Joy Complete

"We write this to make our joy complete"
I John 1:4.

REFLECTION

True knowledge leads to a life of fulfillment. False knowledge is the key to deception, disillusionment and destruction. Partial knowledge of what we have in Christ is good, but full knowledge is better. Academic knowledge of things spiritual panders to spiritual pride and low levels of growth. Experiential knowledge puts us on the path to true growth into Christ-likeness. Experiential knowledge makes us balanced and rounded in the faith.

True knowledge dispels darkness, disputations, and old wife fables. True knowledge brings us into reality. True knowledge of what we have in Christ brings us into the joy of our salvation. This joy cannot be shaken by any outward circumstance or any demonic activity. The joy we have in Christ is not whimsical but is permanent, stable and satisfying. Joy is indeed the fruit of the Spirit and as such is supernatural in nature.

When we understand the bond and our union, our partnership and our participation, in the family of God, and with His Son Jesus Christ, our joy brims over. When we consider that we are seated in the heavenly realms in Christ Jesus, and all that implies, we ought to sit up. When we meditate on us being heirs and joint-heirs with Christ, it should make our joy clock alarm. When we ponder the glory of our future in the eternal kingdom of God, it should put our joy into overdrive.

Have you given serious thought as to what you have in Christ? If you do, it should make your joy complete.

PRAYER

Lord, help me to see better those things that I have in Christ. Amen

WISDOM

In Christ, **we are full.**

187

God Is Light

*"This is the message we have heard from him and declare to you: God is **light**; in him there is no darkness at all"*
I John 1:5.

REFLECTION

Reverence for God is the beginning of **knowledge** (Proverb 1:7) and the commencement of **wisdom** (Psalm 111:10. This is where we must begin if we are to understand God aright. We do not have a multiplicity of gods from which to choose, for there is only one true God. This God, John declares, is **Light**. What a profound thought!

God as Light has no flaw or moral imperfection in His being. Habakkuk tells us that God is holy and intolerant of all evil (Habakkuk 1:12, 13). He cannot wink, ignore, or overlook evil but must judge and condemn evil in all its forms.

Our moral imperfections put us in the dark and away from the light of God's moral perfections. We live in an evil world where compromise with morality is the norm. However, should we view ourselves in the light of God's righteousness; we would discover we are all culpable and unclean. The God of Light exposes us for being corrupt, depraved and exceedingly sinful.

No one can stand in the light of His holy gaze and not be consumed. I Timothy 6:16 (A.S.V.) tells us that God dwells *"in light unapproachable"*. It is difficult for sinful humanity to grasp God's absolute righteousness, holiness and purity. John got a glimpse of it and fell at the feet of Jesus as dead (Revelation 1:17). Isaiah had a vision of it and immediately saw his uncleanness (Isaiah 6:5).

Do you know God as Light?

PRAYER

Lord, help me to grasp the truth of who you are. Amen

WISDOM

Light reveals; sin conceals.

Light Or Darkness?

"If we claim to have fellowship with him yet walk in darkness, we lie and do not live by the truth"
I John 1:6.

REFLECTION

It is easy to be a pretender. We can make all kinds of fancy claims in the spiritual realm but if our lives are in conflict with them then our claims are worthless. It is impossible to walk in the light and in the dark at the same time. The kingdom of darkness is controlled by the devil and his hordes. The 'moral' values of the 'darkness' are in conflict with those of the 'Light'. The two can never be harmonized.

Jesus said we are either for Him or against Him. There is no middle or neutral ground. The temptation to indulge in the things of the dark is a challenge to our spiritual walk and must be firmly resisted on a moment-by-moment basis. For example to lie, to lust, to be enticed by filthy lucre, to curse, to swear, or to give into our temper takes us into the camp of 'darkness'.

Fellowship with God demands a new lifestyle, consistent with the new nature we received when we surrendered our lives to Christ. Our lives must demonstrate much more than the mere chatter of words, or the reciting of a catechism that means nothing to our behavior, but must be a life that is lived out in the power of the Spirit and guided by the principles and practices of the Word. We must walk in sincerity and in obedience to the revealed truths of the Word. Otherwise, we will be walking in the dark.

Are you walking your talk?

PRAYER

Lord, help me to walk in fellowship with you consistently. Amen

WISDOM

Truth exposes.

Walking In The Light

"But if we walk in the light, as he is in the light, we have fellowship with one another, and the blood of Jesus, his Son, purifies us from all sin"
I John 1:7.

REFLECTION

True Christian fellowship cannot be realized apart from godly living. Christians who don't enjoy Christ are not comfortable in the presence of those who do. The Apostle Paul warns the Corinthian Christians against participating in affairs where the influences of demons are active. We should not allow our feet to enter unsanctified places, or our hands to handle that which is impure, or our eyes to view the putrid and our ears to become engrossed with the vulgar.

To enjoy Christian fellowship we must make a choice between two tables around which we can 'feast'. There is the 'table of demons' and the 'table of the Lord'. We cannot artfully combine the two for they are mutually exclusive. Walking in God's light, is the only correct path.

John is very careful as to what light he has in mind for there are many pretenders flashing their peculiar 'lights' and are attracting multitudes. The devil himself, we are told, can appear as an angel of light. His followers are ever ready to lure the unsuspecting to their condemnation. Note carefully that any teaching that does not have Jesus at its center, as the very Son of God and that does not present salvation through His blood shed on the cross, is false. Therefore, such teaching has no ground for Christian fellowship. Such teachings contradict our faith and so should be rejected, for there is no light in them. We should turn away from such doctrines, for they are seducing and demonic.

Have you examined the doctrines of your church?

PRAYER

Lord, help me to walk in Your Light. Amen

WISDOM

Sound teaching builds sound Christians.

Purified By Christ's Blood

*"But if we walk in the light, as he is in the light, we have fellowship with one another, **and the blood of Jesus, his Son, purifies us from all sin"***
I John 1:7.

REFLECTION

God demands blood-sacrifice. There can be no salvation without the shedding of blood. Under Law the blood of certain animals and birds was permitted in sacrifice to God, to temporarily cover sin. The penalty for sin is death, but God permitted animals in that dispensation to die in the place of the offender. Then, a sinner was required to kill an animal at the place appointed by God to have his sin atoned for.

Sin is a very serious matter that unfortunately we take so lightly today. We can have no communion with God if sin is in our lives. The book of Hebrews in the New Testament tells us that sin cannot be irrevocably put aside by the blood of bulls and goats. Those sacrifices had to be repeated over and over for they were only "a *shadow of the good things to come"* Hebrews 10:1 (A.S.V.). But the sacrifice of Christ changed all that. He is the One that gives reality and fulfillment to the Old Testament sacrificial system.

Christ as sacrifice for our sin is God's special provision. It was necessary for Jesus to become a member of the human family for it was only through His perfect life and the shedding of His precious blood that eternal salvation could be secured and purification from all our sin, be it positional or practical, judicial or historical, be realized.

Are you rejoicing in the purifying work of the blood of Jesus in your life?

PRAYER

Lord, help me to praise you daily for your cleansing blood. Amen

WISDOM

Christ's blood removes guilt and restores our fellowship with God.

Deceiving Ourselves?

"If we claim to be without sin, we deceive ourselves and the truth is not in us."
I John 1:8.

REFLECTION

Sinless perfection is not possible. No matter how hard we try or how committed we are to Christ we will always be sinners. This does not mean we should abandon a life of holiness and give ourselves over to the vices of the flesh. It does, however, mean, that we are going to fail and that we will have to deal with the sins we commit. To pretend otherwise is to indulge in self deception. Yet we must never cease from striving to be more and more like Jesus, the perfect human.

Solomon tells us that there is no human who does not sin. We sinned before we came to Christ and we have sinned since we came to Christ. Before we got saved sin was the norm. We were enslaved, and chained to it and this led us into countless vices to our own hurt. Salvation broke that chain of bondage to sin. However, salvation did not take away or eradicate Adam's sin-nature in us. Salvation did, however, give us a 'new nature' alongside that of the old.

So the old nature is still in our flesh and we have daily struggles with it. The inner conflicts are real and from time-to-time we fail to put these desires of the old nature to the 'sword' or have them crucified. This struggle can be likened to Israel entering the land of promise and had to conquer it to possess it. What struggles they had! To pretend we have arrived at total conquest of all the passions and evil desires that reside within, is a myth, and just put us on a collision course with the truth.

Self deception is deception at its worst. If you think you have arrived, then you need to have a reality check in your life!

PRAYER

Lord, help me to see myself as I really am. Amen

WISDOM

To accept falsehood is to reject truth.

Confess Sin

"If we confess our sins, he is faithful and just and will forgive us our sins and purify us from all unrighteousness"
I John 1:9.

REFLECTION

'Confession is good for the soul', is a popular saying and it is right on target. Confession is the admission or acknowledgement of our sins. When we confess our sins we should not seek to make light the offense or try and rationalize the action of our wickedness or justify the offense. We must call the sin by its proper name and with deep contrition ask God's forgiveness.

Confession of sin should not be general, but specific. God wants the facts, all the details. We must even reveal our motives in the presence of Him who searches the heart. Confession must be much more than a mere routine religious exercise. Confession must be a purging of filth from the soul. Confession will be painful, and debilitating. The sins in our lives that we tend to overlook are the very ones that make us weak, impure, sulky, guilty and mean in disposition. All these must be admitted.

There are sins we have committed against our fellowmen that we must confess **to them** and **then to God**. James tells us we are to confess our faults one to another, and at times this can be a very difficult exercise, but one that is absolutely necessary if we would obtain the forgiveness of God. There are lurking, well camouflaged sins that need to be exposed, flushed from our system and renounced. Some sins seemed welded to the soul and we no longer see them as evil, but these too must be confessed if we would have cleansing and victory in our lives.

What are some of the sins I need to confess?

PRAYER

Lord, help me to see the dreadful nature of sin and confess it. Amen

WISDOM

Confession restores.

God Is Faithful

"If we confess our sins, he is faithful and just and will forgive us our sins and purify us from all unrighteousness"
I John 1:9.

REFLECTION

The God to whom we honestly, sincerely acknowledge our sins is a reliable God. He will uphold His end of the 'bargain'. He is not willy-nilly, unstable, capricious or unkind. His provision for forgiving us is based on the sacrifice of His Son Jesus. He accepted that wonderful and eternal sacrifice that Christ offered once for all. The foundation of our forgiveness is solid and God will always honor it. We need not have any fear in our hearts about God not acting favorably to our confession.

The righteous demands of the Law have been fully met through the shed blood of Christ and God cannot but honor what that sacrifice accomplished. It is with boldness that we come to the Throne of God for therein will we find grace and mercy to help us in our need (Hebrews 4:16). We can only approach God on the merits and worth of our Lord Jesus, and, on that premise, God will be faithful and just in dealing with our sins.

Sin defiles and makes us unholy. But sins confessed to God are forgiven and the debt cancelled. He replaces the rottenness of our wickedness with purity and holiness. Sin is a heavy burden to be borne, but forgiveness gives us freedom and happiness. Purity elevates our spirit, puts a song in our hearts, a spring in our steps and adds purpose to our lives.

There is power and blessedness in God's forgiveness.

PRAYER

Lord, help me to appreciate the gift of your forgiveness. Amen

WISDOM

No confession, no forgiveness.

Sinless? Nuts!

"If we claim we have not sinned, we make him out to be a liar and his word has no place in our lives"
I John 1:10.

REFLECTION

God's claim upon our lives must always have priority. When our claims conflict with the Word of God, we are in opposition to God. Any claim that opposes the Scriptures has its origin either in the flesh or the Evil One, who is the father of lies.

To claim we are sinless is to make void the sacrifice of Christ on the cross for us sinners. To make that fanciful claim is to indulge in a dangerous theology that will draw us away from God and the truth. To pursue such stupid beliefs, no matter how high sounding and idealistic it might seem, is to pave a path to hell.

To despise the revelation of God through the Word is to insult God. Any 'New Light Theology' that runs counter to the Word must be rejected. The Bible declares all men to be sinners stumbling in the dark and cut off from the light and life of God. There are no 'good' people in our world. By this I mean none, whose goodness could find favor with God. Sin has contaminated man's entire nature and made it warped and crooked. This is true from the time we were conceived in our mother's womb and for any person to claim sinlessness is ridiculous. But, of course, there are many ridiculous persons in our world and many of them are 'well educated'.

As Christians, we must always side with God and confess that He is true and that every man is a liar. If any person is 'honest' with his own heart and listens to it, it will surely reveal to him that he is a sinner and that he needs the Savior.

PRAYER

Lord, help me to live a life that is pleasing to you. Amen

WISDOM

To claim sinlessness is to utter foolishness.

The Truth Or The Lie?

"If we claim we have not sinned, we make him out to be a liar and his word has no place in our lives"
I John 1:10.

REFLECTION

Religious people can be alienated from God's truth. Religion that is based on self-opinion is at best, built upon a foundation of sand. Religion based on mere feelings or dreams of the carnal mind or the reasoning of the 'flesh' or listening to voices from the spirit world are contrary to the truth of the Kingdom of God.

Jesus said, *"Every one that is of the truth heareth my voice"* John 18:37b (A.S.V.). There is nothing more important in this life than spiritual truth. This is one area in life we cannot afford to be in grave error. We despise, ignore, put on hold, or put off God's truth, at the peril of our souls. We must not dilute, twist, manipulate, or corrupt God's revelation. Corrupt lives gravitate to corrupt teachings and practices. Those who embrace false teachings have no appetite for God's truth.

Like those who opposed Jesus, they will contradict, gainsay, criticize, belittle and persecute those who today uphold the truth. When God is no longer the centre of our theology, we expose ourselves to deceiving spirits and will embrace doctrines taught by demons (I Timothy 4:1).

The spirit of error will never lead us to truth. Instead, it will lead us to confusion and spiritual mischief. Religious persons who reject the truth of the Bible are nothing more than wolves in sheep clothing. They may look like sheep but they speak with the voice of dragons.

Do you love God's Word? How often do you read and apply it?

PRAYER

Lord, help me to have a burning desire for truth. Amen

WISDOM

Pursue truth; eschew lies.

Don't Sin

"My dear children, I write this to you so that you will not sin. But if anybody sins, we have one who speaks to the Father in our defense – Jesus Christ, the Righteous One."
I John 2:1.

REFLECTION

A Christian should purpose not to sin. There will be temptations to sin, some more attractive than others, but they must be resisted through the power of the indwelling Spirit. To overcome temptation we must begin by depositing God's Word in our hearts. By that means, when confronted to sin, we have a resource to resist.

When Jesus was tempted to deviate from the will of God, He countered the temptation by using the living Word of God. When Joseph was tempted by Potiphar's wife to have sex with her, he fled from her presence as she applied sensual and physical pressure.

Paul advised Timothy not only to flee youthful lust, but also to follow after righteousness, faith, love and peace from a pure heart (II Timothy 2:22). This is a very filthy world and to live a holy life demands the full armor of God, knowledge of the Word, watchfulness and prayer.

Some sins have a residual effect. Such sins have stigma and stench that linger long after they are buried. There is no need for us to experiment with sin to find out for ourselves what it will do to us. Sin is destructive. Paul reminds the believers in Romans 6 that when we received Christ we died to sin. If you died to sin then it should no longer have an appeal to you.

Are you dying daily to sin?

PRAYER

Lord, help me to keep my heart pure. Amen

WISDOM

Play with the fire of sin and you will be burned by the fire for sin.

So You Sinned

"My dear children, I write this to you so that you will not sin. But if anybody sins, we have one who speaks to the Father in our defense – Jesus Christ, the Righteous One."
I John 2:1.

REFLECTION

Maintaining a life of purity is challenging, but can be achieved only by depending on the Spirit. Under the Law, God made provision through the sacrificial system whereby a person who sinned against Him could be restored to fellowship. The two most significant sacrifices would be **the sin** and **the trespass** offering.

Under the Dispensation of Grace, the temple and its animal sacrifices came to an end through the death of Christ on the cross. The very moment Christ died, the curtain in the temple in Jerusalem, which separated the Holy Place from the Most Holy, was supernaturally ripped, from top to bottom, signifying that access into the very presence of God through the sacrifice of Christ was now a reality.

Christ by His one sacrifice forever secured our perfect salvation. If there was any lingering doubt on the matter, His resurrection is proof that His sacrifice was accepted by the Father.

So today, when we sin, Jesus' presence in heaven makes possible our forgiveness. His pierced hands, feet and side constitute evidence that today and forever, full payment was made for sin. Of course, His presence as our advocate does not give us license to sin with impunity, but should be an inspiration for us to live holy lives. His Spirit enables us to live victoriously over sin.

Are you living the victorious Christian life?

PRAYER

Lord, help me to live a pure life. Amen

WISDOM

A pure life is achievable but formidable.

Jesus? Who Is He?

"My dear children, I write this to you so that you will not sin. But if anybody sins, we have one who speaks to the Father in our defense – Jesus Christ, the Righteous One."
I John 2:1.

REFLECTION

How do you see Jesus? Some see Jesus as a great teacher, or a prophet, or archangel or even the first of God's creation. It is important that we have it settled in our minds as to who Jesus really is. The Jews of His day understood the nature of His claims of being **"The Christ"**, and **"The Son of God"**.

His claims to being God are clear and strong in the Bible. We read, *"For a good work we stone thee not,"* replied the Jews, *"But for blasphemy; and because that thou, being a man, makest thyself God* John 10:33 (A.S.V.). On another occasion the Jews tried to kill Him because He *"called God his own Father, making himself equal with God"* John 5:18 (A.S.V.). The Bible is emphatic that if Jesus is not "The Christ", "The Son of God," which means, of the same essence with the Father, then, He is but a charlatan or a lunatic.

Jesus, who is God, blessed forever, the eternal "I AM", stepped out of eternity into time to become our Savior. God acknowledged Jesus as His Son at His **Baptism** and on the Mount where He was **transfigured.** Finally, His **resurrection** was proof that He is the Son of God (Romans 1:4). In Hebrews 1:6 God commanded His **angels** to **worship Him**.

If Jesus is not God, then worshipping Him would be improper. Jesus can be worshipped, God permitting, only because He is on an equal footing with the Father. Indeed, Jesus is the Righteous One in the absolute sense. Let's give Him all the praise.

PRAYER

Lord, help me to acknowledge Jesus to be God. Amen

WISDOM

Jesus is God.

Salvation Secured Through Christ

"He is the atoning sacrifice for our sins, and not only for ours but also for the sins of the whole world"
I John 2:2.

REFLECTION

The greatest need of the world is spiritual. The greatest problem that the world has is sin. All the issues of mankind are sin related. The greatest solution is the removal of mankind's greatest problem – sin. The Bible informs us that Jesus solved man's greatest problem when he died on the cross. His substitutionary death on the cross makes it possible that every man, woman, boy, or girl can be saved – can have his or her sins forgiven and be made a child of God.

His death for us met all the just demands of God. As our Redeemer He paid the full price for our sins. As our High Priest, He ensures our acceptability to God the Father. So, the remedy for sin is available to all who believe. All that is necessary is to trust in the merits of what Christ accomplished on the cross.

God offers salvation as a gift to be received by faith. It is for you. It is for me. It is for whosoever desires it. John sums up this fact beautifully: *"For God so loved the world, that he gave his only begotten Son, that whosoever* (that means you or me) *believeth on him should not perish, but have eternal life"* John 3:16 (A.S.V.).

My claim to being a Christian is based on the fact that I received Him into my heart and He has forgiven me my sin and made me into a new person. If you too, receive Him, you too, will become a new person. He loves you, and died for you, so that you can have eternal life. Take God's offer of salvation now, for there is none like it. You will rejoice if you do.

PRAYER

Lord, help me to receive you today. Amen

WISDOM

Faith secures; the blood redeems.

Unswerving Obedience

"We know that we have come to know Him if we obey his commands"
I John 2:3.

REFLECTION

If you know Christ as Savior you should be obedient to Him. God requires full obedience - zealous, enthusiastic, steadfast, faithful, true, unquestioning and overflowing with love. A mere profession of faith is not enough, but that confession of faith must manifest a connection to the Vine and hence a life of fruitfulness. This is the character of true Christianity.

There is no place in Christ's Kingdom for superficial Christianity. True Christianity must be marked by more than ritual conformity. Lukewarm Christianity sickens the heart of God. 'Christianity' that vacillates between the world and God is nothing short of being despicable. God wants us to respond to His **"Come"** positively and to His **"Go"** warmly, willingly, and instantly.

The obedient Christian delights in doing the will of God from the heart. Can a Christian be other than obedient? The inner springs of true Christian motive will be pure and crystal clear. His hands should be clean, his heart undefiled, his lips anointed with a Biblical message, and his ears perpetually open to the voice of the Lord. The true Christian will be broken, submissive and willing at any cost to obey, with eyes always fixed on the Lord and the heart filled with God's Spirit.

Are you a Christian burning with zeal for the Word and for the work? Or are you one that has not found your direction for life? A heart yielded to the Lord will immediately get you on course.

PRAYER

Lord, help me to be obedient to you in all things. Amen

WISDOM

Obedience is better than sacrifice.

Do You Know Him?

"The man who says, "I know him," but does not do what he commands is a liar, and the truth is not in him."
I John 2:4.

REFLECTION

Our claims are important. We can make grand claims as to who we are, but if our claims, when examined, find us wanting, we will be classified as imposters. We might be able to pull the wool over the eyes of others by pretense but we will not succeed with the God who searches the heart, and who knows everything about us.

In the Book of Acts, chapter 5, Ananias and his wife Sapphira, tried to pull a fast one on Peter and the church, but God exposed their lie and they suffered the extreme penalty for their clever scheme.

If your "Christianity" is a face-card, a sham, devoid of any spiritual reality, then the Word calls you a liar and you have no part or lot in Christ's Kingdom. You are in the same category of Judas the traitor. You belong to those who solemnly say, "Lord, Lord," but have no appetite for the things of God. Like Simon the sorcerer *"your heart is not right before God"* and you are a *"captive to sin"* (Acts 8:21a, 23b)

God does not take light phony Christianity for such people are destined for the Lake of Fire. Are you playing games with your faith?

How sincere is your claim to being a Christian?

PRAYER

Lord, help me to walk before you in sincerity. Amen

WISDOM

Insincerity is demonic captivity.

Love And Obedience Interlocked

"But if anyone obeys his word, God's love is truly made complete in him. This is how we know we are in him"
I John 2:5.

REFLECTION

Church activity is not necessarily spirituality. We can be engaged in all types of spiritual activity without being energized by the Spirit. Motive for action is very important. Motivation can spring from the flesh, as it can from the Spirit. When motivation is from the Spirit, God is the center of all our actions.

We cannot love God and not be obedient to Him. When we are obedient to God, we are in harmony with God. There can be no area of tension or conflict between our will and the will of God.

For us to please God, we must constantly search the Scriptures diligently to discern the will of God. As truth is discovered about God, about us, about our mission, about our sanctification, then it should be applied wholeheartedly to our situation, not merely from a sense of duty, but from a heart that delights in doing those things that are pleasing to God.

No sacrifice is too great, no task impossible, no time inconvenient, for showing love. Wherever, whenever and by whomever love is demonstrated, it generates its own reward and satisfaction. As we open our hearts to God, we will soon discover that we have entered into the storehouse of His limitless love and that truly fulfills and makes us complete.

If you love God, truly love Him, you will obey Him.

PRAYER

Lord, help me to enjoy your unlimited love. Amen

WISDOM

Love and obedience are twins.

Live The Claim

"Whoever claims to live in him must walk as Jesus did"
I John 2:6.

REFLECTION

John's epistle has some statements that are simple, yet profound and very weighty. John sees the Christian life in black and white, with no gray areas. If our conduct does not match our claim, John implies, we are simply pretenders. If we profess to belong to Christ, then our life- style must depict the behavior of Christ. There should be no contradiction or tension between what we say and what we do. There is only one universal standard for Christian conduct and that is to walk as Jesus did.

The Apostle Paul exhorts the Corinthian believers to follow him as he follows Christ (I Corinthians 11:1). Christian conduct should be recognized no matter what nationality, language, tribe, or shade of pigmentation we might have. The same Christ that indwells you also indwells me. The same Holy Spirit that indwells you indwells me. God is not partial. Therefore, if we are committed to Jesus then we must keep in step with Him.

We must not behave like headless chickens, for Christ is our head. We are no longer in the dark, but are children of the day and of the light. We are no more clothed with the filthy garments of sin, but we are adorned in robes of righteousness. We are no longer handicapped by a lack of power, for we are now anointed of God. We are no longer devoid of love for the love of God is now poured into our hearts by the Holy Spirit.

Have you the life of Christ in you?

PRAYER

Lord, help me to demonstrate daily the life of Christ in me. Amen

WISDOM

Love is talk plus walk.

Reminder

"Dear friends, I am not writing you a new command but an old one, which you have had since the beginning. This old command is the message you have heard"
I John 2:7.

REFLECTION

Reminders are excellent means to reinforce important truths. Time does not change, modify or alter truth. Truths of yesterday are just as valid for us today. Reminders are good means of stoking the flames of memory and so keep the 'coals' burning brightly.

Time has a way of stealing the passion, zeal, enthusiasm and love we had when we first came to Christ. Take for instance the Church at Ephesus at the time when John wrote the Book of Revelation. Here was a church that was full of activity, yet it lacked the singular most important ingredient for successful Christian living and that was love. Just think of it, if we have everything in the realm of the Spirit, yet fall short on love, all those other things amount to nothing.

Love is the hallmark of Christianity and when that element is missing from our lives, from our families, and from our churches we are deficient disciples, merely going through the paces of a faith that for us, has lost its bottom; a faith cut off from its root. The writer of Hebrews says, *"And let us consider one another to provoke unto **love** and **good works**"* Hebrews 10:24 (A.S.V.).

Getting 'back to basics' could not be more important, for should we fail to exercise love to God and to one to another, we fail. In that condition we are disoriented and our Christianity is numb and worthless.

Is God's love the driving force of your life?

PRAYER

Lord, help me to seek your love above all else. Amen

WISDOM

Reminders of God's love remove blinders to His grace.

205

Love Conquers

"Yet I am writing you a new command; its truth is seen in him and you, because the darkness is passing and the true light is already shining"
I John 2:8.

REFLECTION

In this first Epistle of John we read of *"a new command"*. What is it? The Gospel of John tells us very clearly what this new command is. *"A new commandment I give unto you, that ye love one another; even as I have loved you, that ye also love one another"* John 13:34 (A.S.V.). Christ, by His first coming into the world, demonstrated the character of the love He wants us as His children to show.

The love that Christ gave was unsparing, sacrificial, and pure. It embraced all mankind. It was redemptive; it was practical, caring and sought the very best for us. This love He deposits in the hearts of all those who put their trust in Him through the person of the Holy Spirit (Romans 8:35).

We can never be separated from this love (Romans 8:35). There is no greater power in the world than this love, and when we allow this love of Christ to flow through us, it transforms us in a radical or revolutionary way.

This love enables us to bridge the generation gap, create the atmosphere for forgiveness, and dedicate ourselves in service to God. If each of us who knows Christ were to exercise this love, on a daily basis, churches, cities and nations would be changed dramatically, morally.

How exactly is the love of Christ working in your life?

PRAYER

Lord, help me to show your love to someone today. Amen

WISDOM

Love of Christ generates love for Christ.

The True Light Is Shining

*"Yet I am writing you a new command; its truth is seen in him and you, because the darkness is passing and **the true light is already shining**"*
I John 2:8.

REFLECTION

Jesus is the Light of the World. He is the Messiah of whom the Old Testaments foretold. He has brought hope for those living in despair and joy for those living in spiritual bondage, and light for those in darkness. Indeed, He is the *"True Light that gives light to every man"* John 1:9.

This one man, Christ Jesus, has forever changed the course of history. Indeed, He has given history a positive direction. Now, as a result of the witness of Jesus, men may walk with confidence in God. We need no longer stumble in the darkness of moral confusion or as to how we can find God, for He, indeed, is the Light of the world. All who seek truth find Him to be its very personification.

His greatness may be seen too in the fact that He has overcome the evil one – the Prince of Darkness - and has given us power over all evil forces. From that obscure Roman colony, Israel, the light that Christ brought to earth is now shining all over the world, changing lives, institutions, cultures, governments, laws, and elevating the status of women.

The single seed He planted centuries ago has become a large tree and the birds of the air are nesting in its branches. Truly the darkness is passing and the true light is shining. The children of God are children of the light and it is through the church, the body of Christ, the light of God will spread to all the nations of the earth.

PRAYER

Lord, help me to be a light in this dark world. Amen

WISDOM

Spiritual light dispels moral darkness.

Which? Light Or Darkness?

"Anyone who claims to be in the light but hates his brother is still in darkness"
I John 2:9.

REFLECTION

A fake diamond cannot stand the scrutiny of a diligent jeweler. Fake gold cannot withstand the refiner's furnace. A forged dollar bill cannot deceive the keen banker. Many things look real until they are closely examined. Then their phony nature is revealed.

In the spirit realm, there are many counterfeits. Outwardly, they appear genuine, until their true character is exposed. Then, the scoundrels become evident. John, in His first epistle, gives us guidelines as to how we can unmask pretenders. Here is an example of such a trait. A man who harbors hate in his heart against a fellow believer is a pretender. Such a man is still in the dark.

Malice, hate, bitterness, or any type of hostility does not become those who are walking in the light. These attitudes belong to the 'kingdom of darkness' and cannot be tolerated in the hearts of those who profess to be walking in the light. These attitudes are incompatible to the teachings and practices of our Lord Jesus who told us to love our enemies. Can we truly love our enemies and have injurious feelings to our brother who shares our common faith?

Vice has no part or lot in the hearts of those who profess to belong to God's Kingdom. If, in our hearts, **hate finds a nest**, we need to examine ourselves as to whether we belong to the Light. John is very clear in our text that such a person is walking in the dark.

Are you walking in the Light?

PRAYER

Lord, help me to walk in the Light. Amen

WISDOM

God's light has no shadows.

Light And Love

"Whoever loves his brother lives in the light, and there is nothing in him to make him stumble"
I John 2:10.

REFLECTION

God's love is for all seasons. Love is not dependent on the social status, health, wealth, charm, skin color, culture, educational standing or on anything that is external. God's love is not inflated by what it sees, for physical beauty can be altered in an instant by an accident.

God's love must flow from the heart. It is not influenced or engineered by any external benefit or reward that it may obtain. It is initiating love, as Jesus has demonstrated, and it is responding love, of which even the heathen are capable.

The deep nature of God's love is to give of itself without reservation; to sacrifice and not to count the cost. It is easy to talk about love but it is quite another thing to live it. Peter boasted of what he would do for Christ, should a crisis arise. Peter was willing to sacrifice his life if the occasion should arise. The opportunity for such a crisis was not long in coming and he had three opportunities to make good his boast, but in that moment of crisis he discovered his love for Christ was just a puff of smoke.

To love in fair or foul weather is to be dwelling in the light. To love without hypocrisy, with consistency, integrity and sincerity is to be genuine. True love is like fine flour devoid of any lump or any quality of coarseness. Its texture is even throughout. Hence, there will be no ground for disappointment.

Is your love for Christ burningly brightly?

PRAYER

Lord, help me to love fervently in all seasons. Amen

WISDOM

When Christ reigns, love prevails.

Know Where You Are Going?

*"But whoever **hates** his brother is in the **darkness** and walks around in the darkness; he does **not know where he is going**, <u>because</u> the darkness has blinded him"*
I John 2:11.

REFLECTION

Hate must never control or direct Christians. Anyone who hates another belongs rightly to the kingdom of darkness rather than to the Kingdom of Light, even if such a one holds an exalted post in a local church. Being a member of a local church does not mean you are destined for heaven. If your heart is governed by hate you are likely not a Christian.

A heart possessed by hatred devalues human worth. Such a heart becomes mean-spirited, bigoted and seeks to justify its own evils. Hate turns off all the lights in our hearts and leaves our 'houses' in darkness even darkness that can be felt.

Hate puts our life in confusion and without direction. Hate distorts judgment, feeds on itself, stunts spiritual development and puts us in the vortex of a spiritual 'black-hole' from which we may never recover.

As long as hate is the focus of our lives, it gives opportunity for the devil to take control of our lives. Hate can be overt or it can be covert. When it is covert, it is more subtle, complex, insidious and deadly.

Unattended hate will become a deadly cancer in the soul that will utterly ruin the life of its victim.

Have you got hate in your heart for anyone?

PRAYER

Lord, help me love and not to hate. Amen

WISDOM

Love builds; hate destroys.

Keep In Touch

"I write to you, dear children, because your sins have been forgiven on account of his name"
I John 2:12.

REFLECTION

Three groups of Christians in a local church attract the special attention of John in this epistle (2:12-14). He characterizes them as: "dear children", "fathers" and "young men". First he deals with "dear children" (I John 2:1). The term is possibly an expression of endearment by a teacher for his disciples. Jesus' disciples were precious to Him and He called them "my children" (John 13:33).

"Dear children" is suggestive of the importance of there being a solid bond between a teacher and his students. A good teacher should be approachable, as Jesus was – gentle and humble in heart. When a teacher loves his disciples he wants to impart everything he knows to them and will guide them into the truths of God's revelation.

John was not present in person among those to whom he wrote but his love and concern for their spiritual development constrained him to write this epistle, which now forms a part of our Bible.

John had something that he wanted to share with them and he cared enough to write. Today you have access to a telephone or e-mail, why not show your concern by getting in touch with that student who has been absent for sometime now, and hear how he is doing physically, emotionally and spiritually?

What is the relationship between you and your Sunday School Class or your Good News Club or your Bible Class?

PRAYER

Lord, help me to care diligently and lovingly for those you have brought into my sphere of influence. Amen

WISDOM

Caring means sharing.

Forgiven Through Christ

"I write to you, dear children, because your sins have been forgiven on account of his name"
I John 2:12.

REFLECTION

Until someone confesses Christ, that person is a sinner, doomed to a lost eternity. The knowledge of sins forgiven for His sake is a precious truth that every child of God ought to be assured of, cherish and fully appreciate.

There are people who don't regard themselves as sinners. They regard themselves as 'good people' and they hope to get into heaven by their good deeds. My mother was one such person. When as a young Christian I told her that she was a sinner, she was deeply offended. The message eventually seeped into her soul, for about three months later, kneeling in her bathroom she asked Jesus in her life and rose up a transformed woman, her sins forgiven, and a recipient of new life. She was "born again".

There is no other way to become a Christian. This is the only way for any human being to enter the Kingdom of God. This is the only way our debt of sin can be removed. We can be saved only when we accept Jesus' substitutionary death for us on the cross. There is no other way that sin can be cancelled. We are told in Ephesians 1:7: *"In whom we have redemption through his blood, the forgiveness of sins, in accordance with the riches of God's grace"*. The same truth is conveyed in Colossians 1:14.

Have you experienced the glorious joy of having the weight and guilt of sin lifted from your soul?

PRAYER

Lord, help me to appreciate more the joy of sins forgiven and assurance of my place in heaven. Amen

WISDOM

Jesus is the only way to God.

Share Jesus!

*"I write to you, **fathers**, because you have known him who is from the beginning. I write to you, **young men**, because you have overcome the evil one. I write to you **dear children**, because you have known the Father"*
I John 2:13.

REFLECTION

Wonderful experiences are to be cherished. One such experience is to have first-hand knowledge of God.

When you experience the grace, power, mercy and the forgiveness of God it is difficult to express your joy adequately in words. The song writer said 'it is more than tongue can tell'. Indeed, we have to agree with the Psalmist when he declared *"For with thee is the fountain of life; in thy light shall we see light"* Psalm 36:9 (A.S.V.).

The "Fathers" in John's epistle had come to know the Most Holy One, without beginning of days or end of life. This same John on the Isle of Patmos was subsequently overawed by the majesty and glory of Jesus' presence that his very breath was taken away and he fell at Jesus' feet as dead. The Samaritan woman Jesus met at the well (John 4) excitedly left His presence to announce to the men that she had an encounter with the Messiah and wanted them to come and meet Him.

Those who know Christ as Savior have an instantaneous desire to share Him with family, relatives, friends and foes. This encounter with Him touches the very core of our being, plants the desire within to share Him with a world that is perishing in sin.

Do you know Him? Are you sharing this good-news so others will come and know Him?

PRAYER

Lord, help me to share with others what I know of you. Amen

WISDOM

We can only share what we have and know.

Youth And Service

*"I write to you, **fathers**, because you have known him who is from the beginning. I write to you, **young men**, because you have overcome the evil one. I write to you **dear children**, because you have known the Father"*
I John 2:13.

REFLECTION

Our youthful years are the best. These years if surrendered to Christ, have the greatest potential for Christian service and achievement. Youth under proper guidance has the energy, strength and vision to tackle and storm the enemy's strongholds and win great victories for the Lord. Youth are not tied down with the responsibility of wives and children. They are able to go at an instant notice in service to the Lord.

If our youth are properly mobilized, communities, towns, and villages could be effectively reached for the Lord. Youth filled with the Holy Spirit, knowledgeable in the Word and trained in the art of personal evangelism would be great 'instruments' in carrying out the Great Commission of our Lord in an effective manner.

David was only a youth when he defeated Goliath, who drove terror in the hearts of all who heard his daring challenge to the army of Israel. He was yet a youth when he was promoted to the place of military commander.

I was a part of a youth group that stormed the city of Kingston in the early sixties and saw thousands come to know Christ. God recognizes the value of our youth. Therefore, don't allow those youthful years to slip by untapped. Make yourself available to God and His work.

What are you doing with your youth, or for a youth?

PRAYER

Lord, help me to make myself available to you always. Amen

WISDOM

Youth is the period for energetic service.

Knowing The Father

*"I write to you, **fathers**, because you have known him who is from the beginning. I write to you, **young men**, because you have overcome the evil one. I write to you **dear children**, because you have known the Father"*
I John 2:13.

REFLECTION

To be a child and not know your earthly father leaves a dreadful void in the heart that nothing in this life seems able to fill. To be a child and not have a father who is there for you leaves you disappointed, hurt and short changed. But to have a dad that patterns the conduct and behavior of our Heavenly Father is indeed glorious for the mental, emotional, psychological, spiritual and social well being of a child.

Now we can only know God as Abba (Father) through Jesus Christ. It is only through the sacrificial work of Christ on the cross that makes God available to us as Father. The Father gave us His son so that we can have redemption. There can be no question that the Father tenderly loves us (I John 3:1). God the Father even cares for the sparrows and feeds them. He adorns the flowers with delicate and splendid beauty.

To know God as Father is the greatest security we can experience in this life and in the life to come (John 10:29). The Father takes special and personal interest in our spiritual development and desires that our lives be fruitful (John 15). There is an intimacy between us and the Father that no one can break (John 17:3) The Father offers us provision, protection and pardon (Matthew 6:11-13).

Worship of the Father is becoming of "dear children" (John 4:23-24). So too is unswerving and dedicated service from an overflowing and grateful heart. Do you truly know the Father?

PRAYER

Lord, help me to appreciate and magnify Your Fatherhood. Amen

WISDOM

Fatherhood builds personhood.

Value Of The Word Stored

SCRIPTURE   August 03

*"I write to you, **fathers**, because you have known him who is from the beginning. I write to you, **young men**, because you are strong, and the word of God lives in you, and you have overcome the evil one"*
I John 2:14.

REFLECTION

John writes to remind the young men of their strength. Physical vigor is one thing, but spiritual vigor is quite another thing. When the two are combined great things can be accomplished for God and His glory.

When we know that it is in God's strength that we stand, then Satan's kingdom will be unnerved. When we dwell in the shadow of the Almighty and learn to be still in the presence of God, then we will see the mighty workings of God and will rest in the confidence that the battle is the Lord's and thus the kingdom of darkness will suffer loss.

Repetition is one means of drawing attention to important truths. Repetition is a method of reinforcing truth in the mind. There are times we may not see the value of Scripture that we have committed to memory. Yet in those moments when our life seems to be spinning out of control, a single word, from the Word becomes the stabilizing force to calm our fears and refocus the mind, spiritually.

The full value of the Word committed to memory 'leaps out of the dark' when we are face-to-face with mortal danger, giving us assurance for this life and the next. There are moments in life when we are about to succumb to sin and the Spirit brings a word of Scripture to mind and so we overcome the evil impulse.

Are you clothed in God's strength?

PRAYER

Lord, help me that Your Word will live in me powerfully. Amen

WISDOM

We overcome evil through God's strength.

The World

*"Do not love the **world** or anything in the **world**. If anyone loves the **world**, the love of the Father is not in Him"*
I John 2:15.

REFLECTION

We read in John 3:16 of God's love for the 'world' and in our text John is exhorting Christians not to love the 'world'. John contends that to have any love for the world is to put ourselves in opposition to God. The Greek word for 'world' (kosmos) has several meanings and only the context can determine which precisely is intended.

The word 'kosmos' originally expressed "the concept of order, congruity, and harmony in the makeup or arrangement of something." The word eventually came "to signify the world or universe, either in whole or of a particular part." Greek scholars tell us that the word 'kosmos' is used at least in six different ways in the New Testament. In I Peter 3:3 we read, *"Your beauty should not come from outward **adornment**"* (kosmos). Second, it is used figuratively or symbolically as in James 3:6, where it speaks of the tongue as a *"**world** of evil".*

Third it is used of the created world as in Acts 17:24 – *"The God who made the **world**".* Fourth, it is used of humanity as in Matthew 5:14 – *"You are the light of the world".* Fifth, it is used of human society with all its institutions, cultures, practices, influences and experiences at both individual and corporate levels in life as is seen in I Corinthians 7:31 – *"For the **world** in its present form is passing away."*

Sixth, it is used morally and ethically of the present evil world order. The sixth meaning is what John has in mind as it relates to our text. This is the system that God wants us to steer away from. The world is like fly bait; it attracts, traps, and then destroys.

PRAYER

Lord, help me to recognize the danger of the 'world'. Amen

WISDOM

To be for God is to be against the world.

Challenge To Godliness

"Do not love the world or anything in the world. If anyone loves the world, the love of the Father is not in Him"
I John 2:15.

REFLECTION

Our present world system is based on self. In effect, this means independence from God. Of course the world's networks of beliefs, values, ethics, attitudes and practices are not God-centered or Theo-centric. They are based upon the self or senses, not spirituality. The system is materialistic. Selfishness, greed, power, lusts, ambition, violence, are integrally associated with this worldliness. It is important to understand this world's system has its roots in man's fallen nature and so is easily exploited by Satan, the prince of this world.

The world system that confronts the Christian and their values, are fundamentally different. The values of the Kingdom of God are diametrically opposed in nature to those of the world and are based upon the principles, precepts and practices of the Word of God. The two systems cannot be bedfellows, or integrated, or compromised, for they are incompatible. To try and unite the two would be like forming a companionship between day and night, truth and falsehood, the authentic and the counterfeit, or God and the Devil.

Should we gravitate to the world we will immediately get signals of disassociation from God. A battle for control of the soul will develop, and in that battle there is no neutral ground. We are either on God's side or that of the world. The stakes are high, the choice clear, and the consequences eternal. You cannot be a good Christian and a good 'worldlian'. Christians are in the world but must not be of the world.

Where do you stand in relation to Christ and in relation to the world?

PRAYER

Lord, help me to make daily choices that will glorify you. Amen

WISDOM

Mastery of the soul is a daily struggle.

Cravings Of The Sinful Man?

SCRIPTURE   August 06

"For everything in the world – the cravings of sinful man, the lust of the eyes and the boasting of what he has and does – comes not from the Father but from the world"
I John 2:16.

REFLECTION

The world's system is contrary to true spiritual values. The conflict between the two is not merely external, but internal, deeply imbedded in our fallen nature. When we became Christians we did not lose our corrupt nature. So, throughout our earthly lives, we will experience constant struggle, sometimes extremely painful, with the desires of the world and the desires of the new nature, enveloping us in spiritual warfare.

In this perpetual struggle for holiness we will experience cravings, lusts and boasts that do not have their origin in God. All these sinful desires and practices are very displeasing to the Father, and should we elect to indulge in them, then our lives will be fleshly rather than spiritual.

This deception takes the line that the flesh can be refined, cultured, educated, be very religious and 'pious'. But all such is still 'flesh' or carnal, or 'worldly'. The fleshly character can become engaged in Christian activity, can even become a leader in the church, without knowing Jesus Christ as personal Savior.

Even some believers are deceived by the religious workings of the flesh as they go about trying to establish their spirituality by carnal means. If there is that desire in you to have your own way, then you are behaving carnally, and you will never achieve spiritual victory until you have surrendered yourself to the Lordship of Christ. How sensitive are you to the promptings of the Spirit?

PRAYER

Lord, help me to abide in The Vine. Amen

WISDOM

The flesh does not rest.

Problem Of Worldiness

*"For everything in the world – the **cravings of sinful man**, the **lust** of the eyes and the **boasting** of what he has and does – comes not from the Father but from the world"*
I John 2:16.

REFLECTION

Love for the 'world' is a major problem in our lives, our families, and in our churches today. Unspiritual attitudes have infiltrated our hearts, our minds and our actions. Some of us are being 'caught' unaware. But despite the general trend, each of us is accountable to God for our actions. On the other hand, there is corporate responsibility, and the responsibility of leaders such as pastors and elders are to establish guidelines for their congregations to avoid worldly values.

People are like sheep and they need the guidance of godly shepherds so that they may follow the path of *"righteousness, godliness, faith, love, patience, meekness"* I Timothy 6:11 (A.S.V.). The typical congregation of many Bible-believing churches displays very little care for each other and for visitors once their meetings are dismissed. As a visitor, I recently experienced that attitude of being 'invisible' in a large evangelical church.

If messages are not tailored to address the deadliness of worldliness that afflicts our souls, then spirituality is bound to decline in our lives, in our families and in our churches. It is about time we take stock of our lives and come to terms with some of the core issues that are sapping us and making us spiritually ineffective. It is so easy to address this matter some other time.

Are you addressing the issue of your worldliness?

PRAYER

Lord, help me to pursue spirituality. Amen

WISDOM

Flaws that we seek to hide are quickly detected by others.

Hold Onto The Eternal

"For the world and its desires pass away, but the man who does the will of God lives forever"
I John 2:17.

REFLECTION

The world system is energized by Satan, who uses for fuel our fallen nature. We strive for great attainments, medals, and accolades. But all such will come to an end whether at the grave or at the rapture. Many are like the 'rich fool' whose life was crowned with worldly success but spiritual failure. He died suddenly, without enjoying the fruit of his planning, and labor, and entered eternity, a lost soul. How tragic!

Worldly attainments entice many, but in truth, the greatest of worldly attainments cannot buy one second of peace in this world or in the world to come. Yet, many are so consumed with temporal things that they have no time for God. They dismiss those who share the message of the gospel with – "Sorry, I don't have time for such things now."

We came into this world with nothing and in the end we will leave with nothing if we don't know Christ as Savior. Any person just living for this world needs to contemplate the question Jesus asked - *"For what shall a man be profited, if he shall gain the whole world, and forfeit his life? or what shall a man give in exchange for his life?* Matthew 6:26 (A.S.V.).

If at the point of death we have no treasures stored up in heaven, then all of our goals in this life would have been misguided. We will be found wanting as we plunge, at the speed of light, into an eternal 'black hole' of no hope of light for eternity.

How are you facing the challenges of the spiritual and the eternal?

PRAYER

Lord, help me to make spiritual things my priority. Amen

WISDOM

Death is certain, therefore prepare for eternity now.

Get It Right

*"For the world and its desires pass away, **but** the man who does the will of God lives forever"*
I John 2:17.

REFLECTION

Always pay close attention to any 'but' in Scripture. A "but" can make an eternal difference. If you would live forever then doing God's will guarantees you that life. Salvation is a gift from God and so cannot be obtained through religious works. True, the manifestation of works is indeed evidence that the gift has been received, but if the gift has not been received, good works, will count for naught.

All the good works of the unsaved persons count for naught towards salvation. Jesus said, *"This is the work of God, that you believe on him* whom he hath sent"* John 6:29 (A.S.V.). Here is an important 'but' in Scripture, *"**But** as many as **received him**, to them **gave he the right** to become children of God, even to them that believe on his name"* John 1:12(A.S.V.).

The values of the Christian life take us beyond the grave. Jesus said, *"Lay not up for yourselves treasure upon the earth, where moth and rust consume, and where thieves break through and steal: **but** lay up for yourselves treasures in heaven, where neither moth or rust doth consume, and where thieves do not break through nor steal: for where thy treasure is, there will thy heart be also"* Matthew 6:19-21 (A.S.V.). Also, *"For we know that if the earthly house of our tabernacle be dissolved, we have a building from God, a house not made with hands, eternal in the heavens"* II Corinthians 5:1 (A.S.V.).

What does doing the will of God mean to you?

PRAYER

Lord, help me to delight in doing your will. Amen

WISDOM

Willing must be the beginning of doing.

The Last Hour

"Dear children, this is the last hour, and as you have heard that the antichrist is coming, even now many antichrists have come, this is how we know it is the last hour"
I John 2:18.

REFLECTION

The prophetic time in which we live is fast coming to an end. We are now living in the interval between the two comings of Christ. At the first coming of Jesus He came as the Savior who gave His life to redeem us from sin. At His second coming, He will establish peace, righteousness and justice over the entire earth. In this present age, God is taking out a people from among the Gentile nations for Himself (Acts 15:14).

During this present period false teachers will arise and oppose the person, works and teachings of Christ. Savage assaults upon true Christians will increase, and, for a brief moment, prevail. The world will be deceived by a leader empowered by Satan and who will be the very embodiment of evil, the Anti-Christ.

This powerful, satanically inspired leader will become the object of worship and the persecutor of all those who worship God. The governments of this world are even now fighting against God, seeking to remove all vestiges of God from the public forum. They are preparing the world, unwittingly, for that superhuman leader who will turn this world into a living nightmare for the true believers in Christ. Satan is at his best when he lies, steals and murders. His man will have mastered his craft and will fully execute the devil's will. Very dark days lie just ahead of us because men are rejecting God's salvation.

Are you making known your stand for Christ?

PRAYER

Lord, help me to shine for you in this dark world. Amen

WISDOM

Evil will reach its nadir or lowest point after the church is raptured.

Association Or Departure

"They went out from us, but they did not really belong to us, for if they had belonged to us, they would have remained with us, but their going showed that none of them belonged"
I John 2:19.

REFLECTION

For Christians to associate closely with non-Christians, in joyful fellowship, is an unworkable position. When the basic beliefs of persons are at variance, tension will be high and conflicts certain. People who disagree concerning the fundamentals of the Christian faith cannot be comfortable with each other.

People who berate Christ, deny His supernatural powers, ridicule the virgin birth, deny His resurrection, treat the Bible as a book of contradictions, deny inspiration of the Scriptures, and who believe that man can save himself will never be at home in a church that believes in contrast, the certainty of all these things.

Once such persons discover the tenets of our faith, they are going to leave our company. People who have not experienced the new birth through Christ will soon discover that association with people with a dynamic relationship with Christ will be like trying to fit a square peg in a round hole. There is no ground for an enduring union and so they will depart from our fellowship.

If you are not prepared to embrace Christ and His values, then Christianity will have no appeal to you. After all, Christianity is a bond and partnership between the believer and Christ. If there is no such bond then a break in fellowship is certain.

Are you 'in Christ"? If so, are you in a congregation of believers?

PRAYER

Lord, help me to draw a little closer to you. Amen

WISDOM

Two can have fellowship only if there is common ground.

A Look At Anointing

"But you have an anointing from the Holy One, and all of you know the truth"
I John 2:20.

REFLECTION

The word 'anointing' is very popular in many church circles today. Christian songs have endeared that word to many hearts. It seems good at this time, therefore, to examine how the word is used in the Bible so we will better appreciate the value of the doctrine that is associated with the word.

The word means literally to paint, to daub, to smear, to pour out, to rub, to massage in and to cover over. The word is used in a variety of ways in the Scriptures so its significance can only be determined by its context. In ancient times anointing the exposed parts of the body, with oil was an effective means of protecting those parts of the body from the fierce heat of the sun. Today skin ointments are big business.

Biblical anointing can be divided into two main categories – one for private use and the other public; one personal and the other religious.

In the Old Testament it was not deemed proper to apply oil to the head during mourning. This is illustrated in 2 Samuel 14:2 and I quote, *"Pretend you are in mourning. Dress in mourning clothes, and don't use any cosmetic lotions. Act like a woman who has spent many days grieving for the dead."* However, in everyday living anointing oil was applied to the body after a bath, for its smell and for skin care (Ruth 3:3).

We too, should take care of the body, God's temple, making ourselves pleasant to be near.

PRAYER

Lord, help me to take care of my body, your holy temple. Amen

WISDOM

We need, ideally a sound mind and a sound spirit in a sound body.

A Look At Anointing

"But you have an anointing from the Holy One, and all of you know the truth"
I John 2:20.

REFLECTION

We are in the process of examining the word 'anointing' as used in the Bible. Mary in John 12:3 honored our Lord by taking a pound of expensive ointment and anointing the feet of Jesus. Those feet of Jesus walked the dusty streets and trails of Israel doing good. Tired feet can always use a good massage from caring hands. Furthermore the right ointment makes a big difference. Nothing we have is too good to lavish on our Lord. Don't mind the 'un-anointed' remarks of the critics for most of them have never loved Him enough to understand or appreciate the significance of her action.

In the time of Jesus, anointing the head of a visitor was a sign of hospitality (Luke 7:46). There was another woman, who was of the night, that Luke in the seventh chapter of his gospel tells us of. She recognized Jesus for who He was and was deeply touched in her spirit. Luke tells us – *"She began to wet his feet with her tears. Then she wiped them with her hair, kissed them **and poured perfume on them**"* Luke 7:38. This woman, taking her place at the feet of Jesus, in humility and with contrition, had the multitude of her sins forgiven.

Recognizing Jesus for who He is will transform our action and produce in us deep contrition, honor and service that befit Him who is King of kings. What place has Jesus in our hearts? Are we treating our Lord with that 'type' of hospitality? Are we taking the lowly place and exalting Him above all else?

Is Jesus the focus of your life?

PRAYER

Lord, help me to give you the first place in my life. Amen

WISDOM

In brokenness we experience

A Look At Anointing

August 14

"But you have an anointing from the Holy One, and all of you know the truth"
I John 2:20.

REFLECTION

In continuing this study of the word anointing we now turn our attention to its religious use. The author of 'sacred anointing' is God. This is clearly stated in Hebrews 1:9, *"Therefore God, thy God, **hath anointed thee** with the oil of gladness above thy fellows"* (A.S.V.). And again this truth is seen in II Corinthians 1:21 – *"Now he that established us with you in Christ, and **anointed us is God"** (A.S.V.).

In the Old Testament, God, who is the author of anointing, used human vessels to actually perform the ritual. We could say that anointing has a divine and human element attached to it. There is the ritual or ceremonial and then there is the reality or the appointment or dedication to a specific office or duty. The two aspects are clearly seen in Samuel the prophet anointing Saul to be the first king in Israel – *"Then **Samuel took** the vial of oil, and **poured it upon his head,** and kissed him, and said, "Is it not that **Jehovah has anointed thee** to be prince over his inheritance?"* I Samuel 10:1 (A.S.V.).

In the installation of the High Priest and all the other priests under the dispensation of Law, a human instrument was used for the anointing of these individuals to their divine duty assigned them by God.

Anointing with oil was not limited to people but was used in the dedication of all the temple furniture that was used in the service of God (Exodus 30:26-28). Even Jacob **anointed the stone** where his head rested after he had that dream of a revelation of God (Genesis 28:18). Everything that God uses He anoints. Are you anointed?

PRAYER

Lord, help me to experience your anointing. Amen

WISDOM

To receive divine blessing we must have divine anointing.

A Look At Anointing

"But you have an anointing from the Holy One, and all of you know the truth"
I John 2:20.

REFLECTION

We shall now turn our attention to the figurative use of anointing. Oil is the means for the anointing, but the work to which God have called us involves the person and ministry of the Holy Spirit. This concept is beautifully illustrated in the life of our Lord Jesus. *"**The Spirit** of the Lord is upon me because **he anointed me** to preach good tidings to the poor: He hath sent me to proclaim release to the captives, And recovering of sight to the blind, To set at liberty them that are bruised"* Luke 4:18(A.S.V.).

At the baptism of Jesus the Spirit of God descended upon Him and shortly after He began His public ministry (Matthew 3:16 & 4:17). All the activities and miracles of Jesus were achieved through the person and work of the Holy Spirit (Luke 4:18, Matthew 12:28).

At the trial of Jesus the High Priest wanted to know if Jesus was **The Christ** – The Son of God. The word Christ means 'anointed' and to the Jews, 'The anointed One' or 'Messiah' had special prophetic significance. The Old Testament Scriptures predicted in great details the coming of this person into our world. Yet in spite of the prophetic facts confronting them, the Jews as a people missed Him (John 1:12) and chose Barabbas, a notorious thief and murderer, and had Jesus crucified.

If you don't have Jesus as your Savior, you, too, is missing the One God has anointed by His Spirit to be the Savior of the world. To miss Him is to miss life eternal.

PRAYER

Lord, help me to acknowledge Jesus as the Christ. Amen

WISDOM

Only Spirit-anointed eyes can behold the Messiah.

A Look At Anointing

SCRIPTURE   August 16

"But you have an anointing from the Holy One, and all of you know the truth"
I John 2:20.

REFLECTION

In our reflection today we will discover that The Holy Spirit of God anoints every believer. This means that every believer is set apart for service to God. *"He anointed us, set his seal of ownership on us, and put his Spirit in our hearts as a deposit, guaranteeing what is to come"* II Corinthians 1:21. In this verse we discover that every believer is anointed and indwelt by the Holy Spirit and so has the potential to do great exploits for God.

It is the anointing Spirit that gives us the appetite for God's Word and the ability to discern spiritual truth. Even a babe in Christ is empowered to see through the clever lies and wiles of Satan because of the abiding presence of the Holy Spirit.

Before the coming of the Spirit to indwell us we were easily led astray by the spirit of error and so we did many foolish things and embraced teachings that were dishonoring to the Lord. But since trusting Christ as Savior God's anointing has put us in a new direction and given us an appetite for the things that relate to the kingdom of God.

The Anointing Spirit now gives us power over the fleshly desires and the ability to cast down evil imaginations and to wage war against demonic forces and to effectively proclaim the Word to those who are held captive in the kingdom of darkness. The success of the early church was wholly due to the anointing work of the Holy Spirit.

Are you fulfilling the task to which God has anointed you?

PRAYER

Lord, help me to function as one anointed. Amen

WISDOM

The Spirit's anointing makes us discerning.

The Beliver Knows The Truth

SCRIPTURE   August 17

*"I do not write to you because you do not know the truth, because you do know it and because **no lie comes from the truth**"*
I John 2:21.

REFLECTION

The truth cannot contradict itself. There is only one Truth and it cannot be circumvented or manipulated to make us say what we want it to say. Jesus is the very embodiment of the Truth and our conscience bears witness to it. Every person born into the Kingdom comes into living contact with the Truth, which is much more than the statement of cold facts, but it embodies a life-style that is living and active and is in harmony with the Author of the universe.

The Psalmist David, after his sin was exposed, cried from the heart, *"Behold, thou desirest truth in the inward parts"* Psalm 51:16 (A.S.V.) Christians are exhorted to speak the truth to each other (Ephesians 4:25). The Bible is the Book of Truth and we should diligently study it and rightly use it for its truth empowers.

Those who seek to twist truth do so to their own destruction for we cannot get a lie from the truth. Many have sought to mix truth with error but it becomes evident to the discerning that such a person is a deceiver and is one with him whom the Bible describes as *"a liar, and the father thereof"* John 8:44 (A.S.V.).

A sanctified life loves the truth and is guided by it. Knowing the truth is the path to freedom and salvation. Avoiding the truth is the sure path to bondage and the wretched state. Truth brings us into light and fellowship with God. Truth known should be embraced and obeyed.

Are you walking and talking in the spirit of the truth?

PRAYER

Lord, help me to love your truth always. Amen

WISDOM

Truth reveals as well as builds.

Get Him Right

"Who is the liar? It is the man who denies that Jesus is the Christ. Such a man is the antichrist – he denies the Father and the Son"
I John 2:22.

REFLECTION

Understanding the person of Christ is crucial to understanding Christianity. Jesus is central to Christianity. For the Christian there should be no doubt as to who He really is. Yet, there are persons who gather with Christians who have not a clue as to His person. Worse, there are even clergy who don't really know Him. Some leaders even speak of Jesus as one of exalted spiritual status, but not as God.

The Gnostics, a cult in John's day, taught that Christ came on Jesus at His baptism and then left Him at His crucifixion. But if like them, we fail to recognize Him for who He is, then our theology is bound to be not only false but dangerous. God the Son did become human and that union is now permanent. Jesus will forever be the God-man.

It is not God the Father who became incarnate as some contend, but God the Son. It was God the Son who gave His life for us on a cross and rose the third day from among the dead and ascended to heaven and is now at the place of all power and authority.

One day very soon, every knee will bow in acknowledging that Jesus is the Christ. If you cannot get the matter of who Jesus is right, then all you will produce is muddled teaching which is but to promote a lie. If you miss Jesus as God's Anointed, then you would have missed who the Father is also. The Bible teaches that there can be no approach to The Father apart from the Son. To be ignorant as to the status of the Son is to be ignorant as to the status of the Father, and the Spirit.

PRAYER

Lord, help me to see the vital connection between each member of the Godhead. Amen

WISDOM

The Trinity is a mystery.

Get Him Right

"Who is the liar? It is the man who denies that Jesus is the Christ. Such a man is the antichrist – he denies the Father and the Son"
I John 2:22.

REFLECTION

The Bible presents a unique relationship among members of the Godhead – the Trinity - God the Father, God the Son and God the Holy Spirit. Failure to grasp the Son's eternal relationship with the Father leads us away from a relationship with the Father. Jesus said, *"No one cometh unto the Father, but by me"* John 14:16 (A.S.V.). So to ignore or treat the Son with scant regard is to do the same to the Father. *"For there is one God, one mediator also between God and men, himself man, Christ Jesus"* I Timothy 2:5 (A.S.V.).

Jesus said, *"I and the Father are one"* John 10:30 (A.S.V.). The Jews of His day understood him to be claiming equality with God the Father (John 10:33), and that is exactly what He was claiming. Jesus' response to Philip's request to show them the Father was, *"He that hath seen me hath seen the Father"* John 14:9 (A.S.V.).

Jesus is not a rival God competing with the Father but is of the same essence with the Father. We do not try to explain divine mystery by human reasoning, but accept the revelation revealed in the Word that gives us insight into the being and nature of God.

Jesus is the key to any meaningful relationship with the Father. Remove Him from the equation and you end up with spiritual rubble.

What is your opinion of Jesus?

PRAYER

Lord, help me to accept readily and fully all the revelation about you in the Bible. Amen

WISDOM

Faith discovers what reason cannot discern.

Get Him Right

"No one who denies the Son has the Father, whoever acknowledges the Son has the Father also"
I John 2:23.

REFLECTION

All the great monotheistic religions of the world, except Christianity, recognize a 'lesser' Jesus. In truth, they that ignore, or disdain, or despise, or deny Jesus or put him on the backburner do not acknowledge Him as equal to God the Father.

Denying the Son of God His rightful place in our lives and in our hearts is to be in league with a theology that is empty no matter how high sounding. Jesus Christ is the Chief Cornerstone; He is the very foundation of theology if we are to have a right understanding of God, so necessary for experiencing a blessed and meaningful life.

To deny the divinity of Jesus is to produce a Christ of our own creation and one that contradicts fundamentally, the Biblical presentation.

Jesus is eternal as the Father. He never came into being. The Son is to be honored to the same degree as we honor the Father. If the Son is not honored, then the Father is not honored (John 5:23). It is only in Jesus we see the true nature and attributes of God fleshed out (John 1:18). *"For God was pleased to have all his fullness dwell in Him"* Colossians 1:19. This is telling us that that entire qualities essential to the very nature of God are to be found in Jesus Christ in all its completeness. If Jesus is not God, then who is He?

Your relationship with God the Son will determine your relationship with God the Father. Do you know the Son?

PRAYER

Lord, help me to know you through Your Son. Amen

WISDOM

Jesus is God.

Hold Fast To Sound Doctrine

SCRIPTURE   August 21

"See that what you have heard from the beginning remain in you. If it does, you also will remain in the Son and in the Father"
I John 2:24.

REFLECTION

Sound doctrine empowers a healthy life-style. To deviate from pure teaching is to deviate from divine truth. Sound teaching must never be diluted or expediently explained away in order to engage in questionable practices. The source of our teaching is important. There are many who are not honest servants of the Word and who will not hesitate to mingle truth with error in order to ensnare and corrupt the minds of the simple and the unsuspecting.

The source of our beliefs is critical. John, the Apostle, who was a faithful servant of Christ, exhorts believers to hold fast to those doctrines and make them settled convictions to live by. Paul, another Apostle of Christ, writing to his friend Timothy says, *"And the things which **thou hast heard** from me among many witnesses, **the same commit to faithful men**, who shall be able to teach others also"* II Timothy 2:2 (A.S.V.). It is important that the transmission of truth from one generation to another must not suffer any defects or misunderstandings or corruptions.

Time or circumstances or even culture does not alter God's eternal truth, which is forever settled in heaven. Today we have all of God's truth for us in the Bible. Hence, this book is the standard by which all sacred Truths must be measured and evaluated.

Are you a discerning listener of God's Truth?

PRAYER

Lord, help me to be true to the teachings of Your Word. Amen

WISDOM

The Word is essential to all that's fundamental.

Don't Slip

*"See that **what you have heard** from the beginning **remain in you**. If it does, you also will remain in the Son and in the Father"*
I John 2:24.

REFLECTION

To despise or ignore warning signs is to live dangerously. Many, indeed, have disregarded warning signs in the physical world and are no longer around for they have paid the price with their lives. The spiritual world is also marked with warning signs and should we choose to ignore them we too will pay the price.

Heeding warnings must be a constant practice. The one time we throw caution to the wind might just be enough to leave us maligned and scarred beyond recovery as far as this life is concerned. Caution signs are warnings designed to preserve and protect us against danger and dreadful pitfalls. They are not designed to create mischief but rather to protect us from misfortunes that might destroy us.

Here is a Biblical example of a caution, given to the nation of Israel, *"Only **be careful** and **watch yourselves** so that you **do not forget** the things your eyes have seen or **let them slip from your heart** as long as you live"* Deuteronomy 4:9 (A.S.V).

When driving, the amber light cautions us to get ready to stop. In life God gives us His amber to warn us. To disregard His flashing amber is likely to lead to serious loss in our vital living. To disregard those critical amber lights will endanger your relationship with the Lord.

How do you respond to the cautions of the Scriptures?

PRAYER

Lord, help me to pay heed to all the warnings of the Bible. Amen

WISDOM

To be forewarned is to be forearmed.

Hold To The Precious

"See that what you have heard from the beginning remain in you. If it does, you also will remain in the Son and in the Father"
I John 2:24.

REFLECTION

We should never tamper with the foundation of our faith. If we disturb the foundation the superstructure will be endangered. It is important, therefore, to have a firm foundation of faith. We must know *"the certainty concerning the things wherein we are instructed"* Luke 1:4. We must never waver or be in doubt as to the authenticity of those foundation truths.

Listening to, or reading arguments that challenge our faith from learned men can sometimes unsettle simple believers, not grounded in the faith. The writer of the Book of Hebrews warns, *"Therefore we ought to give the more earnest heed to the things that we have heard, lest **haply we drift away from them***" Hebrews 2:1 (A.S.V)

Paying close attention to the core values of our faith is not a matter to be taken lightly. We are encouraged in Scripture to meditate on these matters day and night if we would experience success in our spiritual lives (Psalm 1:1).

Paul commends the Corinthians for **holding fast** to the teachings he had passed on to them (I Corinthians 11:2). Also he exhorts the Thessalonians to embrace the teachings that were passed unto them by word of mouth or by letter (II Thessalonians 2:15). The Word established and embraced ensures a solid relationship with God.

How many hours do you spend daily studying God's Word?

PRAYER

Lord, help me to relish Your Word daily. Amen

WISDOM

Obeying is the key to growing.

Promise Of Eternal Life

August 24

"And this is what he promised us – even eternal life"
I John 2:25.

REFLECTION

This world is filled with broken pledges and promises. Are we not all guilty at one time or another of not honoring our word? However, the God of the Bible never fails to honor His promises. The God who promises has the ability to bring to pass what He promises. Peter tells us that God's promises are great as they are precious (I Peter 1:4).

If we would see the blessing of God in our lives then we must obey the Word of God from the heart. This means we must keep in step with the Holy Spirit. Of course, some of God's promises are conditional. Here is such a conditional promise taken from the life of Jeremiah – *"Thou therefore gird up thy loins, and arise, and **speak unto them all that I command thee**: be not dismayed at them, lest I dismay thee before them"* Jeremiah 1:17 (A.S.V.).

The lesson to be learnt from conditional promises is that if we shrink or shirk from our Christian responsibility, we will look likes fools in the eyes of the world.

God also makes unconditional promises and holds Himself wholly responsible for the end results. For example, God is the One who promised us eternal life, and so obtaining or retaining eternal life is not dependent upon any effort whatever on our part. Jesus said, *"And **I give them** eternal life and **they shall never perish, and no one can** snatch them out of my hand'* John 1:28 (A.S.V.).

Are you resting securely in the work of Christ for your redemption?

PRAYER

Lord, help me to appreciate the completeness of your provision for my salvation. Amen

WISDOM

God cannot break an unconditional promise.

Promise Of Eternal Life

*"And this is what he **promised us** – even **eternal life**"*
I John 2:25.

REFLECTION

God has promised eternal life to all those who put their faith in Jesus Christ. What is eternal life? Jesus in His high priestly prayer said, *"And this is eternal life, **that they should know thee the only true God, and him whom thou didst send**, even Jesus Christ"* John 17:3 (A.S.V.).

We obtain life by process of birth – New Birth – that imparts to us the divine nature (II Peter 1:4). To obtain this nature we have to be born into the family of God. Our fallen and sinful nature, inherited from our parents by natural generation makes necessary the New Birth.

The corrupt nature inherited from our parents can never produce anything that is acceptable to God. However, when Christ comes into our hearts by faith, we obtain a new nature that is created *"in righteousness and holiness of truth"* Ephesians 4:24 (A.S.V.).

Therefore, we must not view eternal life as mere duration of life without an end, for it is much more. Eternal life is a quality of life that overflows with joy unspeakable, satisfaction devoid of anxiety and unparalleled peace in the heart.

It is like a river flowing with limitless freshness, purity, power and life with an eternal purpose. Eternal life will never grow stale for it has an eternal fragrance of sweetness that will never diminish.

Do you have eternal life?

PRAYER

Lord, help me to receive eternal life now. Amen

WISDOM

What we value most we pursue most.

Beware Of Erroneous Doctrine

SCRIPTURE   August 26

*"I am writing these things to you **about those who are trying to lead you astray"***
I John 2:26.

REFLECTION

The spirit of error has plagued the church almost from its very birth. Even Jesus had a betrayer among the Twelve He chose to be His apostles. The sons of perdition, with their distorted doctrines, egocentric life-style and love for money are to be found in every local church. Jesus warned His disciples of false prophets and even of those who would claim to be the Messiah through whom many would be deceived.

Paul warned the church of Ephesus saying *"**savage wolves** will come in among you and will not spare the flock. Even from your own number men will arise and **distort the truth** in order to draw away disciples after them. So be on your guard"* Acts 20:29-31a. The wolves, whether they come from without or from within the congregation, share a common motive, which is, to lead the saints into doctrinal error and a life-style that is not honoring to the Lord.

Both the Old and New Testaments have many harsh statements against false prophets. Both denounce the messages of false prophets as demonic. When men or women deviate from the orthodox doctrines clearly taught in Scripture and put a spin on it, beware of those deceivers. Knowing your Bible is a good safeguard against such deceivers who cunningly mingle truth with error. Don't be gullible but listen with a 'discerning spirit' so that you do not become one of their victims.

PRAYER

Lord, help me to see through the errors of false prophets. Amen

WISDOM

Holiness insulates against falsehood.

Anointing Preserves From Error

"As for you, the anointing you received from the beginning remains in you, and you do not need anyone to teach you. But as his anointing teaches you about all things as that anointing is real, not counterfeit – just as it has taught you, remain in Him"
I John 2:27.

REFLECTION

All Christians have the Holy Spirit indwelling them. While Jesus was still living with his disciples physically, He promised them that He would send The Spirit who would lead them into all truth. The truth that the Spirit gave the Apostles is now embodied in our New Testament record.

Of course it takes a spiritual mind to understand spiritual truth. The truths of the New Testament are infallible because those truths are from the Holy Spirit. He is not only the author of the New Testament Books but also those of the Old Testament. Peter tells us *"For prophecy never had its origin in the will of man, but men spoke from God as they were carried along by the Holy Spirit"* II Peter 1:21.

As Peter makes plain, especially prepared men wrote the Bible. The Bible does not owe its origin to man's intellect. God is the source of their messages and they were under the supervision of the Holy Spirit. God preserved them from error so that the end product, the Bible, is all that God intended for us to have – His inspired Word. Any teaching or so called 'revelation' that runs counter to what the Bible says, is to be regarded as spurious and is to be rejected.

Knowing the word will save you from many heart aches.

How much time do you spend daily studying the Bible?

PRAYER

Lord, help me to hunger and thirst more for Your Word. Amen

WISDOM

No matter how clever the imitation, it is still a counterfeit.

A Look At Anointing

"As for you, the anointing you received from the beginning remains in you, and you do not need anyone to teach you. But as his anointing teaches you about all things as that anointing is real, not counterfeit – just as it has taught you, remain in Him"
I John 2:27.

REFLECTION

Relying on a gifted teacher of the Word is no substitute for your anointing from the Holy Spirit. You need to open your mind to grasp spiritual truths, for only then will true learning take place. No Theological Seminary or Christian Education program can substitute for a believer who is taught by the Holy Spirit. Filling our heads with knowledge is not the same as having our hearts filled with truth imparted by the Spirit of Truth.

A babe in Christ, submissive to God's Spirit, will not be deceived by some clever agent of Satan masquerading as a Christian. There is divine guidance given the believer that no man can impart. The mind of the believer is opened to God's truth and is clearly able to discern the devil's lie.

Does this mean that believers should not read their Bible? Should Christians not read Christian books since the anointing teaches Christians all things? No, for the Holy Spirit will be using the material from the Scriptures, to guide the mind into God's truth. Therefore, the Word of God should be faithfully studied for it is in those critical moments when we need guidance that He will bring to our minds the appropriate Scriptures. Reading books written by faithful teachers of the Word also does has its place in Christian development.

Are you relying on the Spirit for understanding Biblical truth?

PRAYER

Lord, help me to pay heed to the voice of the Spirit. Amen

WISDOM

The Word fuels the Holy Spirit's power.

A Look At Anointing

"As for you, the anointing you received from the beginning remains in you, and you do not need anyone to teach you. But as his anointing teaches you about all things as that anointing is real, not counterfeit – just as it has taught you, remain in Him"
I John 2:27.

REFLECTION

Some believers do hear from God while others seem to be out of touch with him. A branch that is severed from the vine will never bear fruit. Abiding in Christ or walking in step with the Spirit and obedience to the Word are key factors in being Spirit taught. We can block the channels of communication between ourselves and the Lord through carnality and by unconfessed sin.

A Christian living in disobedience has jammed His communication with the Lord and is setting himself up for chastening. Samson was one such careless 'free spirit' that awoke one day devoid of divine power for he had broken his covenant with the Lord. If we continue to tinker with the flesh then that 'still small voice' will not be heard above the clarion call of our fallen nature.

On the other hand we can be like Samuel whose ears were attuned to the voice of God and possessed a heart that was willing to obey. Therefore, if we would hear from God, then we must remain in Him for there is no substitute for a life of obedience. It is the obedient who are Spirit taught.

Are you Spirit taught? Are you truly anointed?

PRAYER

Lord, help me to have my ears attuned so that I can distinguish between the voice of the flesh and that of the Spirit. Amen

WISDOM

Do not resist the Spirit's call.

Continue In Him

*"And now, dear children, **continue in him**, so that when he appears we may be confident and unashamed before him at his coming"*
I John 2:28.

REFLECTION

Consistency in good conduct builds character. There is a difference, however, in character established on the principles of the flesh and one that is established by the Spirit, even if the same virtue is being pursued. We can have the appearance of being outwardly serene and upright in behavior but inwardly there is decay and death.

We can be involved in Christian service; yet, Christ is not the centre for our living nor is He the theme of our hearts. We do not like to be in the presence of committed Christians nor do we enjoy their conversation since it is all centered in Christ. The Apostle Paul said that living for Christ was the only purpose of his being and his life was centered on how to please Him. There can be no area of our lives that Christ should be excluded –*"Whether therefore ye eat, or drink, or whatsoever ye do, do all to the glory of God"* I Corinthians 10:31 (A.S.V.).

Peter tells us we ought to establish Christ as Lord in our lives at all times (I Peter 3:15). We will be tempted to cheat, become ill tempered, be sour in disposition under pressure, be unkind, and become 'cocky' due to job promotion, treat our children unjustly, not honor our word, despise the poor, or neglect to read our Bible.

Today let us resolve to renew our covenant with the Lord and pattern our lives after Him who is meek and lowly in heart.

Are you ready to covenant with God for dedication?

PRAYER

Lord, help me to be consistent in my devotion to you. Amen

WISDOM

Consistency generates confidence.

Check Your Motive

*"And now, dear children, continue in him, so that when he appears **we may be confident and unashamed** before him at his coming"*
I John 2:28.

REFLECTION

The threat of death helps us to make a quick assessment of what is really worthwhile in this life. It is also at this time our confidence or our lack of readiness to meet our Savior becomes a stark reality. If we have covered our tracks and have kept secret our sins, it will be at the point of death they will be aroused by an accusing conscience and confessions made that should have been made years ago.

The terror of death, like a mad dog, is unleashed and your wasted life, even though it may have been crowned with great worldly success, suddenly becomes worthless. God had not been on your mind when you had health and strength and now, as a Christian, having to face your Maker you are grievously ashamed.

But then, you may have been a very active Christian but your motive for service was self serving and not done to the glory of God. You too will be ashamed that your service to God was not pure and single in purpose. God is the Judge of all our motives and while we can deceive others by our actions, we cannot deceive Him who knows the secret motives of our hearts.

All pretense and sham on that great day will be exposed in the penetrating light of His presence. On that day, many shall be ashamed.

Are you truly living for Him?

PRAYER

Lord, help me to judge my motives for all my actions. Amen

WISDOM

God brings to light the deep and hidden things.

Ready For His Coming

September 01

*"And now, dear children, continue in him, so that when he appears **we may be confident and unashamed before him at his coming"***
I John 2:28.

REFLECTION

The Apostle Paul, shortly before he was beheaded, writing to his friend Timothy, had these words to say, *"But be thou sober in all things, suffer hardship, do the work of an evangelist, fulfill thy ministry. I am already being offered, and the time of my departure is come. I have fought the good fight, I have finished the course, I have kept the faith: henceforth there is laid up for me the crown of righteousness, which the Lord, the righteous judge, shall give to me at that day: and not to me only, **but also to all them that have loved his appearing"** II* Timothy 4:7-9 (A.S.V.).

Faithful service to the Lord will receive its reward and every Christian that so desires, can have his crown of righteous. The greatest motive force for Christian service is to live in the consciousness of our Lord's soon return. To conduct ourselves in light of the glory of that event, will keep us on the straight and narrow way. We will have no desire to deviate to the left or right of that path but will have our ears attuned and our eyes focused upon the One who gave His life for us.

We will seek to keep short accounts with our Lord and let not the world, the flesh and the devil run roughshod over us. If we fall we shall not stay down but arise to do battle for our Lord. Let us rid our lives from the stain of all known sin and walk honestly before God at all times.

PRAYER

Lord, help me to live in the light of your soon return. Amen

WISDOM

Live as those who are accountable to God.

Rebirth And Righteousness

*"If you know that **he is righteous**, you know that everyone who does what is right has been born of him"*
I John 2:29.

REFLECTION

John in his epistle declares Jesus Christ as the "Righteous One" (I John 2:1). This knowledge is more than mere intellectual accent, but it is the knowledge that flows from the experience of the heart cleansed from sin. No person who has experienced the forgiveness of sin through the sacrificial work of Christ can help but acknowledge that our redemption could only be achieved by the holy spotless Lamb of God taking our place on the cross.

Paul in I Corinthians 1:30 tells us that Christ Jesus became our righteousness and again in Philippians 3:9 (A.S.V.) he states *"and be found in him, not having a righteousness of mine own, even that which is of the law, but that which is through faith in Christ, **the righteousness which is from God** by faith."* The righteousness of Christ that is put to our account is based upon the merits of His sacrifice and that is what secures our eternal salvation.

Now from the life that flows from our new birth there ought to flow behavior that patterns the life of Christ. That new behavior is proof that indeed a wonderful change has taken place in our lives. The overflow of a life of righteousness is spontaneous and has now become the value system that is worked out daily in our lives.

If this new life is not being evidenced in your daily conduct you need to examine yourself.

PRAYER

Lord, help me to allow Christ to live His life through me. Amen

WISDOM

Birth determines the nature of our behavior.

Lavished By God's Love

"How great is the love the Father has lavished on us that we should be called children of God. And that is what we are! The reason the world does not know us is that it did not know him"
I John 3:1.

REFLECTION

We can never appreciate the greatness of the love of God until we grasp the magnitude and horror of our sins. Sin has wormed itself into ever fiber of our being. We were despicable to behold. We were hateful and performed hateful things. There was nothing attractive about us for we were defined as creatures fit for the outpouring of God's wrath. Isaiah's graphic picture of us is that of a very sick man whose horrible wounds have been left unattended.

There was the stench of rotting flesh and there was the evidence of gangrene from the head to the very soles of the feet. There is nothing morally and spiritually healthy about sinful man. The Apostle Paul tells us that we were dead – slain by our sins and transgressions. There is nothing innocent or pure about mankind and the evidence is manifest in us and all those around us. Bad news is the order of the day evidenced in outward violence and inward corruption.

Mankind's fall has robbed us of all goodness that is acceptable to God. All who would seek to glory in their 'goodness' has not yet understood the universal depravity of the human mind and its incurable state.

It is to this people that this great love of God has been lavished. It is to the ungodly, the lost, and the perishing this great love of the Father has been revealed.

Have you experienced in your life this great and wonderful love?

PRAYER

Lord, thank You for Your great love manifested for us in Christ. Amen

WISDOM

Love spared no cost to

Lavished By God's Love

*"How great is the **love the Father has lavished on us** that we should be called children of God. And that is what we are! The reason the world does not know us is that it did not know him"*
I John 3:1.

REFLECTION

There is no greater force than the power of God's love. That great love of God was not dependent upon what it saw in us. We were unattractive, ugly and utterly repulsive. Yet God loved us in spite of what we were.

That love stooped to supply our need and lifted us from poverty, impurity, and corruption and made us children of God. That great love of God was unsparing in its generosity and made every blessing available to us on a scale that is incomprehensible.

That love chose us, adopted us into the family of God, forgave us our transgressions and have now seated us in heavenly places in Christ Jesus. We are now God's peculiar possession sealed with the Holy Spirit with the promise of a life of eternal bliss. God's love has imparted to us spiritual life and has duplicated in us the very nature of that love.

Well, has the world rejoiced in this great love of God? Was it not the world that greatly hated Christ and nailed Him to a cross? Just as Christ was rejected by the world, the believer too is rejected by that system. They did not recognize Jesus for who He was and, you as a Christian will become the target of their hate.

We too were a part of that God rejecting world when the love of God overwhelmed us and won our hearts. Isn't God simply amazing?

PRAYER

Lord, thank You for Your love that overcame all my resistance. Amen

WISDOM

God's love, once set in motion, is irresistible.

Wonderful Changes Just Ahead

*"Dear friends, now we are children of God, and what we will be has not yet been made known. But we know that when he appears, **we shall be like him, for we shall see him as he is**"*
I John 3:2.

REFLECTION

Is the Christians hope a pie in the sky? Is God's promise a myth or will it be a reality as it relates to the future prospects for those who have put their faith in Jesus? The scoffers of our day are *"walking after their own lusts, and saying, "Where is the promise of his coming? For, from the day that the fathers fell asleep, all things continue as they were from the beginning of the creation"* II Peter 3:4 (A.S.V.)

Now it is either God is a liar or the scoffers are. I believe that God's promise will be fulfilled. The scoffers are saying that history is going nowhere. To the Christian, history has a predetermined destiny that will be implemented by the Father's fixed plan and purpose. We live in an age of instant gratification, but with God a thousand years are like an evening past.

In our present age God is taking out a people for His name from every tribe, nation and tongue to form a part of the mystical body of Christ – The Church, the bride of Christ. When that task is accomplished He will take His people out of this world, and in an instant, what God has promised His church will be realized in us. God has given us His prophetic Word and it contains pointers to God's over all programs. These pointers are appearing at a rather rapid rate indicating that something major and wonderful is about to happen in this world.

Are you ready for that event?

PRAYER

Lord, help me not to lose sight of my spiritual purpose and the blessed hope for those who love your name. Amen

WISDOM

The best days for believers are yet ahead. Be patient, and wait for them.

Ready For His Coming

*"Dear friends, now we are children of God, and what we will be has not yet been made known. But we know that **when he appears**, we shall be like him, for we shall see him as he is"*
I John 3:2.

REFLECTION

In this present life, our lives are to become more and more Christ like, but in spite of our noblest efforts there are many failures and shortcomings in trying to achieve that goal. On that day when Christ shall have come for His bride, the Church, the great transformation will be completed.

The hurdles, the struggles, the infirmities of the flesh, the impurities of the heart and the accusing finger of conscience will be in the archives of our history as the full effects of Christ's salvation will be realized and then the church will be radiant, stainless, without wrinkle, or any sort of blemish. She will be holy and blameless on that day. She will be adorned in fine linen which is symbolic of the righteous acts of the saints (Revelation 19:8).

The nature of the bodies we will possess will be like that of our Lord Jesus. The limitations of this present body will be replaced with a body that will never experience disease or death or any type of physical disorder. That new body will be capable of moving through space at speeds we cannot now comprehend and passing through solids will not be a problem.

There will be no more emotional traumas, mourning, crying or any sort of pain for all those things will have passed away. We echo the cry of John in Revelation 22:20 – *"Come, Lord Jesus."*

PRAYER

Lord, help me to live in light of the glorious prospects that lie ahead. Amen

WISDOM

Our future is more glorious than we can ever think or imagine.

Hope Purifies

"Everyone who has this hope in him purifies himself, just as he is pure"
I John 3:3.

REFLECTION

Nothing has a more sanctifying effect on our conduct than the blessed hope of Christ's coming for His church. A good steward will work not only when the Master is around, but will be just as faithful when the Master's eyes are not on him. If you have to be monitored to perform at work, I can tell you, you are not prepared for the coming of Him who will judge our motives. We can sit at our desks and appear to be working and fool the boss, but we cannot deceive God by shoddy preparation for Sunday school. Our bodies may appear to be enjoying worship, yet our minds maybe occupied with mundane things.

A proper sense of accountability helps to put our life in perspective. A man who is looking forward to His Lord's return cannot divide his life into that which is sacred and that which is secular for all of life is sacred. A man who is longing for his Lord's return will not entangle himself in sinful indulgences and makes excuses for the flesh to fulfill its lusts.

The recipe for a pure life is to have a heart that is undivided and full of love for the Savior. If love for Jesus is not uppermost in the affection then service to Christ becomes routine, mundane and will be performed out of a sense of mere duty. When service is motivated by love, then service becomes a delight as was the case of Jacob laboring for seven years for the hand of Rachel. The labor *"seemed unto him but a few days, for the love he had to her"* Genesis 29:20 (A.S.V). Are you looking forward to Christ's return because it truly motivates and sanctifies?

PRAYER

Lord, help me to live with a consciousness of your soon return. Amen

WISDOM

When hope fires the mind it also sanctifies the heart.

Sin Is Breaking The Law

"Everyone who sins breaks the law; in fact, sin is lawlessness"
I John 3:4.

REFLECTION

There was a rich ruler in the Bible that inquired of Jesus what he must do to inherit eternal life. Jesus pointed him to that section of the law that dealt with his moral responsibility towards his fellowmen – *"Do not commit adultery, Do not kill, Do not steal, Do not bear false witness, Honor thy father and mother"* Luke 18:20 (A.S.V.).

His response to this was that he was obedient to the law from his childhood yet there was still a void in his life. Jesus told him to sell all he had and give to the poor and then become a disciple of His. Jesus by doing this was exposing the moral defect of this man's life, for his love of money was the real god of his life. So the man who thought he had kept the law was only doing so superficially, for self was still the supreme ruler of his life.

This man left the presence of Jesus sad for he was not prepared to give up his wealth, the idol of his life, and be committed to follow Jesus. There is no man, no matter how sincere, who has not violated the letter of the law and also its spirit. Consider carefully what James says, *"For whosoever shall keep the whole law, and yet stumble in one point, he is become guilty of all"* James 2:10(A.S.V.).

A man who violates the law of God is not to be trusted and Paul says we are all violators and have fallen short of God's holy demand. When we sin, John says we are lawless. Sin puts us in opposition to God and that is a serious matter. Thanks be to God, that matter can be resolved through Christ. Have you come to terms with God's solution?

PRAYER

Lord, help me to see the true nature of sin. Amen

WISDOM

All men are lawbreakers.

He Took Away Our Sins

SCRIPTURE   September 09

"But you know that he appeared so that he might take away our sins. And in him is no sin"
I John 3:5.

REFLECTION

The coming of God's Son into the world was to take away our sins. Adam's one act of disobedience brought rebellion, death and destruction to all mankind. Adam's nature is now transmitted to all his off springs and has brought condemnation to all men (Romans 5).

No matter how hard we try, we can never attain the righteousness that God demands. Our sinful nature is a natural barrier between us and God. Well, God's solution to man's sin problem was resolved by the appearing of Jesus Christ, the seed of the woman. Now Jesus was God taking on human nature in order to reverse the curse that Adam's disobedience involved us in. Jesus, we must emphasize, is much more than a mere man. He is the God-man.

As the God-man it was impossible for him to sin. There are those who contend that it was possible for Him to sin. But if that is so, what is to prevent Him at some time in the future from becoming a sinner? John is very emphatic and states, *"And in Him is no sin."* Being sinless does not mean that the temptations were not real but they were bound to fail because there was nothing in His nature that answered to sinful vices.

It was this sinless One who became our substitute on the cross and took the full penalty for our sins, thus opening the door for us to become God's children. We can now be clothed in Christ's righteousness. It is a righteousness that comes through faith. It is the only righteousness that God will accept. All you have to do is open your heart to the Savior and His righteousness is credited to you. Will you do it now?

PRAYER

Lord, help me to see the wonder and beauty of your salvation. Amen

WISDOM

Christ's salvation is perfect and valid for all eternity.

Knowing Him And Sin?

*"**No one who lives in him keeps on sinning**. No one who continues to sin has either seen him or known him"*
I John 3:6.

REFLECTION

A spiritual encounter with Christ makes a powerful difference in our lives. It impacts on every part of our being for good. It ushers in a new level to living and creates new desires for holiness. Coming to Christ does create the desire for righteousness, truth and justice. No person receiving New Life in Christ has an appetite or longing for sin.

The miracle of the new birth makes **new creations** of us and the pull to evil is given a deadly blow. Once our lives are **committed to Christ** our motto becomes that of the Apostle Paul, *"For to me to live is Christ"* Philippians 1:21 (A.S.V.).

If after professing to receive Christ as your personal Savior you still have a craving for evil and there has been no change in your former life style then it could mean that your profession was not genuine and you are yet in your sins. One cannot be living for Christ and at the same time be holding unto the ways of the devil. That is grotesque.

Paul the Apostle writing to the Corinthian Christians says, *"You cannot drink the cup of the Lord and the cup of demons too; you cannot have a part in both the Lord's Table and the table of demons"* I Corinthians 10:21. A life style of habitual sin demonstrates that there has been no meaningful change within, that such a one is still a **stranger to grace** and Jesus Christ and that encounter, was at best, superficial.

Is sin still your master or do you have the mastery over sin?

PRAYER

Lord, help me to hate sin in all it manifold manifestations. Amen

WISDOM

To love sin is to despise righteousness.

Sin Can Never Be Justified

"No one who lives in him keeps on sinning. No one who continues to sin has either seen him or known him"
I John 3:6.

REFLECTION

There were certain Gnostic teachers that lived in the time of John who taught that matter was evil and only spirit was good. Therefore to engage the material part of our being in sinful acts was no big thing, since they reasoned, the material was already evil. That lie depreciates the truth that God, who is pure Spirit, became a man. It also makes a mockery of our sanctification.

John insists that the incarnation was physical and that sanctification is valid proof that we are truly born of God. Jesus makes the spiritual rebirth the only qualification of either seeing or entering the Kingdom of God. Sin is the great barrier that must be torn down if we would have fellowship with God. Therefore to indulge in sin covertly or overtly would become the acid test as to whether we belong to Him or not. Paul declares that our bodies are the temples of the Holy Spirit and therefore must be kept pure.

No amount of manipulation or twisting of the truth can ever justify a life of sin. Willful participation in evil betrays the lies of those who claim they belong to the family of God and in practice are not. This passage is not advocating sinless perfection in this present life, but it gives no comfort to those who live for sin in spite of their pretended profession of having Christ as Savior. Knowing Christ means a changed and transformed life. If there are no quality changes in your life then you are lost and still in your sins.

Your nature determines your behavior. What is your behavior?

PRAYER

Lord, help me to die daily to sinful passions. Amen

WISDOM

Sin resisted is sin denied.

Living Right From The Heart

*"Dear children, do not let anyone lead you astray. **He who does right is righteous,** just as he is righteous"*
I John 3:7.

REFLECTION

There is no period in the church's history that she has not had false teachers in her midst. In every period their goal has been the same – to lead astray. These pretended 'shepherds' want to catch us off guard and lead us into error and into a life style that is unlike Christ's. Don't be sucked in by these con artists with their clever talk but whose theology and oft times, their life styles, tend to expose them. Right living becomes the believer.

Now there are those who are reformists who try to emulate the right, but have never experienced the transforming power of the cross-work of Christ. They are trying to establish righteousness based upon works of law and not by the sanctifying power of the Holy Spirit. They, like Israel, have missed the righteousness of God by faith and are trying by means of the fallen nature, to please God.

All Christian attainments are accomplished by and through faith, for as the Scriptures says, *"The just shall live by faith"* Romans 1:17 (K.J.V.).

Christianity is much more than trying to imitate Christ. It is allowing **Christ to live through us** (Galatians 2:20). It is the same kind of righteousness that Christ possesses that we must have flowing through us. Jesus said, *"For without me ye can do nothing"* John 15:5 (K.J.V.).

Is Christ operating through your life in a manner that is spontaneous and yielding precious fruit?

PRAYER

Lord, help me to live a life that is righteous and pleasing to you. Amen

WISDOM

Right living is proof of your conversion.

Sin Is The Devil's Work

"He who does what is sinful is of the devil, because the devil has been sinning from the beginning. The reason the Son of God appeared was to destroy the devil's work"
I John 3:8.

REFLECTION

The devil is the father of sin. It was he who got our first parents into trouble in the Garden of Eden. Eve was deceived by the devil's lie. He gave her a story that put God in a 'bad light'. He reassured Eve that God was withholding the best from her. She took the bait and sinned. On the other hand Adam's sin was deliberate. He knowingly went against the will of God.

If we are deceived, sin ignorantly or sin deliberately it puts us on the side of the devil. It makes no difference to Satan as to how, why or where we sin. His mission is to get us to sin. When we sin we may become ashamed, and proceed to conceal it, or brag about our nefarious acts of sin. Some indulge in sin, in terror of their conscience, while others have their conscience stifled.

No sin can ever be justified for all sins are rebellion against the Laws and person of God. Some persons make their living off sinful acts, others use it to make a profit and yet others use it to cover their misdeeds. Whatever our reason might be for sinning it makes us collaborators with the enemy of God. We can plan to sin or we can with fixity of purpose determine to live for God.

The challenge to sin is a moment by moment affair. We can give in, cave in or run into it or we can elect by God's grace to honor Him by a righteous response. How are you handling the matter of temptation?

PRAYER

Lord, help me not to keep company with the devil for any reason. Amen

WISDOM

Sin blights the life.

The Devil And His Destiny

"He who does what is sinful is of the devil, because the devil has been sinning from the beginning. The reason the Son of God appeared was to destroy the devil's work"
I John 3:8.

REFLECTION

Who is the devil? Does he have an eternal existence? Is he a rival god? In our world he seems to be having the upper hand for evil seems to be mushrooming everywhere. Wickedness seems securely seated on the throne and righteousness appears soundly defeated and retreating in disarray.

Is the God of the Bible taken off guard by the cunning wiles of the master of deception? Well, to begin with, the devil or Satan is a creature with very limited powers. He was not always bad. He may have been the most powerful angel in heaven. He was created with a will and so had the power of choice. Isaiah 14:12-15 gives us insight into his sin which was pride. He was trying foolishly to usurp the authority of God by replacing God with himself and of course this brought to pass his downfall.

He is now the arch enemy of God. He is not omnipresent, nor omnipotent nor omniscient. He had a large following in heaven as a third of the angels joined in the revolt against God (Revelation 12:3). He has an enormous following on earth and is recognized in Scripture as the 'god of this world' (John 14:30). God is going to allow evil to peak in this world and then dramatically crush it and temporarily confine its chief architect to the abyss and then permanently to the Lake of Fire.

Who is the architect of your daily conduct?

PRAYER

Lord, help me not to become involved in the devil's work. Amen

WISDOM

The devil and evil will not ultimately triumph, God will.

Jesus Defeated The Devil

*"He who does what is sinful is of the devil, because the devil has been sinning from the beginning. **The reason the Son of God appeared was to destroy the devil's work"***
I John 3:8.

REFLECTION

In spite of the outward success of the devil, he has been given a fatal blow by the coming of Christ to the world. The area of his domain that has been struck and left shattered is in the realm of death (Hebrews 2:14). The devil once had the key of death, his most prized possession.

With one master stroke Jesus destroyed the power base of the master of deception, had him 'tied up' and immediately began spoiling his goods. Jesus did this when the devil thought he had the upper hand. The deceiver was 'deceived' by his own cunning. When he had Jesus crucified, he did not realize it was the undoing of his realm.

The cross work of Christ accomplished much more than the devil bargained for. It is through the cross man was reconciled to God. Sin can now be forgiven, it being the cause of man's condemnation and physical death. Eternal life is available to all who put their trust in Christ as well as the impartation of righteousness through faith thus bringing to an end the matter of spiritual death.

But horror of horrors, his most prized victim, whose tomb was well guarded by Roman soldiers and legions of demons, brought panic to his realm when Jesus rose from among the dead. The devil was numb with fear as Jesus unceremoniously grabbed the keys of death from his grasp. The day is coming when He will empty every tomb to the chagrin of Satan. Jesus has defeated Satan and we need not fear him. Give glory to Jesus.

PRAYER

Lord, help me to realize in my experience that Satan is defeated. Amen

WISDOM

The master mind of evil is routed and that will soon become evident.

Jesus Deafeated The Devil

*"He who does what is sinful is of the devil, because the devil has been sinning from the beginning. **The reason the Son of God appeared was to destroy the devil's work**"*
I John 3:8.

REFLECTION

The devil is on a leash. The historical defeat of evil in principle was accomplished by the death and resurrection of Jesus Christ. It appears today that 'Goliath' still challenges the people of God in daring and hostile tones and still causes deep concern in the camp of 'Israel'. If the enemy is defeated why death, disease, misery and destruction?

God's plans are fixed and certain and the events of the present are all a part of His program. God is today taking out a people for His name from the very camp of the enemy and when that is accomplished the harvest of the first resurrection unto life will empty the graves of the redeemed in the twinkling of an eye. The Bible tells us, *"For the Lord himself shall descend from heaven, with a shout, with the voice of the archangel, and with the trump call of God: and the dead in Christ will rise first"* I Thessalonians 4:16 (A.S.V.).

Not only will He raise the dead saints, but millions 'in Christ' at His coming for His Church, will never taste death. It is an event that this wicked world will never forget and Satan and his horde will be powerless to do anything about it. *"And the God of peace shall bruise Satan under your feet shortly"* Romans 16:20 (A.S.V.). As God's plans come into full swing it will become evident that Christ has indeed **destroyed the works of the devil**.

Are you living today in the spiritual victory that Christ secured for you?

PRAYER

Lord, help me to see beyond the present to your ultimate defeat of evil. Amen

WISDOM

Every knee will one day bow to the Christ who is King of kings.

Cannot Go On Sinning

*"No one who is born of God will continue to sin, because God's seed remains in Him: **he cannot go on sinning**, because he has been born of God"*
I John 3:9.

REFLECTION

Sinning cannot be the life style of those who have been redeemed by the precious blood of Jesus. Those who are born of God find sin repulsive and undesirable. They have no appetite for stealing, lying, fornicating or any other menu of the flesh. When we trusted Christ as Savior we died to sin. If we died to it, then it can no longer have a hold on us. It is impossible to die to a thing and still be under its dominion. We are therefore no longer under its spell or under its sphere of control.

Christianity is not a natural religion, but one that is supernatural from its inception to its 'end'. Christianity is an infusion of life, a life that has its origin in God and its manifestation are in a life lived in righteousness and truth. To live the Christian life demands we live in union with Christ on a moment by moment basis.

A disciple of Christ is pictured as a branch attached to the Vine. The branch is dependent on the vine for its survival and productivity. There is nothing superficial about its linkage for the relationship is spontaneous and the fruit it bears reflects the very nature of the vine. Therefore we cannot be 'in Christ' and not reflect the characteristics of His behavior in our daily conduct. A life style of sin is incompatible with Christianity for the two cannot coexist. Holiness becomes the Christian.

What does your life style portray?

PRAYER

Lord, help me to remain in you in all my ways. Amen

WISDOM

Those born of God are assured of victory over sin.

Christian Distinctives

*"This is how we know who the children of God are and who the children of the devil are: Anyone who does not **do what is right** is not a child of God; nor is anyone who does not **love his brother**"*
I John 3:10.

REFLECTION

Christians are known by their conduct. We can say we are Christians, but if our lives stand in stark contradiction to our confession, we are, according to John, children of the devil. John, in our text, gives us two characteristics of a true Christian. The first, which we will consider today is, he does what is right. Doing the right flow from the heart of one who is born of God. The motive for doing the right is not to please himself or be a 'man pleaser' but rather to please God.

Because 'proper conduct' is not always indicative of pure motives, we can deceive others. Even criminals can feign good behavior to shorten their term of confinement and once they are out, they revert to regressive behavior that shortly puts them back in the slammer. Doing right can become the ground of boasting or the basis for humility. Doing right must come from a heart that is conscious of God knowing the motive for my every action.

Therefore, if my relationship with God is on shaky ground and my communion with Him is not sweet and consistent, then the sincerity of my action will not stand before the penetrating gaze of Him whose righteous eyes are like a blazing furnace.

Are your actions springing from a heart that is in tune with God?

PRAYER

Lord, help me to look unto Jesus the Author and Finisher of my faith. Amen

WISDOM

Keeping the distinction between the children of God and those of the devil is critical for our spiritual separation and development.

Love The Brethren

*"This is how we know who the children of God are and who the children of the devil are: Anyone who does not **do what is right** is not a child of God; nor is anyone who does not **love his brother"***
I John 3:10.

REFLECTION

John gives us two distinctives of a genuine Christian. The first is that a Christian must practice what is right which we briefly examined yesterday and the second is equally important and that is to love our brothers.

It is easy to love people we don't see in the flesh, but it is quite another matter to love that brother or sister that just seems to rub you in the wrong direction every time, or that brother who is ill mannered that when you see him approaching you seek a detour to avoid contact with him. Or it could be a needy sister coming in your direction and your heart sinks because she is going to make demands that will touch your billfold.

The world and the church are filled with all sorts of individuals and loving each one as an individual might be quite an undertaking. Love is not partial. We must love the brethren no matter what their social class might be, or the nature of their temperaments, or their educational status or the status of their health.

Love is boundless. Therefore in our relationships we must avoid putting up invisible shields to avoid those folks we feel uncomfortable being around. We must work on our attitudes so that we do not disfellowship anyone from our minds. Is your love discriminating or does it abound to all?

PRAYER

Lord, help me to love people because they bear your image. Amen

WISDOM

Showing love reflects my relationship with God.

Love One Another

*"This is the message you heard from the beginning. We should **love one another**"*
I John 3:11.

REFLECTION

Love is the foundation upon which Christianity is built. John 3:16 tells us the Father loved the world. This love was demonstrated to us by Jesus giving His life for the sins of the world. Love is much more than verbalizing an emotional sentiment, even though at times our verbal expression of love can be reassuring and necessary.

Love is much more than romantic passion between a man and a woman. Love is caring for each other, even enough to give our very life for the other person should the need arise.

Love is at times just giving another who maybe going through a crisis in life, your undivided attention. Yes, it's making your shoulder available for someone to cry upon. It is extending patience, kindness and mercy to those who need it. Love is full of eyes, but it is willing to forgive and to put a grievous matter behind it. Love indeed covers a multitude of sin. Love is greater than the defects we see in others and is able to work with another in spite of that. Love has anger under control and uses it sparingly and wisely.

Love sees the needs of others and without calling attention to it meets those needs. Love does not parade itself, yet when it is shown all will see it. Jesus said, *"By this shall all men know that ye are my disciples, if ye have love one to another"* John 13:35 (A.S.V.).

Are you showing this love to those you know?

PRAYER

Lord, help me to show your love to others in meaningful ways. Amen

WISDOM

Love is the greatest gift we can give.

'Growing Cain?'

SCRIPTURE September 21

"Do not be like Cain, who belonged to the evil one and murdered his brother. And why did he murder him? Because his own actions were evil and his brother's were righteous"
I John 3:12.

REFLECTION

The spirit of Cain is alive and growing in our world at an alarming rate. We as Christians are called upon not to emulate Cain. Cain gave his heart to Satan and Satan filled it with evil desires. Cain was jealous of his brother Abel whose worship God found acceptable.

Once jealousy and envy enter the human heart it will stop at nothing to settle the score. Abel was not in competition with his brother, for all Able desired was to honor God by doing what was right. But right action by others irritates those whose life style is displeasing to the Lord, and this will lead them to desperate and vicious action.

There is a tension between evil and good men. The first murder committed in the human family was committed by a brother. One person excelling in anything becomes the very ground for being targeted by the less successful person. It could begin by belittling the person's performance, or by back stabbing or smearing and fostering hate in the heart. Hate will never be satisfied until the other person is 'eliminated' at an opportune time.

Was not Christ crucified because his opponents could not stand to see His great success with the people? He was winning the hearts of the people by His love and powerful actions; His opponent's animosity and hatred of Him could not be concealed and their envy eventually won the day. Who are you patterning your life after – Cain or Abel?

PRAYER

Lord, help me to fashion my life after good and not evil. Amen

WISDOM

It is wisdom to love right and eschew evil.

Hated By The World

SCRIPTURE   September 22

*"Do **not be surprised**, my brothers, **if the world hates you**"*
I John 3:13.

REFLECTION

A Christian is a stranger and pilgrim in this world. The 'world' will never embrace the Christian's value system of doing the right and hating falsehood. The system of the world is based on the behavior of Cain who is of that wicked one. We are in a system that we have to rebuke and testify against. It is a system based upon our sinful nature.

Just as how it is impossible to marry day to night, right to wrong, ungodliness to godliness, Christ to the devil, so it is impossible to unite this evil world system and Christian values. This world is going in the opposite direction and therefore we cannot get a piggy back ride on it and expect to reach our destination. So we ought not to compromise with it for there is an inbuilt hostility of the world towards us.

James warns that being a friend of the world is to be an enemy of God. This hostility will lead the worldly man to ridicule our beliefs, hold us in contempt, despise and persecute us for we are an offense to the system.

If the occasion arises, they will put us to death as is happening in many countries across our globe. Christ is an offense to the world and those who belong to Him are fair game for the world's hatred. Jesus said, *"If the world hateth you, ye know that it hath hated me before it hated you. If ye were of the world, the world would love its own: but because ye are not of the world, but I chose you out of the world, therefore the world hateth you"* John 15: 18, 19 (A.S.V). Are you surprised?

PRAYER

Lord, help me not to look to the world for comfort or relief. Amen

WISDOM

Don't pitch your tent towards the world for it cannot be a true companion.

In Love Or In Death?

*"We know that we have **passed from death to life, because we love** our brothers. Anyone **who does not love remains in death**"*
I John 3:14.

REFLECTION

A changed life style must accompany our salvation. A profession of faith that does not result in quality changes on the inside and is not evidenced by an outward display of those inward changes is a sham. There is a wise old saying that says that the proof of the pudding is in the eating.

Now if a person professes to have passed from spiritual death to spiritual life and yet possesses no love for his brothers and sisters in Christ then no true transformation has taken place. If a person says he belongs to the family of God and does not love and care for the children of God, such a one is still in his sins.

Christianity is the transmission or the infusion of the life of Christ into your being. If your life is not transformed, then you have not crossed over the bridge of salvation by faith and therefore you are in a state of spiritual death. You cannot be a Christian and it is life as usual for that is not possible. If Christ is in you, then love must flow out from you as it did from Christ.

Christianity is about a supernatural life style that defies the works of the flesh and displays the supernatural fruit of the Spirit. Being a new creation must manifest the characteristics of that life. New life in Christ is not dormant but powerful and all pervasive.

Do you love the brethren?

PRAYER

Lord, help me to grow in your love that transforms. Amen

WISDOM

The proof of Christianity is love.

Love And Life

"We know that we have passed from death to life, because we love our brothers. Anyone who does not love remains in death"
I John 3:14.

REFLECTION

To know a matter with certainty gives great assurance. To know we have eternal life gives us peace of mind and joy that nothing or no one can steal. Salvation is a gift from God. It is not earned by human effort, nor is it maintained by human merit.

However, there are certain credentials that accompany salvation and if they are not realized in our experience then something could be amiss with what we think we have.

John tells us that love is one such credential. The new nature does not come with an unforgiving spirit, hostility or any other negative emotions. Love does not wear the old clothes of the past. Love releases us from that which is morbid into the sterling qualities of the new life. Love has a positive outlook to all of life. Love changes everything it touches and leaves its imprint on those whom it impacts.

Love delights in putting others first and has their very best interest at heart. The very nature of love is to sacrifice and not inquire of its cost. Love is sincere and its motive for action is always pure. A life that loves is a life with purpose and satisfaction and never has a dull moment. There is no force that can transform more effectively than the power of love.

Are you seeing the effects of that great love energizing your life and impacting others?

PRAYER

Lord, help me to understand and assimilate the significance of your love in my life. Amen

WISDOM

Leave love on the front burner.

Hate Is Murder's Twin

"Anyone who hates his brother is a murderer, and you know that no murderer has eternal life in him"
I John 3:15.

REFLECTION

What we allow to fill our hearts will determine the course of our lives. What we are comes from deep within us and if the inward springs are poisoned with evil thoughts, that evil will eventually surface on our countenances and will be betrayed by our actions. Hate is the opposite of love. The storehouses of hate in this world are full and overflowing. We, therefore, can get it wholesale or retail in every community at rock-bottom bargain prices. The demand for the product is great and supply is readily available.

Hate, like a stream of 'polluted water' is transmitted from one generation to another. Its stench is suffocating and its viruses render those affected, virtually incurable. Hate is the mother of wars - cold or hot. The Devil is the father of hate. Hate might manifest itself in physical, psychological, or spiritual murder. The spirit of hate is so pervasive that to hate is as easy as to breathe.

The seed of hate indwells every human heart and just one drop of 'water' will cause it to grow overnight to the size of the miraculous vine that provided shade for Jonah. Hate is dangerous and if allowed to grow unhindered in our lives, will certainly block our passage to the Kingdom of God. Love, which is of God, is the only power to overcome hate and deliver us from its poisonous springs.

If your heart is not right with your brother, you are a murderer. You need to deal with that heart condition right away.

PRAYER

Lord, help me to fill my heart with pure love. Amen

WISDOM

Hate is a sore and love is the balm.

Example Of Love

*"This is how we know what love is: **Jesus Christ laid down his life for us**. And we ought to lay down our lives for our brothers"*
I John 3:16.

REFLECTION

Love defined is not as forceful as a demonstration of what it is and how it functions. Hands-on gives meaning to theory. It breathes life, excitement, and reality into what seems so complex and perplexing. God, as Spirit, seems so distant; as if He is dwelling in a thick dark cloud far beyond our comprehension. He seems to be dwelling in that dark chamber that the High Priest was allowed in once a year.

However, when God took on the nature of a human, it brought Him into a whole new dimension of understanding that has greatly enhanced our grasp of spiritual truth and their powerful realities. Here was God clothed in human flesh raising the dead, cleansing lepers, healing the sick, walking on water, calming a storm by the Word of His power, forgiving a sinful woman, casting out demons out of those who were oppressed by them and sharing the Good News of how men could be born again and thus become children of God.

Some of those who saw Jesus in the flesh came to appreciate the wonders of the incarnation which introduced them to a whole new appreciation of God. Today, the four accounts recorded in the gospels of those encounters with the God-man have ignited and set our hearts aflame with a passion for Christ. Even though removed two thousand years from the event, the Spirit of God still breathes life into them.

Our hearts now pulsate with new life because Jesus came and put a human face on God. Does this excite you?

PRAYER

Lord, help me that my love for you will be excited by your love for me. Amen

WISDOM

Love by example impacts powerfully on our spirit.

The Cost Of Love

*"This is how we know what love is: **Jesus Christ laid down his life for us**. And we ought to lay down our lives for our brothers"*
I John 3:16.

REFLECTION

If we would know what love is, all we need do is study the life of Christ. There is no greater demonstration of love in the history of humanity that can compare with the love of Christ. His Kingdom is built on the very foundation of love, friendship and partnership. Jesus did not build his kingdom on military might or by being an astute politician, but rather on caring for the need of others.

He came to seek and to save those who were lost. His capacity for compassion is boundless. He never despised the sinner, but was among them as their caring Physician, bringing healing to their broken and shattered lives. He was never haughty or arrogant, but was meek and lowly of heart. He was always approachable and He never once turned down the request of someone needing help.

There was not present in Jesus a spirit of condemnation. His life was characterized by forgiveness and kindness and goodness to those who needed Him. Christ has established a standard of love that cannot be surpassed. He, the perfect Lamb of God, sealed His life of love by giving up His life for us on a cross in order to secure our eternal salvation. He did this when we were His enemies and hostile in our minds towards Him. He sent His Holy Spirit to overcome our hostility and to woo and win our hearts.

The same kind of love Christ demonstrated to us, we must now exercise the one for the other. How are you doing?

PRAYER

Lord, help me to appreciate your love that made you give yourself for me. Amen

WISDOM

The power of a good example is persuasive.

Love Follows Through

*"If anyone has **material possessions and sees his brother in need** but has no pity on him, how can the love of God be in him?*
I John 3:17.

REFLECTION

In our world there are abundant opportunities to demonstrate that we care by sharing our material possessions with the less fortunate. Being 'conned' by unscrupulous 'brethren' should not make us develop a philosophy toward life that despises the genuine need of the poor in our congregations.

The passage before us does not imply that it is the poor who makes his need known, but rather the onus is on the person who can render assistance. It is he who should act in concert with his discerning compassion. John poses the question in a somewhat negative manner - a person seeing the need of another, and reacts negatively by closing his bowels of compassion, is demonstrating he is devoid of God's love.

We cannot see, or hear of a need of a fellow Christian and then act in callous disregard or with indifference towards that person. This verse is not necessarily targeting the wealthy in our congregations, but rather any person who has the means at his disposal to help someone less fortunate.

Some are willing to lecture the poor, but not willing to give of their material possessions. It is unthinkable for those, touched by the love of God, to simply ignore them when it is in their ability to help.

What is your attitude towards the poor? A special blessing of God is on those who have regard for the poor (Psalm 41:1-3).

PRAYER

Lord, help me to love in practical ways. Amen

WISDOM

Love responds to seen needs.

Right Attitude To Giving

SCRIPTURE   September 29

*"If anyone has **material possessions and sees his brother in need** but has no pity on him, how can the love of God be in him?*
I John 3:17.

REFLECTION

Paul writing to the church in Rome tells us the attitude we should have when we give: *"he that giveth, let him do it with **liberality**"* Romans 12:8 (A.S.V.). Giving should not call attention to itself. There is no need to call the press or other media outlets to make public our generosity. Let our giving be done with sincerity and don't allow pride to have a piggy back ride on the occasion. Give with humility. Give with a thankful heart for it is God who gave you the ability to acquire wealth.

We should be eager to help the unfortunate. Our generosity must not be in word only, for it is easy to make a promise and not honor it, but our action must either be equal to the promise or in excess of it. Giving should not be done with regret in the heart, or complainingly as though it is a bother. It should not be out of a spirit of shame or embarrassment or for that matter, in competition with another.

The Apostle Paul warns us in I Corinthians 13:3 (A.S.V.): *"And if I bestow all my goods to feed the poor, and if I give my body to be burned, but do not have love, **it profiteth me nothing.**"* The motive for giving is important. If generosity springs from self serving motives, don't expect to reap any reward in the hereafter, for you have already had your reward and have duly robbed God of His honor in this life.

Give cheerfully and sacrificially. Ananias gave deceitfully and died as a consequence. Let our giving proceed from a heart surrendered to God as was the generous giving of Barnabas. Practice these and you do well.

PRAYER

Lord, help me to give unselfishly. Amen

WISDOM

A generous heart abounds with blessing.

Tongue Love!

"Dear children, let us not love with words or tongue but with actions and in truth"
I John 3:18.

REFLECTION

James, in his epistle, warns about the danger of the tongue and its corrupting influence on our lives. There is no member of the body that gives more trouble than an unsanctified tongue. James calls it *"a restless evil, it is full of deadly poison"* James 3:8(A.S.V.). Love must go beyond the promise of the tongue and persuasive words, for that is comfort only to a fool.

There is the real danger of the tongue giving the hapless a sense of hope and something to look forward to, but fails to implement any meaningful action either sooner or later. We can fall into the trap of engaging our lips into useless and empty chatter and become known for it; it will not be long before people learn that whatever we utter has to be taken with a pinch of salt.

Actions speak louder than words. Words dishonored leads to a life of hypocrisy. Let us engage our mind before we utter a word. Let Christ be Lord of our lives, for that will ensure that the words spoken by us will be followed by genuine action.

Jesus tells us that our words will either justify or condemn us. One day we will all be accountable to God for every utterance that proceeds from our lips. Therefore let us make every effort to coordinate our speech with our action and thus promote the truth.

Weigh your words before you speak today.

PRAYER

Lord, help me from uttering empty expressions. Amen

WISDOM

Let there be no conflict in what we say and what we do.

We Belong To The Truth

*"This then is how we know **that we belong to the truth**, and how we set our hearts at rest in his presence whenever our hearts condemn us. For God is greater than our hearts, and he knows everything"*
I John 3:19-20.

REFLECTION

Jesus declared Himself to be the very embodiment of the truth (John 14:6). Jesus before Pilate, the governor, states, *"Every one that is of the truth heareth my voice"* John 18:37(A.S.V.). Moral and spiritual truths are more than the mere statements of facts, or a creed of beliefs, but must be the vigorous life style and practice of the redeemed. It is the encounter with the "Living Truth" that makes us free.

The Holy Spirit is the Spirit of truth and He indwells us - *"Seeing ye have purified your souls in your **obedience to the truth**"* I Peter 1:22 (A.S.V.). To the Christian truth is not an appendage but that which is indispensable. We are not detached, or merely associated, or have an acquaintance with the truth, **but we do belong to the truth.**

We belong to the truth as a bird belongs to the air, as a fish belongs to water, as the stars belong to the sky, as the lung needs air to survive. Truth is not an option. We live and move in the realm of truth.

When our lives are governed by the truth we will never be hypocrites. When we live and speak the truth our relationship with God will be healthy. There is an unbreakable bond between truth, love, righteousness and holiness. We cannot build godly character without truth. Truth is the very essence of our Christian faith and impacts on all facets of the fruit of the Spirit (Galatians 5:22-25).Do you belong to the Truth?

PRAYER

Lord, help me to love truth in the inward part. Amen

WISDOM

Truth liberates.

Truth The Sanctifier

"This then is how we know that we belong to the truth, and how we set our hearts at rest in his presence whenever our hearts condemn us. For God is greater than our hearts, and he knows everything"
I John 3:19-20.

REFLECTION

Living in harmony with God demands that our lives conform to God's truth. It is the truth that exposes sin, and storing it carefully in our hearts protects us from sin (Psalm 119:11). The truth provides light for our pilgrim journey and the path to purity (Psalm 119:9).

In Psalm 24 the Psalmist asks the question about those who are qualified to stand in the presence of God and then proceeds to give us the answer. If there is one word that sums up what he has to say it would be the word "truth". Truth pervades our action, sets the tone for our inward man; it impacts upon our worship and is the corner stone of our speech.

If truth becomes the missing component in our lives then corruption, dishonest gain, abuse of others, and falsehood will have the ascendancy. Any step we take will surely be marked by misery and ultimately damn our souls to hell without any hope of recovery.

Ah! How wonderful to obey the truth for it is the source of peace for our minds. It is God's truth that purges our consciences from dead works and guides our steps in the paths of righteousness. There are many facets to righteousness and God's eternal truth uncovers them so that our fellowship with God can be assured.

Truth is the key to fellowship. Are you walking in it?

PRAYER

Lord, help me to be guided by your truth no matter how it hurts. Amen

WISDOM

God's truth purifies the heart.

Are You At One With Conscience?

SCRIPTURE   October 03

"This then is how we know that we belong to the truth, and how we set our hearts at rest in his presence whenever our hearts condemn us. For God is greater than our hearts, and he knows everything"
I John 3:19-20.

REFLECTION

Conscience is a wonderful moral monitor that either approves of our behavior or gets its thumb down. It is not wise to go against conscience for its accusing voice is not easily stilled and to violate it can make life a living hell. Conscience can be like a dart, an arrow or a dagger, a sword that pierces with righteous indignation or painfully probe deeply into any action that violates the laws of God.

Provoke it, and it becomes our dreaded enemy; cherish it, and it is your beloved companion that seeks the very best for internal harmony. Conscience is greatly enhanced through the reading of God's Word. There is no greater tool for sharpening and refining it than the Word.

Tamper with it and it becomes dull and even insensitive to moral issues. The Bible speaks of a seared conscience (I Timothy 4:2). It tell of a corrupt conscience (Titus 1:15). It speaks of a stricken conscience (I Samuel 24:5), and of a sensitive conscience that is troubled over matters that are morally neutral. It is termed in Scripture as a weak conscience (I Corinthians 8:7).

Then the Bible speaks of a conscience that has been cleansed from sin and renewed to serve the living God (Hebrews 9:14). As wonderful as conscience is, it is not the final arbiter of things moral – God is. Do you listen to conscience and is your ear open to the voice of the Spirit?

PRAYER

Lord, help me to walk in step with conscience and with Your Word. Amen

WISDOM

Keep conscience undefiled.

God Is Judge

*"This then is how we know that we belong to the truth, and how we set our hearts at rest in his presence whenever our hearts condemn us. For **God is greater than our hearts, and he knows everything**"*
I John 3:19-20.

REFLECTION

God is the final judge of our thoughts and all our actions. God knows everything and He keeps precise and accurate records of all our actions for which we shall on that day give an account. For the Christians it will be at the Judgment Seat of Christ (II Corinthians 5:10). This will take place after the church is snatched away (I Thessalonians 4:13-18).

It is the time when God will reward His saints for faithful service, but for those who wasted the opportunities they had to serve; it will be an embarrassing event. No one will lose his soul at the Judgment Seat, for salvation is not the issue at stake, but service to God.

The Great White Throne Judgment (Revelation 20:11) which is at least 1000 years removed from the Judgment Seat of Christ, is for the damned. It is for those who rejected Christ. They loved the wages and the rewards of sin and rejected the way of life. The ungodly will be judged by those things recorded in the Books. They will be damned to the Lake of Fire and there will be weeping and lamentations forever.

The God who is Judge knows our thoughts and searches our hearts and knows the motives for our actions. He is a God of compassion, and knows we are dust. He is our Savior and loves us. God probes deeper than conscience for everything is naked before Him, with whom we have to do. Let us therefore walk in truth and humility before God.

PRAYER

Lord, help me to walk in reverence before you. Amen

WISDOM

It pays to serve God.

Undefiled

*"Dear friend, **if our hearts do not condemn us,** we have confidence before God and receive from him anything we ask, because we obey his commands and do what pleases him"*
I John 3:21 -22.

REFLECTION

These two verses give us the key to a successful prayer life. If we would prevail with God then understanding the conditions and abiding by them is the foundation for spiritual power and enrichment of our lives. The first condition is to live in harmony with conscience.

A poor memory, or one that is selective, or that suppresses evil done, or excuses it will not qualify us for a dynamic prayer life. If we are not prepared to search our hearts and deal faithfully with evil in all its forms and manifestations in our lives, then we are not prepared to be transparent before God.

If there is duplicity, carnality, an unforgiving spirit, any type of malice and nursed anger, then we must first own up to them and with deep humility and a spirit of repentance and honest confession, bring these to the Lord and renounce and forsake them.

When the heart is pure and undefiled, committed to unswerving loyalty to the Lord and is prepared to deal with all acts of disobedience, and to tear down all imaginations that exalt themselves against the authority of Christ, only then are we ready to do business with God. Only then are we ready to be ushered into the presence of God to speak with Him in prayer.

Is your conscience clear of all dead works?

PRAYER

Lord, help me to keep the channel of my heart free from sinful obstructions. Amen

WISDOM

The path to holiness is singleness of life.

Praying In Confidence

*"Dear friend, if our hearts do not condemn us, **we have confidence before God** and receive from him anything we ask, because we obey his commands and do what pleases him"*
I John 3:21 -22.

REFLECTION

Approaching God with confidence cannot be overstated. To be bold and dare to ask God for what is on our hearts and not leave until we are assured of a definitive answer shows there is intimacy in our relationship with our Lord. Our confidence to approach the Father is not based upon our merits, bur rather upon what Christ achieved for us by His death and resurrection.

It is Christ who secured the freedom for us to talk and relate to God. The Father has accepted the vicarious work of His Son and we now stand complete and whole in Him. If God accepts what His Son did, and I have the Son, then it stands to reason that He has accepted me and this gives me boldness and plainness of speech in God's presence.

This, by no means, gives me the right to be irreverent, or cocky, but it does mean that I can lay claim to the promises of God set forth in His Word and expect God to honor them.

Prayer is not an exercise in futility. It is not a religious tread-mill that we daily practice, not expecting anything extraordinary to happen. Prayer, indeed, makes a path in the sea, brings water out of the rock, and stays the sun in its course, moves mountains and stills the tongue of the enemy. Prayer provides food in the wilderness. You cannot put a limit on God when you pray. Anticipate an answer when you pray and you will receive oft times far more than your expectations. Do you have confidence in Your God?

PRAYER

Lord, help me to see the largeness and generosity of your heart. Amen

WISDOM

Prayer makes God available.

Prayer - A Life Style

October 07

*"Dear friend, if our hearts do not condemn us, **we have confidence before God and receive from him anything we ask**, because we obey his commands and do what pleases him"*
I John 3:21 -22.

REFLECTION

Prayer is work and it is not for the spiritually slothful. There is no 'magic' in merely verbalizing a petition that is not truly directed to God. If our prayer life is like that of the Pharisee, in the parable of the Pharisee and the Tax Collector (Luke 18:9-14), then we are engaged in talking to ourselves and using the medium of 'prayer' to inflate our ego and of course that is an invalid spiritual exercise.

The Pharisee got no response from heaven and neither will we. Those who doubt when they pray will fare no better. James in his epistle, tells us of another category of persons who don't even bother to pray. They never turn their needs into a prayer and therefore obtain nothing. *"Ye have not, because ye ask not"* James 4:2 (A.S.V.).

Paul calls prayer labor (Colossians 4:12); it demands earnestness, consistency, persistency, and watchfulness. It is intercession; it is a life style lived in the presence of God. Prayer is then the heart's desire and passion. We see the intensity, passion and agony of prayer demonstrated by Christ in the Garden of Gethsemane – *"And being in anguish, he prayed more earnestly, and his sweat was like drops of blood falling to the ground"* Luke 22:44.

Christ, as a life style, spent many a night in prayer. On other occasions he got up early in the morning to commune with His Father and what a remarkable life of power and wonders came as a result. How is your prayer life? Is it meaningful? Are you getting what you ask for?

PRAYER

Lord, help me to discover the value and power of prayer. Amen

WISDOM

Prayer is an important key to spiritual success.

Prayer And The Person

"Dear friend, if our hearts do not condemn us, we have confidence before God and receive from him anything we ask, because we obey his commands and do what pleases him"
I John 3:21 -22.

REFLECTION

When we delight ourselves in God, then God delights Himself in us. There are Christians who serve God, as it were out of a sense of compulsion and thus in a very servile manner. They serve not as sons, but out of necessity. They serve Him not out of a reverential fear, but out of fear of being punished. It is a begrudging service – "I will do it since you ask me." It is not based upon "I want to" or "I would love to", but on "I have to".

Seeming obedience does not necessarily have to spring from the heart but may issue from mere force of will. Obedience that springs from a heart of love is easily detected. There is something spontaneous about it. There is a spirit of eagerness and a delightful attitude that permeates the whole being by a person so exercised. These Christians never question the will of God, but display a hunger and thirst for God that is insatiable.

You won't find this category of Christians among the complainers, the grumblers and the murmurers. The glow of God is on their faces. They won't wilt under trying circumstances and their entire attitude and disposition is yielded to God. This is the kind of person who has power with God. Their prayers prevail and their lives are monumental in their achievements for God's glory.

Are you a contented Christian who delights in doing the will of God for your life?

PRAYER

Lord, help me to have a heart that delights to do your will. Amen

WISDOM

There is a connection between who we are by God's grace and prayer.

Power Of The Name

*"And this is his command: to **believe in the name of his Son**, Jesus Christ, and to love one another as he commanded us"*
I John 3:23.

REFLECTION

Two important commands are given us in this verse and they are still binding on us to this day. The first is **to believe** in the name of Jesus and the other is to **love one another**. These two commands dovetail into each other. The first makes the second possible.

Now to put our trust in **the name** of Jesus Christ is an all embracing command. In the Book of Acts we begin to see and understand the significance and power of the name, Jesus Christ. A name signifies all that a person is and to invoke that name is to tap into all the virtues and power of that person. It is in the name of Jesus Christ, the crippled man at the gate called Beautiful, is healed and life becomes beautiful for him from that moment on (Acts 3:6).

We can become associated with or identified with the person bearing that name as those Jews did on the day of Pentecost – *"Repent ye, and be baptized every one of you **in the name of Jesus Christ unto the remission of** your sins"* Acts 2:38 A.S.V.).

The name of Jesus carries great weight in heaven. As a matter of fact His name is above every name (Philippians 2:9) and every knee shall bow to Him who bears that name. Salvation is through the name of Jesus (Acts 2:21, 4:21). All Christian activity is to be done in the name of the Lord (Colossians 3:17). Anointing the sick for healing is done in the name of the Lord (James 5:14). We are to pray in the name of Jesus (John 16:23-24). To the Christian the name of Jesus is precious and indispensable. Are you committed to that name?

PRAYER

Lord, help me to appreciate the value of your name. Amen

WISDOM

What's in a name? Everything!

Love One Another

"And this is his command: to believe in the name of his Son, Jesus Christ, and to love one another as he commanded us"
I John 3:23.

REFLECTION

There is nothing more important to practice in our Christian lives than love, faith and hope and these three will endure for ever, but love is the greatest of the three, so says the Apostle Paul (I Corinthians 13:13). Some local churches lay great emphasis on the gifts of the Spirit, but should they fall short on love, they would have had a misplaced emphasis that would result in zero profit. Now there is nothing wrong with having the gifts of the Spirit for they are great and not to be despised.

The problems of gifts are centered in the earthen vessels that use them. It is better to have a few gifts and an abundance of love than to abound with gifts and be devoid of love. The ideal is to have both in balance.

Can you imagine a church where there is no gossip, backbiting or meddling in another person's affair? A Church where each person looks out for the welfare of his fellow-believer and where each person is loved as we love ourselves? A church where the interests of the poor are catered to and social distinctions are not noticed? A church where widows and orphans are not left to fend for themselves? A church where members honor each other and the household of faith are united and where visitors feel welcomed and loved?

Love must begin in the heart of the individual for that is what will make the difference in our lives and in the places where we worship.

How do you measure up to Christ's command to love?

PRAYER

Lord, help me to allow love to adorn my life. Amen

WISDOM

"Love covers over a multitude of sins" I Peter 4:8.

284

The Indwelling Presence

SCRIPTURE   October 11

"Those who obey his command live in him, and he in them. And this is how we know that he lives in us: **We know it by the Spirit he gave us**"
I John 3:24.

REFLECTION

Those who have experienced the New Birth know, with great assurance, the reality of the indwelling Christ. This presence elevates us to a new dimension we could never hope to attain by virtue of mere human effort. There is an inward consciousness of the divine presence that affects every aspect of our being, conduct and communion. That presence is as real as our thoughts, yet is distinct from them. That presence has no physical properties, yet affects our physical behavior by ordering our steps in the right direction and protects our bodies from becoming instruments of sinful acts.

Just as how a demon spirit controls the one he occupies by making that person behave in a devilish manner, so it is when Christ is Lord of our lives, the indwelling Spirit of God empowers us and enables us to do those things that are pleasing in God's eyes. There is no tension between our wills and that of the Holy Spirit when Christ is Lord of our lives, for all our desires and affections are set on glorifying Him through our lives.

The behavior of a transformed life is observable. That was the case of Saul, the hostile and vicious persecutor of Christians, who, after his encounter with Christ, was dramatically changed and became the greatest promoter of the Christian faith and its values. This miraculous change was initiated in concert with the Holy Spirit who now indwells and controls our lives. Is the Spirit in charge of your life?

PRAYER

Lord, help me to give you the controls of my life. Amen

WISDOM

The Holy Spirit is God's gift to us.

Be Discerning

"Dear friends, do not believe every spirit, but test the spirits to see whether they are from God, because many false prophets have gone out into the world"
I John 4:1.

REFLECTION

We should not be gullible with regards to spiritual issues but we should be discerning. A person who is well attired, very polite and well mannered, and armed with a Bible should not take us off guard for he could very well be a messenger of Satan and could be more dangerous than a man with legions of demons.

We instinctively avoid the legion-type of person, but with the suave and cultured, we tend to drop our guard, especially if he uses the same biblical expressions we use but very cunningly and slyly add a bit of poison now and then.

Deceiving and lying spirits work through human beings, especially the religious type. The lying spirits, in my judgment, are far more dangerous than the raving maniacs. Satan operating as a messenger of light has damned more souls to hell than when he displays himself as the old dragon. When he puts on the sheep clothing of pretense and poses as a prophet, he is able to perpetrate his hellish doctrines for centuries with millions of followers in his train.

You and I may never meet the human master minds behind these lies. But we certainly meet their devoted disciples in our schools, colleges, universities, in books and magazines and of course at our doors. These disciples seek to spread their poisoned doctrines.

Be on your guard.

PRAYER

Lord, help me to be alert and not swallow what is false. Amen

WISDOM

Satan as a roaring lion or, as an angel of light, is equally dangerous.

Test The Spirits

"Dear friends, do not believe every spirit, but test the spirits to see whether they are from God, because many false prophets have gone out into the world"
I John 4:1.

REFLECTION

We Christians must apply the litmus test to all teaching we encounter, be it at our gates, over the radio, or television, on CDs or tapes, or books or even from the very pulpit. The enemy is a master of camouflaging error, packaged and gift wrapped in elements of truth. He has errors that cater to every taste and style you can think of and new ones are being conceived, with the intent to deceive. He will modify the old lies and adopt new methods to effectively get his message across.

Recently I was at the bank changing some foreign exchange and the teller examined every note I gave her to make sure that each one was authentic. They were not checked randomly but each one was carefully examined under the light for it is the light that exposes the true from the false. There is only one standard for discerning truth from error and that standard is the Word of God – the Bible.

Merely possessing a Bible will not protect us from the spirit of error. We must know our Bible from cover to cover. The deceiving spirits know the Bible too, but are intent on distorting its message. They twist, dilute, take a teaching out of context, pervert and adulterate the Word. They read meaning into a text by 'spiritualizing' to uncover a 'deeper' meaning that cannot be substantiated by the scientific method of interpretation. Don't be deceived by these clever religious con artists no matter how sincere they may sound. They are nothing but agents of Satan and they are programmed to deceive. Be like the people of Berea and carefully examine the Scriptures to see if what they say is true.

PRAYER

Lord, help me to discern your truth. Amen

WISDOM

Don't give a false prophet your blessing.

Jesus Is God Incarnate

"This is how you can recognize the Spirit of God: Every spirit that acknowledge that Jesus Christ has come in the flesh is from God"
I John 3:23.

REFLECTION

John is now getting into specifics as to how we can uncover the counterfeit prophet. The counterfeit teacher or prophet is not in touch with the Spirit of God and therefore his doctrine is bound to be in conflict with the person of our Lord Jesus Christ whom the Holy Spirit is here to glorify. The acid test of any false teaching is always related to the person of our Lord Jesus and who He is.

If you misrepresent Him then your cover is blown and the other kingdom that you represent suddenly becomes obvious. The false teacher will not exalt Jesus Christ, but will cleverly denigrate His deity and eternity, or make little of His atoning sacrifice, or of God becoming incarnate. When you tear the masks they are wearing from their faces, you will soon discover that they have no love for Jesus, but that in reality they hate and despise Him.

The devil and his human agents are fighting against the Kingdom of God and Christ in spite of their pretended lip service to the contrary. If Jesus does not take centre stage in your theology, then it needs to be examined as to its authenticity. If God did not become human, and died on a cross for our sins, then there is no salvation. Jesus was not a mere man nor was he a phantom. He is the God-man and as such was able to secure for us eternal salvation.

Do you know this Jesus of whom the Scriptures speak?

PRAYER

Lord, help me to recognize the God of glory in Jesus. Amen

WISDOM

If Jesus is not God then He is not good.

The Spirit Of Antichrist

SCRIPTURE   October 15

*"But every spirit that does not acknowledge Jesus is not from God. **This is the spirit of the antichrist**, which you have heard is coming and even now is already in the world"*
I John 4:3.

REFLECTION

Behind God's truth is the Spirit of God and those anointed by Him are instruments and messengers of the truth. Behind false teachers are the devil and his spirit agents and they are used to spread false doctrines that are opposed to God's truth in Christ Jesus.

The devil's mission is to undermine and oppose everything that exalts Christ. That hostile and vicious opposition to Christ is responsible for all persecution of true believers be it inspired by false religions or is state sponsored. It is the same diabolical force that energizes both and its sole intent is to obliterate the name of Christ from the earth.

The spirit of antichrist is very active in our world today and men of high learning, deceived by Satan, are using every so called legal or illegal means to overthrow and to remove the memory of His name from among the nations. The enemy, Satan, hates the person of Christ and a great struggle is presently going on to muster all the forces of darkness to eliminate the knowledge of Christ and all those who embrace Him from the world.

It is only the presence and power of the Holy Spirit working through the agency of the church that is now holding back evil from achieving its goal. This battle is yet to intensify and will become extremely bloody and brutal as man's day draws to its close.

Are you ready for the fight?

PRAYER

Lord, help me to understand the evil times in which I live. Amen

WISDOM

Evil will, for a time get the upper hand, but it shall not prevail.

Dark Days Ahead

SCRIPTURE October 16

*"But every spirit that does not acknowledge Jesus is not from God. This is the spirit of the antichrist, **which you have heard is coming** and even now is already in the world"*
I John 4:3.

REFLECTION

The Bible predicts that righteousness will cover the earth as the waters cover the sea (Isaiah 11:9) but before that takes place evil, like a poisoned cloud, will cover the earth like a mantle. This will come to pass when Satan's strong man, Antichrist, is permitted to rule the world for a period of seven years. This Antichrist will come out of United Europe.

This event will fall between Christ coming **for** His church and Christ coming **with** His church. The presence of the church indwelt by the Holy Spirit is what is now restraining evil from engulfing the entire earth, but when the church, the Bride of Christ, is snatched away by Christ (I Thessalonians 4:13-18), then the lawless one shall be revealed.

"He will oppose and exalt himself over everything that is called God or is worshipped, so that he sets himself up in God's temple, proclaiming himself to be God" II Thessalonians 2:4. He, the Antichrist, will brook no rivals and he will be given power over the people of God at that time to slaughter them by the millions (Daniel 7:25) and in the process will attempt to exterminate the children of Israel.

Jeremiah describes this period as the time of Jacob's trouble (Jeremiah 30:7). This Antichrist or the man of sin will set up an abominable image in the yet to be built temple in Jerusalem and demand that it be worshipped by all. There are some very dark and difficult days ahead for this world, but evil shall not triumph. God will.

PRAYER

Lord, help me to shine my light in this dark world. Amen

WISDOM

Evil when it peaks will be smashed by the power of God.

Reign Of Antichrist

"But every spirit that does not acknowledge Jesus is not from God. This is the spirit of the antichrist, which you have heard is coming and even now is already in the world"
I John 4:3.

REFLECTION

Mankind, since the fall, has always desired to cast aside all moral constraint and throw the knowledge of God on the garbage heap so as to sate the appetites of the flesh to the hilt. This evil day they have been longing for will not be long in coming and it will be ushered in by the world's greatest tyrant who will be Satan incarnate, the Antichrist.

He will first appear as a 'man of peace'. He will possess supernatural powers and will amaze the world by a display of *"all kinds of counterfeit miracles, signs and wonders and in every sort of evil that deceives those who are perishing"* II Thessalonians 2:9-10.

This Antichrist, the beast, will control the world's economy so that one cannot buy or sell unless one has his mark in one's forehead or in one's right hand (revelation 13:16). Antichrist will also be the political and religious head of the nations (Revelation 13:5-8). He will promote Satan worship on an international scale (Revelation 13:4).

Jesus warned us that Satan is a liar, a thief, a murderer and a destroyer and what is true of the old dragon will be true of the kingdom of Antichrist. Jesus warned that during the reign of Antichrist there will be unparalleled distress and that if there was not divine intervention no human being would be left alive. But in spite of Satan's greatest effort, the Kingdom of God will smash the kingdom of evil with one mighty blow and establish His Kingdom of Righteousness forever.

PRAYER

Lord, help me to see that your plans and purposes are on target. Amen

WISDOM

Evil that now appears invincible will be crushed suddenly.

Defeat Of Antichrist

"But every spirit that does not acknowledge Jesus is not from God. This is the spirit of the antichrist, which you have heard is coming and even now is already in the world"
I John 4:3.

REFLECTION

Antichrist will be the very embodiment of evil, and everything that is diabolical. His reign shall come to an abrupt end with the second coming of Christ. During Antichrist's reign more than half the world's population will be wiped out. State terrorism, religious terrorism and economic terrorism will have their day and Jesus, coming in the glory cloud, will overthrow this monster and his evil system with the breath of His mouth and destroy him by the splendor of His coming (II Thessalonians 2:8).

Jesus, the Rock, divine in origin, shall smite the king and his kingdom of that diabolical system with such force that there will not be a trace left behind and He, Jesus, shall set up His Kingdom of righteousness that shall cover the entire earth.

The Bible describes the humiliating end of Antichrist and his false prophet in these words, *"But the beast (Antichrist) was captured, and with him the false prophet who had performed the miraculous signs on his behalf...the two of them were thrown alive into the fiery lake of burning sulpher"* Revelation 19:20. They will be tormented day and night for ever and ever (Revelation 20:10).

Siding with the enemy against God will be short lived and the consequences are dreadful. Receiving Jesus as Savior and Lord is the constructive way to go. Have you taken Him into your life?

PRAYER

Lord, help me to understand that there is no neutral ground in this spiritual battle. Amen

WISDOM

Evil may appear attractive for its barbs are carefully concealed.

Victory Through Christ

*"You, dear children, are from God and have overcome them, because the **one in you is greater than the one who is in the world**"*
I John 4:4.

REFLECTION

When we trusted Christ as our personal Savior it placed us into the family of God. All the rights and privileges of children are now ours. We are no longer orphans or the unwanted of the earth for we now belong to God who is the Creator and owner of all things. We are not brought into the Father's house as slaves, but as sons and daughters of the Living God. In the Father's house we do not have to fend for ourselves, for we all fall under the bountiful provisions of God. We are under His protection and His guidance.

It is our relationship with the Lord that now gives us the ability to be overcomers. In God's house we are all favorites for God is not partial. There is no child of God who cannot have daily victory in his life. There is no child of God who has to live under the devil's lies and deceptions. Are we not children of the light and of the truth?

The enemy who opposes us is a defeated foe. In spite of his pretended show of force, guile, and cunning, he was dealt a lethal blow by our Lord on Mount Calvary. The power he once held over us is broken by the risen exalted Christ who has made a wimp of him.

In our own strength we are no match for him, but through the indwelling power of God, we will always have the victory over the one who is evil's inspiration. We need to learn to focus on God's might and ability in our lives for it is through Him only we are more than conquerors. Remember it is the overcomer who gets the reward.

PRAYER

Lord, help me to look to you for daily victory. Amen

WISDOM

God is greater than the devil and his allies.

Two World Views

"They are from the world and therefore speak from the view point of the world, and the world listens to them"
I John 4:5.

REFLECTION

Have you ever wondered why seemingly intelligent persons embrace high sounding nonsense? A mind that is not redeemed will lock into a lie, embrace it and spend the rest of its life promoting it. The fallen nature in us is very flawed and will embrace philosophies, politics, psychology, policies and programs that are harmful and deadly.

There are two value systems in our world that take us to two diverse destinies. One is destructive and leads us away from God and ends in eternal separation from Him. The godly system is constructive, transforming and issues in eternal life. The systems cover all areas of life. You may travel in them as a first, second or third class adherent.

Most of mankind are followers. They are like sheep without a shepherd and mere education will not prevent them from being duped by a man with a 'vision' or a 'prophetic voice'. If false leaders play a religious, or political 'tune' and it is groovy, it will attract a tail and multitudes will march in their train to their own destruction.

People don't carefully examine their beliefs, but are driven by the herd spirit, that takes them without mercy to their doom. Nations have been targeted and deceived en masse by clever liars who pass off a six for a nine resulting in generation after generation holding unto false religions and superstitions that oppress, pauperize and enslave them spiritually.

Do you know what you believe in and have you ever critically examined its content?

PRAYER

Lord, help me to evaluate my convictions carefully. Amen

WISDOM

It is wisdom to dispose of intellectual and spiritual garbage.

World Listens To Its Own

"They are from the world and therefore speak from the view point of the world, and the world listens to them"
I John 4:5.

REFLECTION

The world is not short of the gullible. There is a natural appeal in our fallen nature to gravitate to the foolish and the perverse. It is the path of least resistance and its appeal seems to gratify the senses. 'The prophet' only has to say, "Crack, cocaine, pot will give you the high", and millions believe him and end up being drug addicts. In spite of the obvious destructive force of drugs, millions more continue to run recklessly to embrace the fleeting pleasures derived from drug use and, they too, become drug abusers.

A Marx, or a Hitler, comes along and multitudes run headlong and embrace their destructive politics that lead to the slaughter of millions. Then there is the man who claims to hear from God, though his teachings are in conflict with the revelation God has given us in the Bible, yet multitudes 'mindlessly' embrace the tenets of his doctrine and drink the poison as if it were milk.

As long as our fallen nature exists there will be those who will lead the simple astray by harmful and dangerous teachings inspired by the devil. The prophets of this world will never be short of an audience upon which to prey and seduce with deceptive words, for the spirit of delusion and blindness is a part of what makes up the world system to which our fallen nature is easily lured. Tell the world the truth and you will be crucified.

We too were once deceived, but were delivered by God's truth. Let us share it with them.

PRAYER

Lord, help me share your truth in spite of the opposition. Amen

WISDOM

A Christian **will never find** companionship in the world.

Mutual Attraction

"We are from God, and **whoever knows God listens to us**; *but whoever is not from God does not listen to us. This is how we recognize the Spirit of truth and the spirit of falsehood"*
I John 4:6.

REFLECTION

Is it not beautiful that an instant bond can be created between two Christians no matter what their tongue, race, nationality, social status or denomination background might be? There is something in our spirits that responds to each other. There is ground for instant conversation, love and fellowship.

We share a common faith, saved by the same Lord, are indwelt by the same Holy Spirit, and loved by the same Father. We all have new life in Christ, a love for God's truth and share a common hope and value system. The very name of Jesus used reverently attracts us to each other be it in a bus, a plane, a ship, an office, a stadium, a park or where ever.

Truth is a magnet that attracts believers to each other, be they educated or uneducated, be they young in the faith or mature, be they theologians or disciples. All true believers love to talk about Jesus and the things of God, for there is nothing in this world that can quite satisfy the desire and yearnings of the redeemed heart more than Jesus. A Christian is at home listening and talking about Christ. Godly conversation always hit a responsive cord in our hearts.

Intimacy with God creates the desire for the things of God and to associate with those who do.

Do the things of God excite you and tug on the cords of your heart?

PRAYER

Lord, help me to always have my heart strangely warmed just talking about you. Amen

WISDOM

People of the same persuasion seek each others company.

Jesus Draws Enemy Fire

"We are from God, and whoever knows God listens to us; but whoever is not from God does not listen to us. This is how we recognize the Spirit of truth and the spirit of falsehood"
I John 4:6.

REFLECTION

When Christ was on earth His greatest antagonist and persecutors were from the religious community. They ridiculed, called Him names, associated His miracles with Satan, spoke disparagingly of his family connections, cast a slur on His legitimacy, tried to set Him up in order to discredit Him in the eyes of the public and charged Him with breaching the Sabbath.

They wanted to stone Him on more than one occasion for claiming to be the Son of God. Jesus had this to say to His opponents, *"He that is of God heareth the words of God: for this cause ye hear them not, **because ye are not of God"** John 8:47 (A.S.V.).*

Being religious does not necessarily take you out of the camp of the enemy, even if you are 'orthodox', for some of these are Satan's greatest missionaries. Jesus is still the acid test for truth and error. He is still the divider of those who are for God and those opposed to God. Everyone who opposes Christ is against Him and is therefore not a part of His kingdom.

Nothing draws fire from the enemy's camp more than a simple presentation of God's truth in Christ Jesus. It makes every 'muscle' in the enemy taut and every emotion tense and certainly exposes the flaws of human nature. There is tension between the Spirit of truth and the spirit of falsehood and there can be no truce. Have you ever experienced it?

PRAYER

Lord, help me to be courageous in sharing my faith in this world. Amen

WISDOM

The man of the 'world, needs the goods news of the gospel.

Love Is The Answer

"Dear friends, let us love one another, for love comes from God. Everyone who loves has been born of God and knows God. Whoever does not love does not know God, because God is love"
I John 4:7.

REFLECTION

Love is the key that unlocks the door to happiness and harmony in our homes, communities, churches, clubs, politics, and businesses. Only love can end blood feuds, end international terrorism, end pollution, end the manufacture of weapons of mass destruction, and give from its storehouses food for the starving. If love filled our hearts rape would never occur, child abuse would be non existent, wars would cease and so would the thousand and one different ills that plague our world. Surely the exercise and daily implementation of love is the answer.

The solution seems so simple, yet it has eluded us and will continue to elude us, for the wicked condition of the human heart has not changed. The murderer will continue to murder, the stalker will continue to stalk, local and international hostilities will continue unabated and the ambassadors for 'peace and love' will continue to wring their hands in despair over the senseless acts of cruelty that are evident in our world.

We find it easy to 'love' those who 'love' us but are intolerant to those who hate us. The demonstration of love we see around us seems so shallow and self-serving and if there are no immediate returns, we quickly end our program and justify our action by saying, "These people are ungrateful", and believe me, that could be the cold truth.

What, however we need, is a love for all seasons, for all people and under all circumstances. We need a love that will overcome all hate and hostility and such a love can only come from God. Do you have it?

PRAYER

Lord, help me to love the unlovely. Amen

WISDOM

Love endures all things.

Love One Another

October 25

*"Dear friends, **let us love one another**, for love comes from God. Everyone who loves has been born of God and knows God. Whoever does not love does not know God, because God is love"*
I John 4:7.

REFLECTION

Every Christian must take to heart John's exhortation to love one another. Love heals, it forgives, it is patient, it does not retaliate, nor does it nurse a grudge. Love is considerate; it is full of compassion and seeks to put itself in the other man's shoe. Love is other centered and is prepared to sacrifice without giving a thought for it's owns self interests or safety.

Wherever there is a need love will find itself in the centre – ministering. Love is much more than hugs and kisses, even though that is necessary and vital. However, a Judas is capable of displaying 'affection' as a means to an end.

The love John speaks of is divine in nature and does not emanate from the soiled nature of our flesh. It is a love that proceeds from God and it is that love that He plants in our hearts through His Holy Spirit.

This love affects our minds and fires the will with an energy that is not of this earth and fixes the affections on things that are pure, wholesome and unselfish. This love brings a compulsion and combustion that conquer negative feelings. It rises above these to see other human beings as created in God's image and loves them for what they are and helps to love them into what they can become through God's grace.

Love does not despair no matter how desperate the condition might be, but it prevails over circumstances. How are you doing in your love life?

PRAYER

Lord, help me to love in spite of the conditions. Amen

WISDOM

Love conquers all things.

All Season Love

*"Dear friends, **let us love one another**, for love comes from God. Everyone who loves has been born of God and knows God. Whoever does not love does not know God, because God is love"*
I John 4:7.

REFLECTION

Love is much more than a nice feeling when things are going well for us. When we have health, wealth and are overwhelmed with golden opportunities, our flow of love seems limitless and our sense of well being and generosity abound.

But should our bodies become riddled with disease, the income is drained dry and life is in a somersault of perplexing and seemingly endless distress, love must not be put on hold, or go on leave of absence but must be just as steadfast in adversity.

We must not allow the grouch in us to come to the fore. We must not allow the spirit of murmuring and bitter complaint to take possession of our lives. The mouth that gave wise counsel in the good times must be just as ready to lovingly help the discouraged and the weak with strength and solace. Love came about as a result of the new birth. Situations and circumstances do not in anyway annul the implantation of love nor should they affect our relationship with the Lord.

Love is not static, but dynamic and grows and abounds in the most hostile conditions that may prevail in our experience. Knowing God made Job worship when he lost his family and possessions in rapid succession. We cannot control what may happen to us, but we are responsible for our response. Let love prevail in our response to life and its trials, its difficulties and its challenges.

PRAYER

Lord, help my love to grow and mature in all the circumstances that life may throw at me. Amen

WISDOM

Love does not wilt in adversity but grows.

No Love - No God In The Life

*"Dear friends, let us **love one another**, for love comes from God. Everyone who loves has been born of God and knows God. **Whoever does not love does not know God**, because God is love"*
I John 4:7.

REFLECTION

The spirit of lovelessness abounds in our world. You don't have to search for it, for it is everywhere in its sordid attire. It is observed on our countenances, evident in our speech and patent in our actions. Lovelessness is passed from one generation to the next like a generational curse.

Lovelessness indicates that there is a disconnection between the individual and God. It is as if the spirit of Cain is stamped on the spiritual DNA and hence there is no desire to change such brutish ways. The loveless are at their 'best' belittling, cursing or lording it over others. They are bitter, resentful, uncaring, without compassion, unforgiving, malicious and insecure. They are like empty and irritating noise makers. They can be pushy, pugnacious, insolent, sulky, and full of self pity, scheming, moody, and saturated with hurt, resentful, seething with malice and bitterness.

There are no strata of society from which they are exempted. There is no temperament group that is not infected by the spirit of lovelessness. They are found in all human institutions. Even in the very church of God these loveless creatures have taken root.

If we don't possess love or allow love to possess us, it means we don't know God. All who know God automatically experience love. We cannot go swimming and not get wet and no way can we say we know God and not love, for God is love.

PRAYER

Lord, help me to love at all times. Amen

WISDOM

Guard your spiritual life for it is the key to consistent love.

Love Is Knowing God

"Whoever does not love does not know God, because God is love"
I John 4:8.

REFLECTION

It does not matter how public and loud our confession of faith might be, if our hearts are devoid of love, that confession is hollow and worthless. If there is no manifestation of love flowing from our lives, then there is no relationship whatever with God. The nature of light is to shine. The nature of love is to give of itself unselfishly.

Once there is a contact with God and a relationship is established through the vicarious death of Christ then love must flow from the life. A water main connected to a reservoir filled with sweet water is bound to convey sweet water. A life in union with God must be possessed with love. If there is no love then there is no connection to God.

Jesus said that the one value that sets his disciples apart from others is their love one for another. If you cannot love, it is reasonable to assume that you do not know God. God is the very personification and embodiment of love. When you think of love you instantly think of God for that is the very essence of His nature. God cannot help but love.

It was God's love that conceived the plan to redeem fallen man. We cannot soar to the height of God's love, nor can we plummet to its depth nor can we find the extent of it breath, but nevertheless we have come to experience the immeasurable love of God in our hearts.

Do you know this wonderful and powerful love of God in your heart?

PRAYER

Lord, help me always to be filled with your love. Amen

WISDOM

We can never have too much of love.

God Showed His Love

*"This is how **God showed his love among us:** He sent his one and only Son into the world that we might live through him"*
I John 4:9.

REFLECTION

Love is not about talk. Love is not philosophy. Love is practical. Love is about sacrifice. Love is having the others person's interest at heart and doing something about it. Love is not about blame and indictment but the display of compassion, mercy and grace. Love is about elevating the miserable condition of the sinner from a state of condemnation and making him a child of God. That was what God's love did.

Love is taking the weak and helpless and miserable and empowering them with righteousness, truth and love. God's method of demonstrating his love among us was not a spectacular display of His awesome power that would have our eyes popping out of their sockets; our jaws open almost to the point of snapping and our bodies quivering with excitement. God's love was revealed in all its glory in giving us His One and only Son to die on a cross for our sins. That, indeed, touches our hearts.

God is love. There was never a time that God did not love. God's love is constant. It has no jars or jerks. There is a bond of love within the godhead that is eternal, but there was a facet of God's love that hitherto had never been displayed for the condition did not exist for it to be put in operation until sin entered the human family. Sin brought to light an aspect of divine love that had been dormant from eternity but was realized in time in the redemption of His fallen creature, man.

God's love is truly amazing. Have you experienced that amazing love?

PRAYER

Lord, help me to appreciate your amazing love for me. Amen

WISDOM

The love of God for us came alive in Christ.

Loved Demonstrated In Christ

"This is how God showed his love among us: **He sent his one and only Son into the world that we might live through him"**
I John 4:9.

REFLECTION

The way that God showed His amazing love was first demonstrated in the incarnation. God, through His Son became a human being and lived among us in the flesh for above thirty three years. God the Son stepped from the adoration of angels to be born in a stable. He was targeted as a babe to be murdered by jealous king Herod. He grew up in an insignificant town called Nazareth and was by profession a carpenter. He did not get a higher education, yet at the age of twelve confounded the learned men of his day.

He chose twelve disciples after He embarked upon His public ministry and multitudes from all walks of life came to listen to Him. He, the undefiled Son of God, was the friend of sinners and the despised tax collectors. He was on a mission to crush the power of Satan and liberate those held captive by him.

He angered the religious authority of His day and exposed their hypocrisy, for they held in greater esteem their traditions above the very Word of God. The religious authority conspired to discredit and then destroy Him.

He was betrayed by one of His own, arrested and executed like a common criminal. But this was part of God's plan to save the world from sin. Jesus had to die as our substitute to bring us salvation. The God-man had to be humiliated so that He could bring us into glory. It is through Christ's blood that we now have redemption and eternal life. Praise be to God for giving us the Son of His love.

PRAYER

Lord, help me to see what your great love for me cost you. Amen

WISDOM

God's love for us made Him give heaven's best – His Son Jesus.

Life Through Christ's Cross

*"This is how God showed his love among us: **He sent his one and only Son into the world that we might live through him**"*
I John 4:9.

REFLECTION

The cross, the symbol of a cruel, painful and shameful death, has now become the symbol of God's love, forgiveness, restoration and redemption of wayward man. The preaching of Christ crucified on the cross, causes the Jews to stumble religiously and to the intellectually worldly wise, it is foolishness. But to those who have experienced its amazing and transforming effects, it is the power of God unto salvation.

The wise of the world cannot grasp God's method of salvation through the cross, but to those who are saved it demonstrates the profound wisdom of God in securing our salvation by way of the cross. It is through Christ's death, victory over death was realized. It was through the death of the Lord Jesus, the devil was disarmed. Jesus took away from him the key of death by way of His resurrection.

When Satan thought He had forever triumphed over the Son of God, for His cold body was now in his domain, he was only to discover he had been taken, his kingdom had been invaded and he was deposed as Lord over death by the resurrection of Jesus.

All who put their faith in the risen Christ now obtains eternal life and possesses the sure hope of being reunited with their bodies at the shout of His command. Salvation is here and it is irreversible and eternal.

Have you experienced the New Life that is in Christ Jesus?

PRAYER

Lord, help me now to receive this new life through Christ. Amen

WISDOM

Jesus is the only way to new and eternal life.

God Loves Us

*"This is love: not that we loved God, but that **he loved us** and sent his Son as an atoning sacrifice for our sins"*
I John 4:10.

REFLECTION

God's love for us is not based on mutual attraction. As a matter of fact, we had no affection for God, but deep feelings of hostility towards Him. His ways are not our ways, nor did we entertain godly thoughts and we had no sympathy towards Him. All our energies were spent in how best we could disassociate ourselves from Him for we saw no beauty in Him.

The Bible clearly teaches that we were enemies of God when Christ died to reconcile us (Romans 5:10). It was for the ungodly Christ died (Romans 5:6). It was the lost sheep that God loved. God loved us even when we crowned His Son with a crown of thorns. God loved us even when we drove the spikes into His Son's hands and feet and pierced His side with a spear. He loved us when we were at our worst.

When we deserved the full fury of God's judgment, His Son Jesus, was drinking, in our stead, the bitter cup of God's wrath for sin and He drained it to the last dregs. There is no love that can come near the love of God for us. And with all that Christ endured on the cross for us, our mind's eyes were still blinded to the truth of this amazing love and we had no desire for Him. In our hearts we still despised Him and had nothing but contempt for Him.

Had it not been for the ministry of the Holy Spirit overcoming the evil within us, not one of us would ever have received salvation. It was God's Spirit that opened our eyes to grasp this great salvation. We can't help but thank the Lord for not giving up on us in our sinful state.

PRAYER

Lord, help me to thank you for loving me and saving my soul. Amen

WISDOM

Love that flowed into us through the cross has it origin in God.

God's Love In Christ

"Dear friends, since God so loved us, we also ought to love one another"
I John 4:11.

REFLECTION

The power of example is a very persuasive tool. Example shows how a particular thing is done and makes it easier to emulate. God's love for us was made manifest when His Son Jesus took on physical properties and showed us, in tangible form, what love is. This love of God was displayed in the mighty healings of those who were sick in body, soul and spirit. Jesus had compassion for the hungry and fed them. He was the friend of the social outcast and gave them hope and a new life. Jesus understood the deep needs and hurts of the human heart.

He forgave the guilty and repentant sinner and embraced them. He cared for children and was a great motivator for all those who followed Him. He taught His disciples with patience, by precept and, of course, by practice. His life was one of service and even as Master; He was prepared to adopt the servant role when necessary to teach humility. Our Lord was approachable, meek and humble.

The greatest manifestation of His love for us was when He allowed Himself to be taken by vicious hands and, without rancor or railing or any sort of hostility, allowed Himself to be nailed to a cross as our offering for sins. The greatest display of His love was to give His life when we were at our worst, taunting, accusing, mocking, spitting, slapping as we crucified Him the spotless Lamb of God. Our hands dripped with innocent blood. He uttered words of forgiveness as His soul was made an offering for our sin. Christ lived and died love.

How about you? Are you a dispenser of God's love?

PRAYER

Lord, help me to love my brothers and sisters in Christ. Amen

WISDOM

Be a model of love.

God Is Spirit

"No one has ever seen God; but if we love one another, God lives in us and his love is made complete in us"
I John 4:12.

REFLECTION

God, in His essential nature, is Spirit, and as such, is not observable to our eyes. Not even angels who are spirit beings can claim to have seen God in the full manifestation of His essence. God has no limit and therefore is infinite. We are finite and even if we had ability to see 'spirit', to say we have seen God in His completeness, would be ridiculous.

The finite cannot assimilate or comprehend the infinite. What this does to the contemplative is to make them stand in awe of this magnificent person whose power, knowledge and presence are boundless. We cannot put a cordon around God. We catch a glimpse of God's awesome infinity, power and glory when God addressed Job in chapters 38 to 41.

Space and its boundary are awesome, yet they are finite. We measure time in light years and that is mind boggling, how much more the uncreated, invisible God who is the author of the universe?

Yet the Bible states that men have seen God. Is this a contradiction? What men have seen are just wonderful, visible manifestations of God that are comprehended by our senses, but such theophanies do not equate to what John is here talking about. There is nothing we can compare with God, for God is in a class by Himself. And none of us know enough about God to explain Him adequately. What He has been pleased to reveal about Himself, let's study that, but the undisclosed elements of His being, let us leave it alone as a great mystery.

PRAYER

Lord, help me to grasp your greatness as revealed in the Word. Amen

WISDOM

It is wonderful to know this incomprehensible God lives in me.

Love Displays God In Us

SCRIPTURE   November 04

"No one has ever seen God; but if we love one another, God lives is us and his love is made complete in us"
I John 4:12.

REFLECTION

Love is the key to any meaningful human relationship. Love is not motionless but is vigorous and is constantly growing and maturing thus making beautiful people of us. It's a great truth that we should love ourselves, for on that hinges the potential to love someone else.

We cannot be content with the mere potential of being capable of loving others. We must love others just as much as we love ourselves. Their pain must become our pain. Their sorrow our sorrow; their need gives us the opportunity to share what we have with them. The greatest need for many is not material but to be accepted and appreciated. Therefore show them that we care and are there for them.

To demonstrate love is at times simply listening attentively to a brother or sister pouring out the sorrow in his or her heart to you. They just want a friend to understand and empathize and help them carry the burden that seems so heavy to bear.

To give a word of cheer to the downcast, to pray with those who mourn for whatever reason and to just show compassion and love in those circumstances is of more value than much gold. A telephone call at the opportune time can make a world of difference to those who mourn.

There are a thousand and one ways to show love one to another. Just choose one of those ways today and exercise it. The person you reach out to will be touched and God will be glorified.

PRAYER

Lord, help me to express love to at least one person today. Amen

WISDOM

Love given generously is great medicine for healing.

God As Seen In Us

SCRIPTURE   November 05

"No one has ever seen God; but if we love one another, God lives is us and his love is made complete in us"
I John 4:12.

REFLECTION

We cannot see God with the physical eyes and it is not because He is hiding but because He is a spirit being. Yet we can demonstrate who and what this invisible God is like and how He operates by giving love one to the other. Our transformed behavior puts 'a face and body' to the God we cannot see for human behavior is observable.

The New Life that is operating on the inside of us cannot be kept a well guarded secret for long, but will naturally flow out of our being like a refreshing river of living water that causes growth to all those who come in contact with us.

If God lives in us, then His love will flow through us and will fulfill its desired goals through our surrendered lives. People will come to a true knowledge of God because they see the supernatural love of God manifested in our lives.

The principles that govern love are intangible. It is these principles that fuel the furnace of our love and cause it to glow and then flow through our fingers and feet, that cause our faces to radiate and touch our billfolds and make our bodies available in service to others.

The living but invisible God takes form and character and becomes a dynamic force through these mortal bodies of ours when love flows unhindered through us. We are an important link in the chain of salvation that demonstrates to the world that God is love.

PRAYER

Lord, help me that your love may flow unhindered through me. Amen

WISDOM

God's love becomes tasteful through our lives.

God Gives The Spirit

SCRIPTURE   November 06

"We know that we live in him and he in us, because he has given us of his Spirit"
I John 4:13.

REFLECTION

No Christian can function without the Holy Spirit. Without Him we have no life. Each person in the trinity plays a vital role as it relates to our salvation. It was the Father who loved us and gave us His Son. The Son gave His life for us upon the cross to secure our eternal salvation. Now it is the Holy Spirit that applies that salvation to our hearts. He was the One who made us uncomfortable in our sins; showed us our lack of righteousness and warned us of the impending hell that awaited us if we rejected Christ as Savior.

It was the Spirit of God that illuminated our darkened minds with the truth of the gospel and introduced us to Jesus Christ, the friend of sinners. He was the One who made the appeal to God's call irresistible and effectual. We would not have been able to come to Christ and receive the gift of eternal life had it not been for the Spirit.

The Spirit imparts new life and indwells each believer. Our bodies are His temples. We would have no assurance of salvation or knowledge that we belong to God apart from the indwelling Holy Spirit.

We don't have to speak tongues to know that we have the Spirit. Some have spoken in another tongue and still don't have Him. We know that a man is drunk by his behavior or that a person is demon possessed by his behavior and so too we know a person who is indwelt by the Spirit.

It is the Spirit of God who brings sweeping and dynamic changes in our lives by the fruit that He produces in us. Are you bearing fruit?

PRAYER

Lord, help me to be controlled daily by Your Holy Spirit. Amen

WISDOM

The Holy Spirit is the source of true spiritual power.

God Gives The Spirit

SCRIPTURE   November 07

"We know that we live in him and he in us, because he has given us of his Spirit"
I John 4:13.

REFLECTION

God has deposited the Spirit in our hearts and He is the seal that guarantees us His eternal salvation (Ephesians 1:13-14 & II Corinthians 1:21-22). Eternal security is not dependent upon me, but upon God (John 10:28-29). Paul said, *"Being confident of this very thing, that he who began a good work in you will perfect it until the day of Jesus Christ"* Philippians 1: 6 (A.S.V). God is not a flip flop God but honors His pledge to us.

If salvation were based on our faithfulness and not upon His then none of us would make it into paradise. It is reassuring to know that *"God's gifts and his call are irrevocable"* Romans 11:29. Christ is the source of eternal salvation (Hebrews 5:9). The indwelling presence of His Holy Spirit assures me this is so. To be in doubt about such an important matter would steal peace from my mind and make me full of anxiety not knowing for sure, at any moment in time, if I am in or I am excluded.

It is true that *"if any man hath not the Spirit of Christ, he is none of his"* Romans 8:9 (A.S.V.). But for those born of the Spirit there will be no separation for the countless ages of eternity.

Eternal security does not promote careless behavior for such conduct is contrary to those who are led by the Spirit. The Spirit will never lead us into sin but rather into a life of holiness.

Are you walking in holiness?

PRAYER

Lord, help me to walk in a way that is always pleasing to you. Amen

WISDOM

The Holy Spirit is the seal that God truly owns us.

Jesus Is The Savior Of The World

SCRIPTURE   November 08

"And we have seen and testify that the Father has sent his Son to be the Savior of the world"
I John 4:14.

REFLECTION

The human origin of Jesus is not clouded in mystery, nor is it based upon myth, or silly fables, but upon well documented facts recorded in four historical documents known as the Gospels of Matthew, Mark, Luke and John. The records are based on eye witness accounts and can stand the most rigorous historical tests to validate their authenticity.

Matthew and John were Disciples of Christ and belonged to the inner circle know as the 12 Apostles. These men were intimately associated with Jesus and did not get their information from other sources but were eye witnesses and were involved in His program. They saw first hand His miracles, supernatural signs and wonders and were convinced that this Jesus was the Messiah of which the Old Testament Scriptures predicted would come into the world.

Scripture after Scripture point to Him as indeed the authentic Savior of the world. Matthew carefully documented many Old Testament Scriptures that Christ fulfilled at His first coming. Isaiah predicted the miraculous conception of Jesus by a virgin (Matthew 1:22-23). Micah predicted the place of His birth (Matthew 2:6); Jeremiah spoke of the slaughter of the innocent by wicked king Herod (Matthew 2:18); Isaiah spoke of His forerunner, John the Baptist (Matthew 3:3). His triumphant entry into Jerusalem was predicted by Zechariah (Matthew 21:5). Were these mere accidents? I think not, for there was never a man like Christ who actually died and was vindicated to be the Son of God by His resurrection from the dead. He is alive today.

PRAYER

Lord, help me to accept you as my Savoir today. Amen

WISDOM

The bodily resurrection of Christ sets apart Christianity as being unique.

Father Sent The Son

*"And we have seen and testify that **the Father has sent his Son** to be the Savior of the world"*
I John 4:14.

REFLECTION

There is no person, no matter how great, who can be compared with Jesus. All the great and mighty men of the world were and are sinners. The mission of Jesus was to deliver mankind from sin and this He did by going to the cross as our substitute. Jesus did not come to do His own will, but the will of the Father. He was on a mission commissioned by the Father.

God in times past commissioned men to be prophets but not one of them had He asked to give his life for the world for none was qualified for such an undertaking. The relationship the Son bears to the Father is unique. No prophet or holy man or any angel bears any such union with the Father. The Son has had unbroken fellowship with the Father from eternity.

The book of Hebrews gives us insight into the significance of Christ becoming human. The coming of Christ was strictly redemptive. *"Wherefore when he cometh into the world, he saith, Sacrifice and offering thou wouldest not, but a body didst thou prepare for me; Then said I, Lo, I am come(In the roll of the book it is written of me) to do thy will, O God"* Hebrews 10:5,7 (A.S.V.).

Only Jesus was uniquely qualified to become the Savior of the world, in that, He was God who took on human nature. Only He was good enough to become the perfect sacrifice for our sins. He indeed is the Lamb of God sent to save the world. Do you know Him?

PRAYER

Lord, help me to thank you for your absolute obedience to the Father. Amen

WISDOM

Jesus is the only qualified Savior.

314

Life Comes Through Jesus

"If anyone acknowledges that Jesus is the Son of God, God lives in him and he in God"
I John 4:15.

REFLECTION

Intimacy with God is connected to our relationship with Jesus Christ the Son. There is absolutely no approach to the Father apart from the Son. The Son is the key to the Father's heart.

We can never put the Son in limbo, or on the back burner, or by pass Him and ever hope to attain fellowship with God. *"I tell you the truth, whoever hears my word and believes him who sent me has eternal life and will not be condemned; he has crossed over from death to life"* John 5:24.

Jesus is much more than a great teacher, or a great prophet or a great miracle worker and merely to acknowledge Him is these areas are not good enough. He must be acknowledged as the very Son of God. Peter's famous confession must also become the confession of our lips and hearts, *"Thou art the Christ, the Son of the living God"* Matthew 16:16 (A.S.V).

If you would have a union with God then you must enter through Jesus, the Door. He, indeed, is the way, the only Way to the Father. If we try to get in God's sheep pen some other way, we will be regarded by God as thieves and robbers (John 10:1)

If you would have power and the life of God flowing in you and through you, then you will have to acknowledge Jesus as the very Son of God.

PRAYER

Lord, help me to confess you as the very Son of God. Amen

WISDOM

Jesus is **the key** to my spiritual life.

God, Love And Me

*"And so we know and rely on the love God has for us. God is love. **Whoever lives in love lives in God and God in him"***
I John 4:16.

REFLECTION

Wives who have put faith and confidence in their husbands' love have been disappointed. Husbands who have relied on the integrity of their partners' love have been disappointed by their unfaithfulness. Children have been abandoned by their mothers and their fathers. Friends have betrayed friends. Jesus was betrayed by a friend with an affectionate kiss as a signal to his enemies for His arrest. Peter's love under pressure gave way to His denying he knew Christ.

When inward integrity sags, then character crumbles and love fall victim to selfishness. Human love is flawed, yet it can be as strong as death (Song of Songs 8:6). But when we contemplate the love of God, it is perfect, pure, enduring, sacrificial, unselfish, caring and reliable.

In I John 4:14 we see that love in action securing our salvation in Christ. The path to the cross and the surrender of His life for that mission tell us that God loves us in Christ. God's love is not about talk but is a demonstrative love that touches the very core of our being. Love liberates us from the bondage of sin and is constantly expressed to us in spite of our many failings in daily life.

We who have experienced the love of God know that this love cannot fail. God's truthfulness, faithfulness and integrity are bound up in his love. God cannot help but love and He has deposited this very love into our hearts. It is God who gives us the ability to love and it must become the life style that flows freely from our hearts. Love relates us to God and God to us. We cannot enjoy God without love.

PRAYER

Lord, help me to see the value and importance of love in my life. Amen

WISDOM

Love is the atmosphere in which we live and have our existence.

Love And Judgment Day

*"In this way, love is made complete among us so that we will have confidence on the **day of judgment**, because in this world we are like him"*
I John 4:17.

REFLECTION

It is impossible to be possessed by the Spirit of love and not share it with others. All our action must be stamped with love and we have endless opportunities to show our love for each other. It is possible to become engaged in a host of activities that could involve great sacrifices, yet our motives do not spring from a heart of love.

We must be very discerning when it comes to the matter of motive. Action is not what God will judge on that day, but the driving force behind the action, the reason that provoked the action. Paul warns that the exercise of spiritual gifts, and these are divinely bestowed, must be exercised in love, if not there will be no reward for us at the judgment seat of Christ.

If we are merely playing to the audience and are nothing more than men pleasers then we are prostituting our gifts and there will be no reward in the hereafter. Love does not show off but seek to have the glory of our Lord Jesus as the reason for our action. If there is any display of self in what we do, then we are robbing God of His glory and that gets no reward.

The display of self can be very subtle especially when it is camouflaged by an air of humility and polished with pious platitudes. In every noble endeavor we would embark upon, self is going to want a piece of the action. This ambition must be denied if we would have confidence on the Day of Judgment. Is your motive in sharing love, unselfish?

PRAYER

Lord, help me to be unselfish in giving love. Amen

WISDOM

Pure love is untainted by selfishness.

Being Like Him

November 13

"In this way, love is made complete among us so that we will have confidence on the day of judgment, because in this world we are like him"
I John 4:17.

REFLECTION

To exhibit Christ-likeness in this hostile world where our Lord was crucified is no easy undertaking. Even to live a life of love among the people of God, who have varying degrees of commitment to our Lord is challenging. Dealing with the saints on a one to one basis will test the mettle of our love. Ask any counselor or psychologist how heavy it is to bear the burdens of others. To talk love and to live love are not by any means synonymous.

Loving from a safe distance is easy, but loving at close quarters is quite another story. To allow love to conquer our hearts means an intimate relationship with our Lord on a moment by moment basis. Love is not a burden when Jesus is the apple of our eyes, the darling of our bosoms and the love of our lives. Only He can help us cope with the obstinate, the uncaring, the careless, the wayward, the unfaithful, the carnal, the abusive and the abused and, of course, the unthankful.

But there are also the kind, the compassionate, the obedient, the caring, and the gentle, the merciful who help to lift our spirits and so help us to make our love for each other complete. We must fuel the fires of love and keep the coals touching each other if we would have confidence that our actions are pure and will be rewarded on that day.

Let us be like Him in the here and now.

Are you answering that great challenge?

PRAYER

Lord, help me to love as Jesus loves. Amen

WISDOM

The mastery of love is a life long occupation.

Fear And Punishment

"There is no fear in love. But perfect love drives out fear, **because fear has to do with punishment.** *The one who fears is not made perfect in love"*
I John 4:18.

REFLECTION

Our world is paralyzed by fear. Its vicious and poisonous tentacles reach deep down into many families and immobilize wholesome relationships between husband and wife, father and children and children and mother. Threats, abuse, cursing and the rule of the iron fist or the fanged tooth makes family life for far too many homes, a living nightmare.

Abuse in the homes is the seed plot for much of the evil that is perpetrated in our world. It is from broken homes the tyrants of our world arise and with vengeance set up their death squads and torture chambers to terrorize and inflict horror on their populations. It is from the sewer of broken homes our criminals and gang members seep into our society. Broken homes are the chief cause of our drug problems.

We have manipulated and refined fear into a fine art and use it effectively in our businesses, in our schemes for promotion, in our politics, in our sports and in our educational institutions. We are attired in the mantle of fear. It is so deeply embedded into the warp and woof of our society that we have come to accept this thorn in our flesh as a natural part of life.

Fear of this sort is an evil that must be expelled from our hearts and practices. Fear wants to control or influence or pressure another person into submission by the threat of dire consequences. If you are such a person, you are devoid of love, for love does not foster fear.

PRAYER

Lord, help me to expel fear from my life and replace it with love. Amen

WISDOM

Most fears are deeply rooted in our early childhood.

Dealing With Past Fear

"There is no fear in love. But perfect love drives out fear, because fear has to do with punishment. The one who fears is not made perfect in love"
I John 4:18.

REFLECTION

Children, who are raised on a steady diet of fear, find it most difficult to adjust and become well balanced and integrated individuals as adults. Fear leaves terrible scars on the psyche of a child that time does not erase nor diminish. It is the handmaiden of inferiority complex and low self esteem, and often times, makes it difficult for the victim to relate appropriately with others.

Long after parents have passed away, many still have to struggle with the legacy of fear instilled in their minds and hearts. As a child, I feared my father and cannot recall having had any meaningful dialogue with him. My communication was limited to a few words. My dad was a distant figure, for fear of him kept me at bay. I can't recall being hugged or kissed or having any fun time with him.

I associated father with discipline, authority, berating and a person to be avoided whenever possible. As a young adult I learned to fear all 'father figures' like the policeman, the teacher, the boss. It brought a strained relationship between me and any and every person who had the stamp of authority on them.

Fear produces paralysis and a distorted view to life and living. To live in fear is to live in torture. Have you passed your past and overcome it with forgiveness and love for your 'tormentors'?

PRAYER

Lord, help me to overcome the fears and ghosts of my past. Amen

WISDOM

Love expels and heals the fears of our past.

Love Drives Out Fear

"There is no fear in love. But perfect love drives out fear, because fear has to do with punishment. The one who fears is not made perfect in love"
I John 4:18.

REFLECTION

The coming of Jesus Christ into our hearts is a new beginning to life and living. Jesus introduces us to LIFE and LOVE. Once His love takes a hold of our lives it drives out fear and makes us want to share, with the mom or dad we feared, the message of hope that this compassionate and loving Savior Jesus Christ gives.

Jesus accepts us just as we are, but He does not leave us the way He found us. He gives us the spirit of boldness for our fear. Can you imagine a person such as me, who was terrified of people, now taking on the ministry of personal evangelism – a one to one ministry? Well that's what God did for me. Love conquers fear and drives it out of our lives. This is not to say that there are no struggles with the past and that the flesh does not try to reassert itself in our lives.

Life is a battle against evil spiritual forces that are real but the God who delivered us from our past and its failures is there to give us victory. As long as we leave Him in control of our lives, and are obedient to the Word of God we will have good success and be overcomers.

We cannot have victory if there is not a fight. If love becomes the focus of our lives then progressive changes and adjustments will be the order of the day and we will daily learn how to perfect love in our lives. Love is not motionless, but a force that sweeps all adversaries aside in triumph. Is your love life free from fear?

PRAYER

Lord, help me to give love a chance in my life. Amen

WISDOM

When love is asserted then fear is denied.

God Loved Us First

"We love because he first loved us"
I John 4:19.

REFLECTION

Love is a rare commodity in our world. We sing of its virtues and praise its values but somehow it eludes us in practice. We have even confused love with lust, sex and passionate feelings. Hollywood has glamorized romantic love which is more related to infatuation and sating the selfish animal urges in us than to caring and sacrificially giving of ourselves to another.

A lot of what we call love, leaves us used and defiled and this normally degenerates into a life of immorality and estrangement from God. People are lonely on the inside and are searching for true love. True love can only be found in God. John tells us in his first epistle that God is the only source of love for says he, *"God is love"* I John 4:8, 16 (A.S.V.). We will never have an encounter with love until we have had an encounter with God.

Love proceeds from God and He demonstrated in the most remarkable manner what love is by giving us His Son, Jesus Christ. We measure our love by God's love. It is God who has taught us how to love. If we would appreciate love then we need to examine the life of Christ for in Christ we see the love of God manifested.

We are redeemed because of love. The cross is the greatest expression of God's love for us. God did not spare heaven's best but freely gave Him up for our salvation. *"How shall he not also with him freely give us all things?"* Romans 8:32 (A.S.V.). It is God who first loved us and has opened to us the highway of love. Are you on it?

PRAYER

Lord, help me never to forget your great love to me and for me. Amen

WISDOM

Love lifts!

The Test Of True Love

"If anyone says, "I love God", yet hates his brother. He is a liar. For anyone who does not love his brother, whom he has seen, cannot love God, whom he has not seen"
I John 4:20.

REFLECTION

Humanity is full of contradictions when it comes to what we say and what we do. It is popular in Christian circles to say, "I love God". Even the unconverted will tell us that they love God. However, when our lives are in tension with our statements, we have a serious moral dilemma at hand that cannot be dismissed or shrugged off.

To have hostile feelings towards a brother or sister and to display a total disregard for their person amounts to despising God. Our attitude to the visible and tangible betrays our attitude to the invisible and the intangible. We cannot pretend to love God and at the same time hold our brother in contempt. The degree of love we have for our brother will be the degree of love we have for God. The true test of love for God is measured on the horizontal plane by our love for our fellowman. I know we would 'love' the opposite to be true, that is, to say we love God and have no regard for our brother.

Love for God is not a sentiment; it is not superfluous, and it does not take us into the realm of fantasy or the world of the imagination. For many, God is no more than a myth, a creation of their minds, a figment of the imagination, or a distant deity that has no concern whatever for what takes place on the planet earth. So they do not relate their moral conduct and behavior as though one day they will be answerable to Him. A distorted view of God will produce distorted moral and spiritual values and a false sense of security. Do you know the God you serve?

PRAYER

Lord, help me to love my brother as I would myself. Amen

WISDOM

True love for God is measured horizontally and not vertically.

Loving Those We See

"If anyone says, "I love God", yet hates his brother. He is a liar. For anyone who does not love his brother, whom he has seen, cannot love God, whom he has not seen"
I John 4:20.

REFLECTION

Our action tells us a lot about our theology and to which camp we truly belong. Pious words and loud acclamation of praise and love for God will not gloss over hypocritical action and conduct, but just exposes the fraud we really are. We don't have to speak a lie to tell a lie for our actions have already done that for us.

To harbor hate in our life style makes the task of loving God an impossible one. Hate excludes us from the Kingdom of God and puts us in the camp of the enemy. Hate distorts true religion and makes a mockery of it.

We cannot hate and be a Christian. We cannot parade an unforgiving spirit and be a child of God. We cannot seek to hurt and injure another person and remain in God's camp. Hate is the seed of murder and discord.

Love makes us act morally responsible. It makes us our brother's keeper. It makes us look out for the best interest of the other person. It makes us care for each other in creative, tender and compassionate ways. Loving one another makes us more and more like God and through our actions people will be attracted to the invisible God we serve.

What badge are you displaying by your actions? Is it the badge of love or the badge of hate?

PRAYER

Lord, help me to show love to those who are around me daily. Amen

WISDOM

Our relationship **in Christ** makes it easy to love.

To Love Is A Command

SCRIPTURE   November 20

"And he has given us this command: whoever loves God must also love his brother"
I John 4:21.

REFLECTION

Love is the essence of Christianity. Love to God and love to man are so interwoven and interlocked that we cannot separate them without doing irreparable damage to both. John could not express it more forcibly – *"Whoever loves God must also love his brother."* The nature of love has no 'chemistry' to it. It is not based on natural attraction or beautiful features or my spirit taking a liking to this or that person.

Love is much deeper and more enduring and comprehensive than that. Love is not centered in the emotions for that is not reliable and is subject to mood swings. The love we need to exercise is controlled by the will and the mind. This type of love was deposited in us by the Holy Spirit of God at our conversion. With this love in us, it is possible to will ourselves to love someone. Love then becomes a matter of choice.

If, for example, your relationship with your wife has grown sour, then God's command to you is to love your wife as Christ loved the church. The secret to love is in the will and not the feelings. If your relationship with that wayward child is strained, you can will yourself by the grace of God to love that child again.

Jesus even commanded us to love our enemies and those who hate and persecute us. Do you think you could start by loving God and your brothers as well?

Are you attempting to obey God's command to love?

PRAYER

Lord, help me to fulfill the command given to love. Amen

WISDOM

Love does not discriminate.

Jesus Is The Christ

*"Everyone **who believes that Jesus is the Christ is born of God,** and everyone who loves the Father loves his child as well"*
I John 5:1.

REFLECTION

Entrance into the family of God comes from accepting that Jesus is the person promised in the Sacred Scriptures that would come into the world and be its Savior. If this Jesus is not the promised One then we would have embraced a lie and so be false witnesses of God.

The early church did not have a New Testament when it came into being. The only Bible that existed was the Old Testament Scriptures and it was from these very Scriptures that they proved that Jesus is the Christ. Jesus Himself resorted to the Scriptures to validate His claims as Israel's Messiah. *"How foolish you are, and how slow of heart to believe **all that the prophets have spoken!** Did not the Christ have to suffer these things and then enter His glory" And **beginning with Moses and all the prophets,** he explained to them **what was said in all the** Scriptures **concerning himself"** Luke 24:26-27.*

On another occasion Jesus said, *"You diligently study the Scriptures because you think that by them you possess eternal life. **These are the** Scriptures **that testify about me"** John 8:39. Again Jesus said, "For if ye believed Moses, ye would believe me, **for he wrote of me"** John 5:46 (A.S.V.).*

You cannot read the Old Testament and not see those Scriptures fulfilled in the New Testament. It is safe to put your trust in Jesus for He is indeed the Christ and the proof of it will be realized by a wonderful transformation in your inner man. Are you born again?

PRAYER

Lord, help me to see how central Jesus is to all of your programs. Amen

WISDOM

The coming of Jesus into our world was the fulfillment of prophecy.

326

Jesus Is The Christ – Believe It!

SCRIPTURE   November 22

*"Everyone **who believes** that Jesus is the Christ is born of God, and everyone who loves the Father loves his child as well"*
I John 5:1.

REFLECTION

There is a popular slogan that says, "Belief kills and belief cures". If what we believe is all negative it can have destructive effects on our being. A man is taught that if he sees a certain bird in the day he will die. If this man believes it, sees that particular bird in the day, he will accept his fate and fret himself to death.

Now pinning faith upon that which is false is indeed destructive. It is wisdom to carefully examine what you believe. If your core beliefs are based upon superstitions, myths, fables, or on historical inaccuracies, then you need to rethink and reexamine their tenets and reevaluate your beliefs. There are people who are exposed to solid, scientific, historical, verifiable truth, yet their relationship to it is superficial, casual and merely intellectual. They are simply not committed in heart to those beliefs. From a practical perspective these beliefs are to them a mere appendage and non essentials to their daily conduct, even though in reality they are vital and absolutely necessary.

Let us consider smoking that is bad for our health. There are many who turn a blind eye to the facts and of course suffer the consequences. Or there is that other person who knows that saturated fats are harmful to health but ignores the facts to his own peril. Then there is the person who knows that Jesus is the Christ yet fails to commit his life to Him and dies in his sin and goes to hell. He has no one to blame but himself.

You don't have to procrastinate. You can open your heart to Christ right now and believe in Him and be born again. Will you do it?

PRAYER

Lord, help me to believe that Jesus is the Christ right now. Amen

WISDOM

Salvation is yours for the taking.

Loving God's Children

November 23

*"Everyone who believes that Jesus is the Christ is born of God, and **everyone who loves the Father loves his child as well**"*
I John 5:1.

REFLECTION

Everyone who has experienced the miracle of the New Birth cannot help loving the Father. The Father is very caring and abounds with love for us. We did not initiate this love relationship for that love had its origin in the Father. God has loved us with an everlasting love. It was God's cords of love that drew us to Him.

It was His love that planned our salvation, called us out of our sins, forgave us, embraced and kissed us, put on us garments of righteousness, shoes of peace for our feet, rings of fellowship for our fingers and had the fatted calf killed for an eternal feast in the Father's house. When we consider what God has done for us, we cannot but love Him as Christians. We cannot cease to marvel at God's great love for us.

We must love God with all our hearts, souls, minds and strength. We cannot put a cap on our love for God. We must love God with abandon. However, we must remind ourselves that love to God must issue in absolute obedience to Him. Love takes us beyond words to deeds done in the spirit of truth. Our love for God is further demonstrated in our love for family members of the household of faith. The degree of our love to God is shown by the care we show the one for the other.

Let us not be like the elder brother in the parable of the prodigal son, but let our love be like Paul's love for Onesimus, whom he describes as *"my very heart"* Philemon 12 (A.S.V.). Let us show our love for each other consistently.

PRAYER

Lord, help me to love my brothers and sisters in Christ. Amen

WISDOM

All God's children are special and are to be loved.

The Value Of Love

SCRIPTURE   November 24

"This is how we know that we love the children of God: by loving God and carrying out his commands"
I John 5:2.

REFLECTION

We cannot miss the topic of love as we read the epistles of John. Love is on the front burner of the stove and it is in the cupboards, in the living and dining rooms. It is in the bedroom, bathroom and in the closet and in the carporte. It is in the den and in the entertainment room. It is in the garden, on the walkway and on the mat. Love is the door and love beams through the windows. It is the foundation of our building and its superstructure. Love is the ceiling and it's the roof. There is nothing more important than love.

If John was the author of the Proverbs, I believe he would substitute wisdom with the word "Love": - Love *"(wisdom) calls aloud in the street, she raises her voice in the public square....she cries out in the gateway"* etc. John is consumed with love and all its implications. There is nothing in the Christian life that is greater or more important than love. You miss love and you miss your reason for being. Love is the compelling force of the Christian life.

The day we cease to love is the day we cease to be. Love must be our goal from start to finish. We cannot even for a moment not focus on it. It is our motivator. It is our inspiration. It is our bread and our sustainer. It is our flame and our illuminator. It is our river and our bridge. It is our ocean and our sky. It is the oxygen of our lives. It is our armor and our sword. It is our dream, our vision and our reality. Love has no rivals for all things must be done in love. Has love got the mastery of your life?

PRAYER

Lord, help me that my entire being may be consumed with love. Amen

WISDOM

Love is the key to successful living.

Love And Obedience

SCRIPTURE   November 25

"This is how we know that we love the children of God: by loving God and carrying out his commands"
I John 5:2.

REFLECTION

Our love for each other is bound up in our love relationship with God. If this is not a reality in our lives then we are non starters in this realm of love. Getting to know love does not spring from reading a romantic novel or watching a movie that touches the sentiment of our hearts and gets us all choked up and weepy eyed.

The only source of love is God and to have and give love demand that our hearts are totally yielded to God. To become the vehicle of love or its channel we must be living in the reality of Romans 12:1-2: - *"Therefore, I urge you, brothers, in view of God's mercy, **to offer your bodies** as living sacrifices, holy and pleasing to God – this is your spiritual act of worship. Do not conform any longer to the pattern of this world, but **be transformed by the renewing of your mind**. Then you will be able to test and approve what God's will is – his good, pleasing and perfect will"*.

Love to God demands obedience to all of His Word and not the parts that are merely convenient to us. It means putting the plough through the clods of resistance in our lives and becoming Disciples of Christ in all areas of our lives. This will involve self denial and cross bearing for it is then our alabaster boxes of perfume are broken and our lives become fragrant perfume that glorify God and benefit those who come in contact with us.

To love God and His children and to obey His Word is the only way we should go. Is your life being effective and honoring to the Lord?

PRAYER

Lord, help me to honor you by obeying Your Word. Amen

WISDOM

There is no cutting of corners in commitment.

Obey God

"This is love for God: To obey his commands. And his commands are not burdensome"
I John 5:3.

REFLECTION

We cannot be wayward and serve God. We cannot be living a life of self-will and bring any honor to God. We cannot be dabbling in sin during the course of the week and on Sunday go to church and there profess to love God. John is very specific of how love for God is to have meaning. To love God demands obedience to His Word. We cannot love God and yet our wills are in conflict with His.

If we love God then we must do those things that are pleasing in His sight. We must delight in the things that God delights in. Love is a full time commitment. Love is making ourselves available to serve God. Love is serving God with singleness of purpose for we cannot love God with a divided heart. Love demands inward integrity. Love is intimacy and intimacy is based on an ever expanding experiential knowledge of God.

If we love God, it demands time being spent in His presence expressing our affection to Him. If we love God it must be much more than a nodding acquaintance and a glancing smile. Intimacy with God cannot be achieved in one minute or five minutes devotionals. If we find we cannot fit God into our daily schedule of our lives then we have lost the purpose of being here on earth and therefore we need to scrap our present program and put Him in the most prominent place in our lives.

If God is not first in our lives, then we have our value system disoriented. We cannot love God and not have room in our hearts for Him, for that is a contradiction. If Christ is Lord then He must be loved.

PRAYER

Lord, help me to show my love for you by being obedient. Amen

WISDOM

There is no substitute for obedience.

331

God's Commands Not Burdensome

November 27

"This is love for God: To obey his commands. And his commands are not burdensome"
I John 5:3.

REFLECTION

What God requires of us are things that are beneficial to us. Satan, our former master, was cruel in his demands and made life bitter and burdensome for us. He whipped us without mercy. It was in desperation that we turned to the Lord, who had mercy on us and by His grace took us in and made us a part of His family. Now, were we swapping one bad master for another? No! Our God is the kindest, most generous, and absolutely good God. He is the most understanding Lord that any one could ever hope for. He who is our Lord is also our Father.

Every house has regulations and so does God's house. The most important command in God's house is love. We are to love God and each other. Each member of God's household has been assigned duties that are best suited to his or her abilities. He has further empowered us with special spiritual gifts that are bestowed and energized by the indwelling presence of the Holy Spirit who resides in us.

God has given us His Word that is sweeter than honey, and sharper than a double edged sword. It is that word that illuminates our path and guides our steps. The Word stored in our hearts keeps us from sinning. The Word strengthens; it empowers and fills the heart with delight. Its instructions are not confusing but are clear in order that we might be thoroughly furnished unto every good work.

God requires of us that we get ourselves familiar with His Word and obey it, for it purifies, preserves and satisfies. God's yoke is easy and His burden is light.

PRAYER

Lord, help me to love you and so delight in Your Word. Amen

WISDOM

Things that are done in love make work light.

332

The Word And Victory

"For everyone born of God overcomes the world. This is the victory that has overcome the world, even our faith"
I John 5:4.

REFLECTION

Why are there so many defeated Christians in our churches when we are promised victory through Christ? The promise of God incorporates all those who have experienced the second birth. Then why is it so many Christians are walking around dazed and terrified by the enemy?

Are God's promises not real, or, are church members ignorant of these promises that assure us of victory? I recently asked a class of believers how many of them have ever read the Bible through and the result was unsettling for not more than 10% had done so. These were not babes in Christ but veterans.

If believers do not master their manual for living, how then can they expect to have good success in their struggle against the world? Studying the Bible and educating ourselves with the Word takes a great deal of time.

Joshua was a very busy man for he was the head of Israel's army that was daily engaged in fierce battles against a hostile enemy, yet God's instruction to him was: - ***"Do not let this Book of the Law depart from your mouth; <u>meditate</u> on it day and night, so that you may be careful to do everything in it. <u>Then you will</u> be prosperous and successful"*** Joshua 1:8.

Victory is not promised us by having a Bible on a shelf in our homes, but is assured if we carry its contents in our hearts. To be an overcomer you must know God and obey His Word.

PRAYER

Lord, help me not to make excuses for not studying Your Word. Amen

WISDOM

Bible knowledge assimilated is the Key for victory over the world.

Faith In Operation

"For everyone born of God overcomes the world. This is the victory that has overcome the world, even our faith"
I John 5:4.

REFLECTION

Faith is crucial in the Christian's life. The Christian life begins with faith and is indispensable for its continuance. Now faith is trust in God and in His ability. Our manual on faith is the Bible. Romans 10:17 (K.J.V.) states, *"So then faith cometh by hearing, and hearing by the word of God"*.

It is possible to read the Bible and not believe its message, or we can read it, and the Word comes alive in our experience. We now expect God to honor His Word by acting in accord with the promises made. The believer lives by faith. Since faith is not a nebulous energy floating in the air but is based upon the promises in the Word, it would greatly benefit us to know the Word, for it is from the Word faith is generated by the Spirit.

Faith is explicitly putting our confidence in what God says and expecting God to bring to pass what He has promised. Faith is claiming the promises of God and making them our own. Faith builds a relationship between us and God. Faith is the key that unlocks the power of God and the more it is exercised the more faith grows in our experience.

Faith turns on the ability of God so that the impossible and the supernatural are realized in our experience. We can grow from little faith to great faith in God. Faith is the dynamo for the triumphant life.

Are you overcoming the seducing world through your faith?

PRAYER

Lord, help me to lock in on you through faith and be victorious. Amen

WISDOM

Faith makes visible our hope!

The World

"Who is he that overcomes the world? Only he who believes that Jesus is the Son of God"
I John 5:5.

REFLECTION

The world, we discovered in an earlier study, has a corrupted value system that is inspired and controlled by the Prince of Darkness. That system covers every aspect of life here on this earth. So the 'world' is opposed point for point to all the value systems of the Kingdom of God. Before we trusted Christ as our personal Savior we too were in its orbit and did its biddings. All non Christians are controlled by the world and can only be liberated from its dreadful power through Christ.

To the natural man the world is a very attractive, but seducing and delusive place. The pleasures of sin are very appealing, but before long, these habits become great chains that enslave those who are so deceived. They enter the world system not realizing that it is a prison for life with hard and cruel task masters as companions. Escape from its fortification by natural means is impossible.

How quickly it turns those trapped in its environment into sex and porn slaves, drug addicts, wife abusers, husband haters, child molesters, abusive parents, disobedient children, abusers of power and unnatural relations. Its victims are turned into money launderers, murderers, fornicators, adulterers, swindlers, slaves of religion and the list goes on and on.

The world is a compassionless tyrant. These poor deluded souls are driven to suicide, depression, insanity or a life without true hope and purpose. But there is one hope of escape from its tyranny and that is to be found in **Jesus Christ**. Do you know Him?

PRAYER

Lord, help me to trust in you and be saved from the world. Amen

WISDOM

The world is attractive yet a very powerful and deadly tyrant.

Overcoming The World

"Who is he that overcomes the world? Only he who believes that Jesus is the Christ"
I John 5:5.

REFLECTION

The battle against the world is perennial and if we would be overcomers we must experience a spiritual rebirth. Jesus is central to that birth. We must be committed to His person. He must be in control of the reins of our lives. He must be in the driver's seat. He must be the one who calls the shots. He must be the Commander-in-Chief of our lives.

Knowing and understanding who our Lord is, is of vital importance in this struggle against this powerful, dangerous and deadly enemy. We must know the credentials of the One who is in charge of us. We must have first hand acquaintance with His qualifications for, the matters at hand, have eternal implications and to follow someone who is an imposter or a charlatan would be disastrous.

We must therefore know beyond a shadow of a doubt who we are putting our trust in. How then can we be sure that Jesus is God's Anointed and the Savior of the world? Christianity is an historical reality and the integrity of its founder is impeccable. His credentials are established by scores of prophecies found in the Old Testament Scriptures that have had their realization in Him. The greatest proof that substantiates His claim of being Savior is that He rose from the dead and is now at God's right hand. His resurrection is a fact well attested to in history. To believe that Jesus is the Christ is safe.

Are you living in the blessings of that reality?

PRAYER

Lord, help me overcome the world through Christ, my strength. Amen

WISDOM

The lure of the world is overcome through love for Christ.

Water And Blood

*"This is the one who came **by water and blood** – Jesus Christ. He did not come by water only, but by water and blood. And it is the Spirit who testifies, because the Spirit is the truth"*
I John 5:6.

REFLECTION

Water and blood were vital elements in the Old Testament system of worship. In the courtyard of the tabernacle set up by Moses there were first of all, the brazen altar and then the laver. The altar was where the blood sacrifices were placed. Without the shedding of blood there could be no forgiveness of sin. To enter the sanctuary the priest had to wash himself at the laver and that speaks of our sanctification.

The entire tabernacle, its furnishings and its offerings, were shadows of the reality which would have their fulfillment in Christ offering Himself as God's perfect lamb to atone for our sins. The Book of Hebrews gives us great insight into the difference between the shadow and the substance. It tells us that *"The gifts and sacrifices being offered were not able to clear the conscience of the worshipper. They were only a matter of food and drink and various ceremonial washings – external regulations applying until the time of the new order"* Hebrews 9:9-10.

The historical event that may have given significance to the matter of water and blood of this epistle, could have been when Christ, on the cross, was pierced with a spear "and *straightway there came out blood and water"* John 19:34 (A.S.V.). There are observable events in Scripture that do not immediately take on spiritual significance until sometime after the occasion. John here reverses the order of what he wrote in his gospel. It is now 'water and blood'. Do these symbols mean anything to you?

PRAYER

Lord, help me to grasp that water and blood are symbols of life. Amen

WISDOM

Forgiveness is by Christ's blood, and sanctification is by the water of the Word.

Water And Blood

"This is the one who came by water and blood – Jesus Christ. He did not come by water only, but by water and blood. And it is the Spirit who testifies, because the Spirit is the truth"
I John 5:6.

REFLECTION

The theological implication of water and blood follows the historical event of the sacrifice of Jesus. We seem to be slow in understanding significant historical events as they transpire. Sometimes the meanings of these events are partially lost to the generation that experienced them.

However, the significance of Christ's coming; His death and His resurrection were not left hanging, because Christ explained their value after His resurrection. Once our minds are oriented, a lot of the smaller details will begin to fall in place. Jesus said to His disciples, *"I have much more to say to you, more than you can now bear. But when he, the Spirit of truth comes, he will guide you into all truth"* John 16:12-13.

John had time to reflect on the life of Christ, for his gospel and epistles may have been written some sixty years after the event. Divine truth sometimes takes time to emerge and to crystallize in our minds before they become a driving force in our lives. Maturity of thought is not an overnight experience but is a product of the unconscious and the subconscious mind alerting the conscious mind to the riches of the treasures we have in Christ.

We will never view water and blood in the same way after we have digested their significance in the life of Christ. Have you ever meditated on their true value and applied it to yourself?

PRAYER

Lord, help me to grasp the double cure of your blood and water. Amen

WISDOM

Christ's blood and water are essential for life and living.

Jesus And Water

"This is the one who came by water and blood – Jesus Christ. He did not come by water only, but by water and blood. And it is the Spirit who testifies, because the Spirit is the truth"
I John 5:6.

REFLECTION

John, in his gospel, records several significant uses of water associated with Jesus. For instance, Jesus used water and miraculously changed it into wine. Jesus told Nicodemus of his need to be born of water and the Spirit. Ezekiel said many centuries before *"I will sprinkle clean water on you, and you will be clean...I will give you a new heart and put a new spirit in you"* Ezekiel 36:25-26.

Jesus offers to the woman at the well, a well of living water – yea eternal life, a life of spiritual purity, power and satisfaction. To those who come and put their trust in Him, He promises streams of living water to flow out of their innermost being. This of course speaks of the richness, vitality, freshness and the enduring presence of the Spirit released in and through us (John 7:38-39).

Jesus uses a basin of water to wash the feet of His disciples to teach them a lesson in service, humility and purity. After the baptism of Jesus in water, the descent of the Holy Spirit like a dove on Him was the sign given to John the Baptist that this indeed is the very Son of God (John 1:31-34). Jesus' baptism in water identified Him not as a sinner but rather as the One who would be the sinner's substitute.

Jesus on the cross was pierced by a spear, and out of that wound came blood and water and that speaks volumes to me of His great love for me. He gave His life in order that I might live in union with Him forever. Do you appreciate Him?

PRAYER

Lord, help me to appreciate your death on the cross for me. Amen

WISDOM

Water is life and He is the Water of Life.

Blood And Salvation

*"This is the one who came by water and **blood** – Jesus Christ. He did not come by water only, but by water and blood. And it is the Spirit who testifies, because the Spirit is the truth"*
I John 5:6.

REFLECTION

Jesus partook of flesh and blood to be our Savior. Salvation of man could only be achieved by God, the Son taking on human nature. No sacrifice offered to God was ever stoned to death or strangled but was killed in a manner that all the blood would drain out. The life of the flesh is in the blood and once blood is shed then the life is taken.

Jesus came specifically into our world to give His life for sinners. Scripture predicted that His death would be by crucifixion and so it was. The dreadful penalty for sin is death and so we all deserve to die. The only way that God could save the world of sinners was by finding a perfect, holy, blameless substitute who was man, and who was willing to give His lifeblood for erring mankind.

Sin is a heinous offense and must be punished without mercy. A sinless man cannot be produced through the course of natural conception, for sin is transmitted through natural generation. However, Jesus, the seed of the woman, came by supernatural means and He alone is qualified to be the second Adam. Acting on our behalf He was able to shed His blood on the cross and thus reconcile us to God. It is only through Him we can have peace with God and the peace of God. It is through His blood we obtain forgiveness of sins, reconciliation, sonship, and thus making us heirs of God.

Do you know Him who came by blood?

PRAYER

Lord, help me to be thankful that you came by blood and freely shed it that I might be saved. Amen

WISDOM

Salvation is through the blood of Christ.

Testimony Of The Spirit

*"This is the one who came by water and blood – Jesus Christ. He did not come by water only, but by water and blood. **And it is the Spirit who testifies**, because the Spirit is the truth"*
I John 5:6.

REFLECTION

The ministry of the Holy Spirit in our present dispensation is to glorify Christ and to reveal to us who He is. The New Testament is the product of the Holy Spirit. The revelation in the New Testament completes all God intended for us to have and this sets forth God's program for His Church in this present age.

Spiritual truth that we need for today is found either explicitly or implicitly in the Word. Spiritual truth cannot be uncovered by the natural mind no matter how brilliant. Even carnal Christians have difficulty appreciating spiritual truths. The deeper the commitment is to Christ, the greater the illumination of the Word it will produce This does not mean that obtaining God's truth does not involve labor, careful study, diligent prayers, research and meditation. God will reward the diligent and the industrious; never the slothful. Christ is central to the message of the New Testament as He is of the Old, but it is the Spirit of God who makes Him real to our experiences.

The Word of God is a mine of spiritual treasures and only the Spirit can uncover the Spiritual nuggets that either lie on the surface or beneath it. Only He can take God's truth and let them glow with grandeur. He can take a simple word like 'water' or 'blood' and forever change how we view them theologically and thus forever change our lives as those words become living, active and transforming.

Do you know the Spirit of truth who testifies of Jesus?

PRAYER

Lord, help me to embrace with my whole heart the Holy Spirit. Amen

WISDOM

The Spirit applies spiritual truth to our hearts.

Three Are In Agreement

*"For there are three that testify: The Spirit, the water and the blood and the **three are in agreement**"*
I John 5:7-8.

REFLECTION

The entire ministry of Jesus Christ while He served on earth was under the direct influence of The Holy Spirit. There was no conflict in what Christ came to do and what He did. There was no rebellion in His soul, no disharmony in His program. His baptism initiated His program of redemption and He stayed the course of seeking to save the lost. His baptism identified Him with fallen man, but not as one who needed salvation, but as the One who would take man's sin and bury them forever. There is no charge of sin laid against any who trusts Jesus as Savior. Indeed, he stands justified before God.

The path to the cross was fraught with difficulties, but He did not flinch at the bitter cup that the Father gave Him, but drank the last bitter dreg through the shedding of His blood on the cross. It was through the eternal Spirit that Christ offered *"Himself without blemish unto God"* Hebrews 9:14 (A.S.V.).

The Spirit of God came upon Christ at His baptism, performed works of wonder through Him in His earthly ministry, and was there as His precious blood was shed. It is now the Blessed Spirit that reveals God's truths and gives us understanding. There is no conflict between these three – the Spirit, the water and the blood - they work in concert to secure our salvation.

We too are in agreement with the Spirit, the water and the blood, for it was these three that put us in the ark of safety and to this, we too, do testify. Do you have this testimony too?

PRAYER

Lord, help me to appreciate the instruments of my salvation. Amen

WISDOM

The Spirit applying truth brings conviction and conversion.

God's Testimony Of His Son

"We accept man's testimony, but God's testimony is greater, which he has given about his Son"
I John 5:9.

REFLECTION

The Scripture teaches that the testimony of two or three witnesses is adequate to put a man to death (Deuteronomy 19:15). In the time of David, a man's doom was sealed by the testimony from his own lips (II Samuel 1:6-16). The woman of Samaria testified to the men of Samaria that she had found the Messiah and many believed on Him. (John 4:39). If the words of sinful man can be believed, how much more then, the testimony of God?

Three times in the Gospels Jesus is acknowledged by God with a voice from heaven. The first was at His baptism: - *"A voice from heaven said, "This is my beloved Son, in whom I am well pleased"* Matthew 3:17 (A.S.V.). The Father said three important things about Jesus in His Testimony. First, He acknowledged Jesus as His Son. Second, He expressed His love for Jesus. Third, He delighted in Jesus.

The second testimony recorded in Scriptures was given when Jesus was transfigured. The face of Jesus shone like the sun. His garment became as white as light. This event was witnessed by Moses and Elijah, and Peter, James and John. Suddenly God spoke the same words that were spoken at His baptism with only one additional sentence, *"Hear ye him"* Matthew 17:5 (A.S.V.).

The final testimony was at the week of the Passover feast. It was there Jesus said, *"Father, glorify your name!"* And the Father spoke from heaven in response: - *"I have glorified it, and will glorify it again"* John 12:28. What a powerful testimony God gave of His Son!

PRAYER

Lord, help me to appreciate your testimony regarding Your Son. Amen

WISDOM

To ignore God's testimony regarding Christ is indeed perilous.

God's Testimony

December 09

"Anyone who believes in the Son of God has this testimony in his heart. Anyone who does not believe God has made him out to be a liar, because he has not believed the testimony God has given about his Son"
I John 5:10.

REFLECTION

God's testimony concerning His Son Jesus Christ extends beyond the three vocal expressions recorded in the Gospels. The prophetic Word gives eloquent testimony to this wonderful person.

He is the Seed of the woman (Genesis 3:15); The Passover Lamb (Exodus 12); The Bull for our atonement (Leviticus 16). He is The Commander of the Lord's army (Joshua 5:14); the promised Seed of David to sit on his throne forever (II Samuel 7:16). Isaiah the Prophet identifies Him as Immanuel (Isaiah 7:14). He is the Son that is given who will manage the governments of this world. He is the Wonderful Counselor, Mighty God, Everlasting Father, Prince of Peace (Isaiah 9:6-8). He is the Branch (Isaiah 11:1) He is the coming Prince who dies to save His people (Daniel 9:25-26). His Body in death would not see corruption (Psalm 16:10). He would triumph over all His enemies as decreed by His Father (Psalm 2).

What was prophetically written of His first coming has materialized and we have come into the blessing of His Salvation and grace. Our hearts have been deeply affected and transformed and renewed. He has given us *"a crown of beauty for ashes, oil of gladness instead of mourning, and a garment of praise instead of a spirit of despair"* Isaiah 61:3. Our inner fountain is purified and we are His new creation for salvation is deep and abiding, and we rejoice in the testimony of what God the Father has done for us through His Son.

PRAYER

Lord, help me see Jesus in the Old Testament Scriptures. Amen

WISDOM

The Scriptures are God's testimony about His Son Jesus.

God's Adversaries

"Anyone who believes in the Son of God has this testimony in his heart. Anyone who does not believe God has made him out to be a liar, because he has not believed the testimony God has given about his Son"
I John 5:10.

REFLECTION

Man can oppose God and many have made this their career. People opposed to God love darkness and the wages of unrighteousness. The atheist, the deist, the infidel, the agnostic, the procrastinator, the idolater point their bony fingers in the face of God and dare to deny, repudiate and defy the testimony of creation and the astounding facts of God's historical revelation.

The opponents of God stifle conscience, disregard sound reasoning, embrace the folly of human wisdom and thus damn their souls to an eternal hell which they do not think exist. The Bible declares that not many 'wise' are called, nor many of noble birth, nor many mighty for they regard the spiritual as folly. In their conceit, they view the spiritual as a crutch for the weak and those deficient in intellectual power.

Those puffed up with so called knowledge, rush with gusto into the fray not realizing they will be crushed by the freight train of truth. No one who wars against truth will come out smiling and triumphant. God's truth will either break you or grind you to powder. To oppose the truth is to embrace the devil's lie and many have been so persuaded. Resisting God's truth is a one way to bondage. To cast in your lot with truth is salvation and freedom.

Have you embraced God's testimony concerning His Son Jesus Christ?

PRAYER

Lord, help me never to stand in opposition to your truth. Amen

WISDOM

Truth will defeat all those who oppose her.

Eternal Life

December 11

*"And this is the testimony: **God has given us eternal life**, and this life is in his Son"*
I John 5:11.

REFLECTION

Eternal life is what all men desire, yet it has eluded countless millions. They seek it in a plant, in water, religion and in science with no success. We cannot, by natural means, obtain something that is essentially spiritual in nature. Eternal life is extra terrestrial. It will not be obtained by what we eat or what we drink or through deep meditation. No guru in the East can impart this life to you.

We do not have the nature within us from which this type of life can be coaxed out of us. It is not locked up somewhere inside of us just awaiting the right pass word for its release. No esoteric knowledge, no secret society has an answer to this vital matter of eternal life. Men continue to live and age and then die.

Man, before the fall, would have lived physically forever and would have enjoyed all the bounty and goodness of life. Sin abruptly introduced into the human family, brought death and contaminated the very fountain of life. Sin not only brought physical death, but it stole virtue, righteousness, holiness, purpose and all the dynamics that made life buoyant, joyful and satisfying. Sin brought misery, sorrow, pain in all its manifold manifestations, hopelessness, and despair and, of course, spiritual death – separation from the very source of life – God.

Is eternal life merely then a dream, something that is etched mockingly in our memories but unattainable? Or is God, gracious and merciful, the solution to the miracle of eternal life?

PRAYER

Lord, help me realize that you are the fountain of life and I can drink of you. Amen

WISDOM

Faith in Christ is the Door to eternal life.

Eternal Life Is In Christ

December 12

*"And this is the testimony: God has given us eternal life, and **this life is in his Son**"*
I John 5:11.

REFLECTION

The person whom we have on indefinite hold in our lives is the solution to our problem. God is the author of all life. God is eternal. He has no beginning and He has no end. He has life in Himself. He is the Great "I AM" who lives in the eternal now. God has no genealogy. He has no history of past, present or future for God is timeless. He is sovereign and does what He pleases. He is answerable to no one in heaven or on earth He is before all things and by Him all things consist.

He is integrity. He is truth. He is trustworthy. This God is the giver of eternal life and this life He desires to impart to us. It comes to us as a gift – *"The gift of God is eternal life"* Romans 6:23. Jonah tells us that *"Salvation is of the LORD"* Jonah 2:9. Eternal life comes to us through the mediatory work of Christ. All God's blessings are channeled to us through Christ. The Son of God is the link to the Father. The transmission of eternal life is no exception for this life is in His Son.

The Father, Son and Holy Spirit each have a distinct ministry yet the ministry of each is interwoven and intertwined one with the other. Each has an indispensable role to play in the impartation of eternal life to us.

*"I tell you the truth, whoever hears my words and believes him who sent me **has eternal life**"* John 5:24. Eternal life is not a future gain. It is an entity we receive **NOW** by faith and its blessings become immediately operational in our lives in wonderful and powerful ways.

Do you know if you have eternal life?

PRAYER

Lord, help me to appreciate the gift of eternal life through Christ. Amen

WISDOM

The search for eternal life is realized in Christ.

He Who Has The Son Has Life

"He who has the Son has life; he who does not have the Son of God does not have life"
I John 5:12.

REFLECTION

How is eternal life obtained? God has made this most important matter of getting eternal life very simple to understand, yet many intellectuals have stumbled over God's simple offer of obtaining this precious gift through Christ. The enemy of our souls has wasted no time in making Christ, the Son of God, a rock of offense and a stumbling block, and has perverted our power of reasoning with ill conceived biases.

Isaiah sums it up well: - *"He had no beauty or majesty to attract us to him, nothing in his appearance that we should desire him. He was despised and rejected of men, a man of sorrows, and familiar with suffering. Like one from whom men hide their faces he was despised, and we esteemed him not"* Isaiah 53:2-3. Like Nathanael of old, many will regard this Nazarene with suspicion and low esteem.

Jesus took the place of a servant on His mission to earth and gave His life for us on a cross. He was crucified as a common criminal in spite of the fact that the Roman judge found Him guiltless. However, God's greater purpose was attained, for it was because of His death we now can receive forgiveness of our sins and the gift of eternal life.

Christ not only died, but on the third day triumphed over death by His resurrection. *"Verily, verily, I say unto you, except a grain of wheat fall into the earth and die, it abideth by itself alone; but if it die, it beareth much fruit"* John 12:24 (A.S.V.). Because Jesus is now alive we all can have life – eternal life. Do you have the Son in your heart?

PRAYER

Lord, help me to accept the truth that having Jesus is having life. Amen

WISDOM

All who despise Christ's message of salvation will be rejected.

Do You Have The Son?

SCRIPTURE   December 14

"He who has the Son has life; he who does not have the Son of God does not have life"
I John 5:12.

REFLECTION

The Son of God stands at the crossroads of our lives. Those who receive Him by faith into their hearts receive eternal life. Those who fail to do so for whatever reason will not have eternal life. The non-Christian is already in darkness and in a state of spiritual death or separation from the life of God. We have biological life but the functions of the 'heart' are cut off from everything that is holy, just, right, good and purposeful.

If our hearts follow the dictates of the world and are lured by its charms and fascinated by its seductive pleasures, then we are in eternal danger of losing our souls. There is a way that looks right, for it appeals to our senses and calls us with enticing words and lures us into the trap of self destruction. The tinsels, the parties, the shining lights, success in business, the frolic, the sex, the drugs, the guns, all have a downside that leads to bondage and eternal separation from God's life.

Life in the fast lane has no room in the inn for accommodation, worship and adoration of the Christ. He is not recognized nor honored as Savior and Lord. He may occasionally get lip service, but to all intents and purposes, He is slighted and kept out of sight at our functions. Even at the celebration of His birthday He is upstaged by another. His suffering and resurrection are remembered by our gorging ourselves with bun and cheese and the focus is then on the Easter bunny. Failure to invite Him into our lives is a tragedy we will have all eternity to mourn and be full of unrelieved regret. Is it wisdom then to reject the Son?

PRAYER

Lord, help me to give Christ first place in my heart. Amen

WISDOM

Marginalize Christ and you cheat yourself of eternal life.

Certain Knowledge

December 15

*"I write these things to you who believe in the name of the Son of God so **that you may know** that you have eternal life"*
I John 5:13.

REFLECTION

We take time out of our busy schedule to inform our friends of things that are really important to us and that would be of great interest to them. The hurricane center sends out bulletins of impending disaster to those in the path of a hurricane. We all take an interest in informing our friends just in case they missed the news. People do take these warnings seriously and prepare themselves for that impending disaster.

John is not here writing about a disaster but is sharing the greatest good news that any one could ever receive. Putting your trust in Christ, says John, results in getting eternal life. Can I get this eternal life and then forfeit it? Is this gift conditioned thereafter by my conduct? Can I in the course of one day be saved and then be lost over and over again? Is salvation a roller coaster ride? If that is so, then we can never really know for sure, can we?

Is my salvation, my rebirth, my eternal life, a matter of certain knowledge? Is not this what John is advocating? The veracity of my salvation does not for one moment depend on me. I stand complete in Christ. The charges against me were dropped and I am now justified through Him. God has declared me righteous. God accepts me for what Christ did on my behalf. The God who has given me eternal life will never go back on His promise. He will never retract His word. I can rest in great confidence in the assurance God has given – *"He that hath the Son hath life"* I John 5:12 (A.S.V.).

Do you know you have eternal life?

PRAYER

Lord, help me appreciate the integrity of your promises. Amen

WISDOM

God's promises cannot fail.

Prayer And God's Will

"This is the confidence we have in approaching God; if we ask anything according to his will, he hears us"
I John 5:14.

REFLECTION

The key to successful prayer is praying in harmony with the will of God. All the great men of the Bible were mighty men of prayer and they prayed in unity with God's will and mighty things were done. Not only must we pray in harmony with God's will, but we must also live according to the revealed Word of God. Living and praying requires that we have intimate knowledge of God's Word and that we take the promises of the Word seriously.

The promises of God are not false but are true, enduring and powerful. They are supported by His omnipotent power. Now the attitudes we adapt to these promises are important. Take the case of Gideon. He is commissioned by God to fight the Midianites but he lacks confidence in God giving him the victory, so he resorts to the fleece test. He wants a sign from God to build up his confidence and courage. Weak faith looks for a sign. Invariably one sign will never do as was the case of Gideon. He requested a second sign which God graciously granted.

Prayer is an encounter with God and as such can be transforming. It is in prayer we often times obtain our commission for our life's ministry. It is there we come face to face with the will of God and the task He has for us. It is in prayer we hear 'the voice of God'. Prayer is dialogue. It is a time of communion, and at times, deep struggles. It is getting to know your God. It is a time of intimacy. It is a time of waiting on God's pleasure.

How confident are you when you pray?

PRAYER

Lord, help me to be expectant and confident when I pray. Amen

WISDOM

Prayer is getting to know God.

Prayer And God's Will

"This is the confidence we have in approaching God; if we ask anything according to his will, he hears us"
I John 5:14.

REFLECTION

Prayer is indispensable and therefore is a must for all Christians. We are not born prayer warriors. It is something that is acquired over a period of time. A crisis in our lives can become the means to bring forth the spiritual giant that prayer can produce through us. God has His way of getting our attention in the 'desert experiences' of our lives that enable us to confront the Pharaohs of our world.

One prayer session can become the pivot point that can forever alter our spiritual and prayer life and embolden us to have confidence in our God. Jacob had such an encounter with God at a place he was to call Peniel – 'face of God'. The night of wrestling with God changed his life and his name from Jacob – supplanter or deceiver - to Israel. That night was not to be forgotten as with confidence and in pain he held unto God and said, *"I will not let thee go, except thou bless me"* Genesis 32:26 (A.S.V.) and God answered his prayer and blessed him.

Prayer, is at times, something that God initiates, and when He does, we will find ourselves standing on holy ground with an awesome sense of the divine presence. It is there God reveals His will for our lives and there is oft a struggle and a torrent of excuses why we would have another take our place. But in that struggle God overcomes our excuses and submission to God's will triumph. Such was the experience of Moses.

Are you discerning God's will for your life through prayer?

PRAYER

Lord, help me discern your will in my prayer life. Amen

WISDOM

When we pray, God listens.

Be Specific In Prayer

"This is the confidence we have in approaching God; if we ask anything according to his will, he hears us"
I John 5:14.

REFLECTION

Asking God for anything should not be done in a general way. When we engage ourselves in prayer we must be specific and not vague. We must not blush or be embarrassed to make our requests known to God. Jesus, His Son, emboldens us to ask – *"Ask, and **it shall be given to you"** Luke 11:9 (A.S.V),* and we are assured of the divine response. Peter tells us that God's eyes are on the righteous.

We are of special interest to God. He loves and cares for us. His love for us is greater than the love of parents or special friends. When we have audience with Him in prayer He listens with an open ear and open hands. God delights to listen to His children and longs for us to seek His face. Prayer should not be a burden, a kind of last resort, or an after thought, but should be the consuming passion and the love of our lives.

Prayer encompasses all of life and God is keen that we consult Him in matters small or great. When tempted, pray; when making a major decision, pray; when seeking a life's partner, pray; in an emergency, pray; choosing a career, pray; when you are at wits end corner, pray. If you are unsure of God's will in a particular matter, pray. If you are in doubt as to the direction you should take, pray. If you are committing yourself to a specific Christian service, pray.

Develop dependence on God for that is what prayer is all about. Prayer is beholding the face of your Heavenly Father and drawing close to the heart of God. Prayer is being intimate with God and developing confidence because of our association with Him. Is prayer real to you?

PRAYER

Lord, help me to come close to you in prayer. Amen

WISDOM

Confidence is gained through practice.

God Delivers

"And if we know that he hears us – whatever we ask – we know that we have what we ask of him"
I John 5:15.

REFLECTION

We cannot touch God with our hands no more can we kiss the wind with our lips. Nor can we see the law of gravity with our eyes. The Bible tells us that the things we can see are temporal, but the things we cannot see will endure forever. We pray to the God we cannot see, for God is Spirit, yet we can develop a relationship with Him that is deep, rich, powerful and abiding. God as Spirit does communicate with our spirits and satisfies the deep longings and urges of our inner man.

Our relationship with God does not hinge on the fanciful, or the imaginative, but is real as the air we breathe or the heat we feel from a flame. The God we cannot see brings us to another level through communications with us. All things are under the control of God be they visible or invisible, be they on the earth or under the earth, or under the seas or in the heights of the heaven above us. All things are at His beck and call, be they animate or inanimate, and be they living or dead.

The God we serve is not a distant deity or one who sleeps or slumbers. When we pray it does not take light years to get His attention nor does it takes years or any effort on His part to respond. God is able to handle all the petitions of praying people across the world in whatever language it is uttered and there is no confusion in His responses whereby He gives my answer to someone else. He answers individually and personally and in a fashion that is exactly tailored to our needs. If we pray according to His will the answer is guaranteed every time.

Are you looking for an answer from God?

PRAYER

Lord, help me to appreciate how great you are. Amen

WISDOM

Ask according to God's will and God will grant the request.

Praying With Confidence

*"And if we know that he hears us – whatever we ask – **we know that we have what we ask of him"***
I John 5:15.

REFLECTION

We should never pray and then wonder if God is going to answer our prayer. We approach God in the confidence of faith and lay our petition before Him and we must leave His presence assured that our prayers will be honored in a time that pleases Him. God hears our petitions and some answers are on the way before the prayer is even completed.

Some prayers have material answers, some are for guidance, others for healing, or family related matters. There are prayers for protection and some are related to a deeper, fuller and consistent walk with our God. Some answers are 'no', as was the case of the Apostle Paul when he asked God to remove a particular problem from his life. That particular thorn in the flesh, a messenger of Satan, was designed to keep him humble and dependent on God for the duration of his life here on earth.

There is an application to us in this matter of infirmities. Some might be afflicted with that which God will not remove. Infirmities many times help to keep us close to God. God does not heal indiscriminately. Then there are delayed answers that can vary from days to years. Take for instance praying for the salvation of a spouse, or parent or a relative or friend, the divine response could be short term or long but our task is to prevail upon God and be faithful until He answers.

If we pray according to God's will then it will be done. Prayer outside of God's will get a no for an answer. Don't despair because of delay but hold fast your confidence that your God will answer your prayer.

PRAYER

Lord, help me to trust you in the midst of the storm. Amen

WISDOM

When we pray, doubt must give way to the assurance of faith.

Prayer And A Sinning Brother

"If anyone sees his brother commit a sin that does not lead to death, he should pray and God will give him life. I refer to those whose sin does not lead to death. There is a sin that leads to death. I am not saying that we should pray about that"
I John 5:16.

REFLECTION

Simon, the sorcerer's faith lacked sincerity and depth. He wanted to purchase God's power so he could impart the Spirit on whomsoever he willed for a profit. Peter responded with this inspired remark, *"You have no part or share in this ministry, because your **heart is not right with God**. Repent of this wickedness and **pray to the Lord**. Perhaps he will forgive you for having such a thought in your heart"* Acts 8:21-23.

Simon in terror responds to Peter, *"**Pray to the Lord for me** so that nothing you have said may happen to me"* Acts 8:24. There are degrees of offenses and some of them do have serious consequences in this life. Under the Law, capital offenses were enumerated and most of them recorded were executed by men, but some were executed by God as was the case of Aaron's sons (Numbers 10:1-3). However, there are offenses against God that do not end in instant death as was the case of Miriam. God smote her with leprosy in a moment but Moses, the man of God interceded for her and she was restored after 7 days. Her sin was spiritual jealousy, envy and backbiting.

Uzziah intruded into the functions of the priests and became a leper. Gehazi's greed caused him to become a leper. The sin of taking the Lord's Supper lightly will cause severe weakness in our bodies and sicknesses. In praying for the sick we should determine if the sickness is linked to sin in the life of the afflicted. If so, then confession must be made followed by prayer for healing. What is the nature of your sin?

PRAYER

Lord, help me to keep away from all sins. Amen

WISDOM

It is God's mercy that preserves us all from being consumed.

356

When Not To Pray

"If anyone sees his brother commit a sin that does not lead to death, he should pray and God will give him life. I refer to those whose sin does not lead to death. There is a sin that leads to death. I am not saying that we should pray about that"
I John 5:16.

REFLECTION

How we judge sin is somewhat subjective. How we view it will depend on our personal relationship with our Lord. If we are shallow then our perception of evil will not be severe. If we have spiritual depth then we will view evil as extremely offensive and to be dealt with severely.

Let us consider for a moment the case of incest in the Corinthian church and the lying of Ananias and his wife Sapphira to the infant church in Jerusalem. In our modern churches we would be more severe with the sin of incest and be more lenient with Ananias' lie, but the record of Scripture is that the liar was instantly put to death while the incestuous person was excommunicated.

Sinning presumptuously is often followed by swift judgment. God told Jeremiah the Prophet not to pray for the children of Israel because their cup of iniquity was full and that no amount of praying could deliver them. They were doomed to death. Partaking in the Lord's Supper in a dishonorable way can take us prematurely out of this world. Therefore praying for a brother or sister that has God's sentence of death upon him or her is an absolute waste of time.

Sin is a serious matter that can remove us out of this life into the next in a matter of moments. Let us not tempt the Lord to see how far we can go into sin without His righteous judgment overwhelming us. Let us pray the one for the other to be delivered from such temptations.

PRAYER

Lord, help me to pray that your people be kept pure. Amen

WISDOM

Don't allow presumptuous sins to have dominion over you.

All Wrong Doing Is Sin

"All wrong doing is sin, and there is sin that does not lead to death"
I John 5:17.

REFLECTION

John is very plain and tells us that all wrong doing is sin. Sinful thoughts defile the mind so we must be careful not to allow our minds to be a haven for evil thoughts. All sins have their origin in the mind. Once the mind is committed to a particular course of action then the other members are on roll call and are mobilized to do evil. Our actions just betray and make manifest and transparent the deeds of the mind. It is through the actions of the body we get our hard copy of sin.

The lips 'print out' I am a liar, a backbiter, a slanderer, a deceiver, a tale bearer, a blasphemer, a false prophet, yea, a hypocrite. When sin takes a hold of the body it announces that, "I am a drug addict, a fornicator, a sodomite, an adulterer, a murderer, a thief, a pusher, a prostitute". When it takes a hold of my affections, I am a seducer, a charmer, a Casanova, a pretender, violent in anger, abusive, cold, calculating, unforgiving, unfaithful and lustful.

Sin is sin and all sins are hated by God, but unfortunately not all sins are hateful to us. Some sins we wink at and find them socially acceptable. God finds no sin acceptable and He is the One who sets the standard and declares all sins repulsive and have hurtful consequences. It is the mercy of God that we do not all perish in a moment, but let us not think that because God has spared us that God, in anyway, condones our sins.

Once we become conscious of our sins, let us seek God's forgiveness and then walk in the light as He is in the Light.

PRAYER

Lord, help me that I will not be deceived by iniquity. Amen

WISDOM

All sins bring condemnation.

All Wrong Doing Is Sin

SCRIPTURE   December 24

"All wrong doing is sin, and there is sin that does not lead to death"
I John 5:17

REFLECTION

Because God does not act in instant judgment on our wrongs that gives us no license to continue in sinful habits. Untreated sins, unconfessed sins harden the heart and put fellowship with God on hold. If we indulge in 'safe' sin we are tempting God. No sin is safe.

All sin is bondage. What you may find pleasurable today, and hide and do, will come to light tomorrow and it will bring you nothing but shame and disgrace and great heaviness and distress of heart with regret and remorse.

Sin is deceitful and its consequences are not always immediate. However, sin will ultimately bring you shame in this life or in the life to come. Sin will mar and haunt you as long as it remains unconfessed.

So you have 'survived' your act of sin, but its tormenting impact on your mind makes you wish you were dead. Sin brings in its train a harvest of corruption. If you are tempted to do evil just this once, please think carefully of the irreparable damage and pain one moment of 'pleasure' can bring.

There is evidence all around us of the ugly consequences of sin and yours will be no different in spite of what the devil whispers in your ear.

Increase the distance between your soul and doing wrong for that is right.

PRAYER

Lord, help me to run away from youthful passions. Amen

WISDOM

Hate falsehood for it is a steel trap.

Sanctified Life A Reality

SCRIPTURE December 25

"We know that anyone born of God does not continue to sin; the one who was born of God keeps him safe, and the evil one cannot harm him"
I John 5:18.

REFLECTION

What a blessed promise we have from God for a sanctified life! The struggles we have to keep pure are on going and can have no truce, not even for a moment. Our rebirth gives us a distinct advantage for coming out on top with every encounter we have with evil. The nature God has given us has no appetite or desire for sin.

If this new nature is always in control of our lives then sin would be put on the shelf for keeps, but life at times becomes very complicated for there is another nature in us that simply will not take this matter lying down. It is there to create a civil war or try to take back the reign of government in our lives. The assault of the fallen nature, which, when it is reinforced by the devil, can at times, be very traumatizing and unsettling for the Christian who is unskilled or skilled in spiritual warfare.

We must know the provisions God has given us and learn to wholly depend on them and we will be assured of victory every time. God has given us a new nature. He has given us His Holy Spirit who indwells us, and He wants to fill us and empower us. He has given us His armor and the sword of the Spirit that is the Word of God. He has given us faith to overcome, the blood of His Son to cleanse and the presence of Himself and His Son to bolster and to garrison us against all the attacks of the enemy. We dare to stand and be victorious in Jesus' Name.

PRAYER

Lord, help me to stand in the full compliments of your provisions. Amen

WISDOM

God's provisions are abundant for those who trust in Him.

Kept Safe

SCRIPTURE December 26

"We know that anyone born of God does not continue to sin; the one who was born of God keeps him safe, and the evil one cannot harm him"
I John 5:18.

REFLECTION

We can live in the shadow of what we have in Christ or we can become the very substance of what our faith is. We can be terrified by the enemy or the enemy can shake in his boots because of who we are.

We can learn some valid lessons from Psalm 18 as to how we can have the upper hand in this spiritual struggle that confronts us day and night. Dependence on God is an absolute necessity. Therefore don't depend on your native ability, but wholly on God's might. It is through God's help we can advance against the devil's fortifications, scale the walls that seem impregnable (v.29) and do the impossible. We draw our strength from God who imparts wisdom to us on how to handle the issues that confront us. It is God who empowers and gives the abilities to attain the heights in spite of the difficulties and trials.

Those who attend God's boot camps become skilled in the use of spiritual weaponry and become masters in the use of complex weapons. It is there that we learn that the battle is the Lord's and that God is able to take us out of the difficult situations in life. It is there we learn endurance, tenacity and conquest over the enemy. You give the enemy no quarter, but put all desires of the flesh, with all its carnal ambitions under the sword. There is no place for compromise, bartering or taking prisoners. All evil must be put to the sword. It is only then we are safe.

Are you doing exploits for your God?

PRAYER

Lord, help me to be bold for you. Amen

WISDOM

We are born again to conquer.

Knowing You Are A Child Of God

December 27

"We know that we are children of God, and that the whole world is under the control of the evil one"
I John 5:19.

REFLECTION

God has only children. He has no grand children. He has only sons and daughters and we become His children by spiritual birth. All those regenerated by the Spirit of God are the very children of God. All who try to get into the family of God by some other way will be disappointed.

We do not become children of God by ritual baptism, or by church membership or being a member of a Christian family. We cannot access the family of God by good works no matter how noble, sincere, or how extensive or intensive that work might be. We cannot get into the family of God by 'keeping' the Ten Commandments or even by trying to imitate the life of Christ.

Salvation is a gift of God and He will not alter that to accommodate any sinner who tries to come some other way. The ground at the cross is level and no compromise is possible. All sinners who hope to be saved must get a new nature and that cannot be achieved by reformation, but only through the miracle of the new birth. That is the only way we can know we are children of God. Salvation is gratuitous. It comes through the grace of God and is wholly based on the merits of our Lord's death for us upon the cross.

There is nothing we can ever do in our fallen nature that will ever please God. Trying in the flesh is a hopeless failure. Trusting in what Christ did, indeed, brings us into the family of God and this truly makes God our Father. Do you know if you are a child of God?

PRAYER

Lord, help me to receive you into my heart and be born again. Amen

WISDOM

Salvation is absolutely free and is received by faith.

The Evil One And The World

SCRIPTURE   December 28

"We know that we are children of God, and that the whole world is under the control of the evil one"
I John 5:19.

REFLECTION

There is not a nation on the face of the earth that is not under the influence and control of a sinister power. The master mind behind the daily tragic events we see, hear and have first hand experience with, is Satan. He is clever, brilliant, cunning, and sly and manipulates the nations to attain all his evil designs. He stirs up the nations politically and religiously with strife and tensions. He divides nations against themselves and creates divisions and open hostility. He is the father of racial tensions, bigotry and ethnic divisions. He attacks all social structures, and the media with the intent to confuse and destroy them.

He corrupts the judicial system and justice is denied the innocent. Without mercy he attacks the family with infidelity, spreads terror among family members and wreaks havoc on the individual. He creates economic hardships. He divides management against labor and labor against management. The master mind behind all these woes is a liar, a thief and a murderer and these wicked characteristics he sows in the heart of individuals, and among nations.

He has his spirit agents who assist him in his mammoth schemes and willing human agents who execute his will. They spread his lies, rob the till and rape the world of morality and slaughter those who dare oppose them. The madness we witness in our world is explained by the fact that an evil one is in control of those who know not God.

Have you escaped from being under the control of this evil tyrant?

PRAYER

Lord, help me walk as your child daily. Amen

WISDOM

Satan is the god of this age.

God Known Through The Son

*"**We know** also that the Son of God has come and has given us understanding so that we may know him who is true. We are in him who is true – even in His son Jesus Christ. He is the true God and eternal life"*
I John 5:20.

REFLECTION

We are not on the uncertain ground of guessing on matters that have eternal import and that impact on our eternal destiny. We are not on the slippery ground or confused by uncertain data that has been corrupted or diluted through transmission. We are standing squarely on historical data that is astounding and most significant for our knowing the true God and our eternal salvation.

There is no book in the history of mankind that has been more carefully transmitted to us than our Bible. We can trust the integrity of the Greek and Hebrew manuscripts so when John says, *"We know"* it is from John an eye witness to the events of our Lord's life and ministry. There was never a man like Jesus and there will be none like Him. He is the Son of God and He did what no other could have done. Only Jesus could make this claim: - *"No one has ever seen God, but the Only Son, who is at the Father's side, has made him known"* John 1:18.

Jesus is the very embodiment of the invisible God (Colossians 1:15), for says Paul, *"For God was pleased to have all his fullness dwell in him"* Colossians 1:19. There can be no knowledge of the Father apart from the Son (John 14:6).

Do you know the Son so that you may have certain knowledge of Him who is true?

PRAYER

Lord, help me to know you more through Your Son Jesus Christ. Amen

WISDOM

Revelational knowledge of God comes through the Son.

Know Him Who Is True

"We know also that the Son of God has come and has given us understanding so that we may know him who is true. We are in him who is true – even in His son Jesus Christ. He is the true God and eternal life"
I John 5:20.

REFLECTION

There is nothing speculative about Christianity. Union with Christ brings us into the realm of spiritual reality. It brings us into freedom and spiritual power. Spiritual truth is not our imagination at work but the effectual power of God working in us and transforming us and filling us with joy and peace. Christ in us does not make lunatics of us but makes us sober, righteous and self controlled. The God we serve is not the idols of the nations but the true authentic God who created all things.

The knowledge of this God caused Felix to be afraid and to cry out, *"Go thy way for this time"* Acts 24:25 (A.S.V.). It caused the Thessalonians heathens to turn from idols *"To serve a living and true God"* I Thessalonians 1:9 (A.S.V.). The cutting, piercing message of Peter on the Day of Pentecost had the Jews crying out, *"Brethren, what shall we do?"* Acts 2:37 (A.S.V.).

Man is empty on the inside in spite of his bumptious behavior. We might saturate our lives with the material but that cannot buy one second of true joy for joy comes with the knowledge of the true God. And so does eternal life. Every man's conscience bears witness to the truth of Jesus and finds its fulfillment when the life is surrendered to Christ. It is in that moment that the light of the true God dawns upon the soul and purpose in life is born.

PRAYER

Lord, help me to recognize that you are the sum of life. Amen

WISDOM

Christ gives meaning to all of life.

Get Rid Of The Idols

"Dear children, keep yourselves from idols"
I John 5:21.

REFLECTION

In the previous verse John presents to us the true God. We cannot mix the true worship of God with graven images. The command is very explicit on this matter. *"You shall have no other gods before me. You shall not make for yourself an idol in the form of anything in heaven above or on the earth beneath or in the waters below. You shall not bow down to them or worship them; for I, the LORD your God, am a jealous God, punishing the children for the sin of the fathers to the third and fourth generation of those who hate me"* Exodus 20:3-5.

Israel used an idol as an aid to the worship of God at the foot of Sinai and it did not find acceptance with God (Exodus 32:5-6, 21). Moses called it a great sin. There is no justification to use images or pictures as an aid in the worship of the invisible God. An image takes the mind off the true and living God and puts the focus on the material and the worthless.

There are idols that are not material but take the place of God in our minds and to these we give our undivided allegiance, worship and service. There are the idols of work, house, land, car, bank account, children, wife, husband, sports, television, and pleasure that exclude the knowledge and worship of God in our lives. The world is full of idols and attractions that seduce the soul and intoxicate the mind in serving worthless things. The onus is on us to keep ourselves from idols and to worship and serve the One and only true God.

How are you doing?

PRAYER

Lord, help me to worship you only. Amen

WISDOM

An idol is an insult to the Spirit nature of God.